FINANCIAL STATEMENTS
DEMYSTIFIED

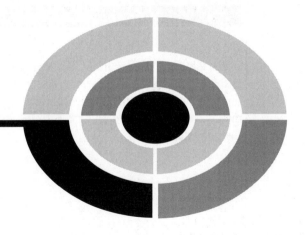

FINANCIAL STATEMENTS DEMYSTIFIED

A SELF-TEACHING GUIDE

BONITA K. KRAMER

CHRISTIE W. JOHNSON

New York   Chicago   San Francisco   Lisbon
London   Madrid   Mexico City   Milan   New Delhi
San Juan   Seoul   Singapore   Sydney   Toronto

3 4 5 6 7 8 9 0   DOC/DOC   1 0

ISBN: 978-0-07-154387-3
MHID: 0-07-154387-2

Printed and bound by RR Donnelley.

McGraw-Hill books are available at special quantity discounts to use as premiums and sales promotions, or for use in corporate training programs. To contact a representative please visit the Contact Us pages at www.mhprofessional.com.

CONTENTS

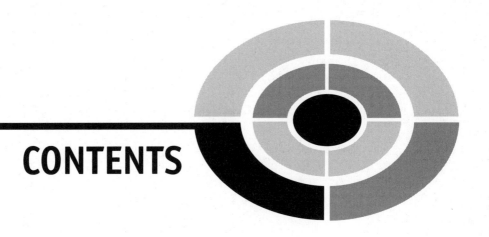

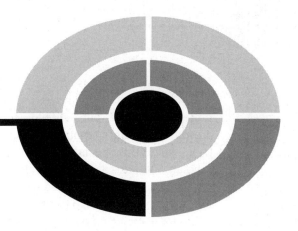

Acknowledgments

From Bonita K. Kramer:

I doubt I would have undertaken this project without the support of my coauthor, Christie Johnson. Christie is an extraordinary writer who has a wealth of information about financial accounting. She has been a faculty member at Montana State University since I was an undergraduate accounting student here many years ago. Then, as now, she had a stellar reputation as an educator, and to coauthor this book with her as a colleague truly has been one of the highlights of my career.

Additionally, however, I could not have written this book without the patience of my husband, Mark, who is my best friend, and our boys, David and Kyle. While my husband never doubted my ability to write this book, he was concerned about the time I would invest in it.

Finally, I want to thank my parents, Rod and Betty Peterson, for their encouragement throughout my life to continue my education and to pursue various professional challenges over the years. They never doubted my abilities and always quietly cheered me on. Yet they also instilled in me a sense of what is truly important in life, and I am grateful.

From Christie W. Johnson:

Bonita flatters me with her remarks describing why our collaboration on this project took place, but I should set the record straight. The opportunity actually arose from Bonita's reputation as an expert in the area of fraud education and contributions to this specialized field and her outstanding reputation as a teacher and scholar. She has garnered numerous teaching and research-related honors during her career as an accounting educator. Bonita is a teaching role model and an incredibly patient and effective mentor when it comes to publishing endeavors. She has a talent for teaching an old dog (like me) some new tricks, and I was honored by her invitation to collaborate. I appreciate and am very grateful for this opportunity, one I probably would not have enjoyed had it not been for Bonita's faith and interest in working with me.

Bonita and I both very much enjoy getting to know our students in person and teaching to a live audience. We are motivated to come up with many different ways to illustrate or explain a concept, knowing that individual student learning styles vary considerably. If we see a few foreheads and eyebrows scrunching, we have a visual cue that our students are struggling to understand a difficult or important concept. In a classroom setting, we can react to these cues, ask and answer questions, and meet with students one on one.

In writing *Financial Statements Demystified,* it was our joint goal to connect with individuals we probably won't meet in person, a prospect both exciting and a bit daunting! We organized this book by presenting the topics and concepts we both felt to be most relevant to your understanding of financial accounting and reporting while avoiding the accounting system details found in most traditional textbooks. We hope that you find our explanations and illustrations provide useful information and that the benefits you gain by reading this book exceed the cost of its purchase!

I too would like to acknowledge my family's support in this endeavor. My husband, Pat, was remarkably patient, especially during marathon writing episodes when I would become so focused and paused just long enough to share the meals he prepared. My daughter, Swithin, plays an important supporting role in my writing and publishing endeavors. In an interesting reversal of roles, I now seek Swithin's input and advice. I think she must take great delight when she has an opportunity to wield a bold-line red pen, much like the one I drew out of my bag and used to critique her written work when she was in junior high and high school.

Bonita's parents and my own instilled many virtues we both appreciate and honor, and they believed deeply in our talents and abilities. While we each grieved over the loss of a parent last year, we knew they would be proud of our collaborative efforts on this book.

INTRODUCTION

This book is intended for people who want to understand the information provided in financial statements. We don't describe all the accounting details of preparing financial statements, which is an approach typically employed in many accounting courses. Since many accounting students, upon graduation, will hold positions requiring that they prepare their employers' financial statements or audit their clients' financial statements, the preparer approach employed in college makes sense for accounting majors. However, that is not our goal here. Instead, we focus on a user approach to understanding financial statements.

Because of the user approach we take in this book, you don't need any accounting courses or background to learn this material. Instead, this book is meant to help people base decisions on the information provided in financial statements.

What kinds of decisions might you be thinking of making in which financial statements can be useful? Well, perhaps you are an investor thinking about your future retirement and are wondering whether you might like to purchase some stock in a particular company. Or perhaps you already own stock in a company and are trying to decide if this is a good time to sell that stock. Or perhaps you are a creditor wondering whether you should lend some money to an organization. Perhaps you are a union official involved in negotiations with a business and want to have a thorough understanding of the business's financial health. Perhaps you own a business and, regardless of its size, want to understand the financial statements compiled by your accountants better to help you make future business decisions. Perhaps you are a manager in an organization that has its own accounting department, which routinely prepares financial statements for your use, and you want to comprehend better the statements they are sending to your office. Or perhaps you are about to enter a graduate business program without an accounting undergraduate degree and want a reference guide to the content and terminology of financial statements.

We hope this book will answer some of your basic questions about financial statements, explain common terminology and concepts, and demonstrate the interrelationships among the four basic financial statements so that you will be better able to understand and make decisions on the basis of the information provided in financial statements.

To accomplish these goals, we first provide a general overview of the four financial statements. Next, we describe some basic concepts and principles that are built into all financial statements. After that, we explain each of the four financial statements and their typical contents in detail, with examples. Armed with this understanding, we then explain how to read financial statements, including the auditor's report, and discuss some common ratios you can compute on the basis of the financial information. Our last section discusses the techniques typically employed by people who are intent on fraudulently misstating their financial statements and gives you guidance on some red flags that might alert you to the possibility that the financial statements should not be replied on.

We encourage you to grab the annual report of any company you are interested in and pore over it as you read this book. We think you'll be surprised and pleased to discover how understandable the financial statements really are!

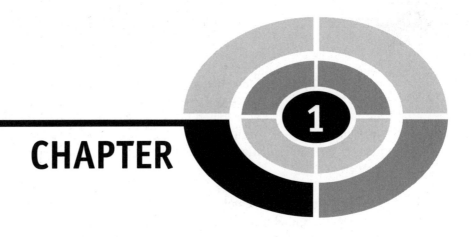

CHAPTER 1

Four Basic Financial Statements

Why Are Financial Statements Necessary?

Financial statements are the output of the accounting process, a formal way of communicating financial information that can be used by a variety of parties in making decisions about a business. For example, understanding financial statements can help you decide whether you want to invest in, lend money to, or grant credit to a company. The owners of an existing business use information derived from financial statements in planning and evaluating business activities. Union officials may use financial statements in their negotiations with management on behalf of the employees. The results reported in financial statements may help a company determine the size of bonuses paid to top management. In short, financial statements are a critical source of information for most business decisions.

In this book, we assume that you know nothing about the accounting process or the different types of financial statements that result from that process. However, even if you already know something about accounting or financial statements, you may find this book useful in providing a more complete view of financial statements, their interrelationships, and the accounting concepts that underlie their preparation.

What will you learn if you read this book? Our purpose is to assist you in understanding financial statements by acquainting you with accounting and financial statement terminology, the underlying concepts on which financial statements are based, and the form and content of those statements and their interrelationships. You will develop skills in reading financial statements, including the accompanying footnotes, and understanding the related auditor's report. Once we have covered those topics, you will be able to develop skills in identifying fraudulently misstated financial statements, a topic covered in the final chapter.

Objectives of Financial Reporting

Before we introduce you to the four basic financial statements, you should understand the overall purpose of summarizing accounting information in formal financial statements. The accounting profession has identified the objectives of financial reporting as follows:

- To provide information that is useful in making investment and credit decisions
- To provide information that is useful in assessing cash flow prospects
- To provide information about the resources of a business, claims to those resources, and changes in them

Note that "to provide information" is the focus of these objectives. In other words, the information provided by financial statements can be useful in answering the following types of questions:

- Is the business profitable?
- Do the operating activities of the business generate sufficient cash flows?
- Has the business grown? Was the growth achieved through its own profits, additional investments by its owners, or borrowing?
- Does the business generate sufficient cash flows to repay amounts borrowed? To return profits to its owner or owners?
- Does the business generate sufficient cash flows to pay its current obligations?

- Is the business likely to continue to be able to pay its obligations as they become due over the long run?
- What are the amounts and types of the resources of the business? What are the amounts and types of claims against those resources?

Many of the answers to these questions can be found directly in the financial statements and indirectly through the relationships between certain items in the financial statements and other information disclosed in the notes to those statements. The answers to these questions can help you decide whether to purchase a business or invest in another business by becoming a partner or stockholder or perhaps help you decide whether to continue to operate or sell your existing business. You may decide whether to lend money or extend credit to a business or determine why it will be difficult or easy for you to get a business loan or establish credit. Financial statement information can help you determine the likelihood of being repaid if you lend money or extend credit or gauge the likelihood of receiving an adequate return on your investment in your own business or investments in others. As you progress through this book, it should become clear that the more you learn about financial statements and the concepts on which they are based, the more understandable and useful they become.

The Four Basic Financial Statements

At this point, we want to introduce you very briefly to the four basic financial statements: (1) the balance sheet, (2) the income statement, (3) the statement of changes in owner's equity, and (4) the statement of cash flows. Later chapters will discuss each type of statement and the underlying concepts in more detail.

THE BALANCE SHEET

The balance sheet presents the assets, liabilities, and residual equity of the owner or owners of a business. It is a snapshot of the business, showing its financial position at a specific point in time. In fact, the balance sheet sometimes is referred to as the statement of financial position.

Assets are the economic resources of the business. They may be tangible—something you can see and touch—or they may represent rights the business possesses. Examples of assets include cash, accounts receivable, inventories of goods to be sold to customers, supplies, prepaid expenses, land, buildings, equipment, investments, and natural resources.

Liabilities are obligations of the business, or creditor claims against the assets of the business. Examples of liabilities include accounts payable to suppliers, customer deposits for goods or services to be provided, salaries or wages payable, taxes payable, rent payable, mortgage notes payable, and interest payable.

Equity is the excess of the assets over the liabilities, or the owners' claims against the assets in the business. Sometimes the terms *net assets* and *net worth* are used to describe the owner's residual interest. Depending on the form in which the business is organized, this residual interest may be called owner's equity (for a sole proprietorship: a one-owner business), owners' equity (for a partnership in which there is more than one owner), or stockholders' equity (for a corporation) (see Figure 1.1).

Figure 1.1   Terms for Equity under Different Business Forms

Business Form	Owners	Equity Commonly Is Called
Sole proprietorship	One owner	Owner's equity
Partnership	Two or more owners (partners)	Owners' equity
Corporation	Stockholders (shareholders)	Stockholders' equity

The balance sheet is based on a basic formula that is called the balance sheet equation or sometimes the accounting equation (Figure 1.2):

Figure 1.2   Balance Sheet Equation

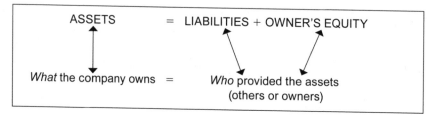

This formula always must hold true; in other words, assets always equal liabilities plus owner's equity. It is probably apparent now how the balance sheet gets its name: It always must be in balance!

A simple balance sheet for a corporation appears in Figure 1.3. Each financial statement includes a heading indicating the name of the business, the type of statement, and the date or period of time pertaining to the statement. Assume the business was formed on January 1, 20x1, with assets, liabilities, and owner's equity, as shown in Figure 1.3.

The assets of this business consist of cash and supplies, which are economic resources of the business. The liabilities consist of a single note payable, which is an

Figure 1.3 Example of a Balance Sheet, Beginning of Year

SDK Consulting
BALANCE SHEET
January 1, 20x1*

ASSETS	
Cash	$1,800
Supplies on hand	200
Total Assets	$2,000
LIABILITIES	
Note payable	$ 800
OWNER'S EQUITY	
SDK, Capital	1,200
Total Liabilities and Equity	$2,000

*In this book, we use the notation 20x1 for the financial statements of the first year; subsequent years will be dated 20x2, 20x3, and so on.

obligation (debt) of the business. At this point, owner's equity consists of one account called SDK, Capital.

Because this is a new business, it appears the owner contributed $1,200 that makes up part of the cash balance and possibly was used to purchase the supplies and that the remainder of the cash was obtained through borrowing. It is also possible that all the cash contributed by the owner went into the company's cash account and the money borrowed was used to purchase supplies, with the remainder going into the cash account. The balance sheet does not tell you exactly which assets each party contributed, but that's not necessary to understand the company's financial position. Instead, you can tell that there are two claims against the $2,000 of assets of the business: the claim of the party who lent the business $800 and the residual claim of the owner of $1,200.

Note that total assets of $2,000 are equal to the sum of the claims against the assets, which total $2,000; Assets = Liabilities + Owner's Equity ($2,000 = $800 + $1,200). Stated another way, total assets minus the creditors' claims against the assets equals owner's equity ($2,000 − $800 = $1,200).

THE INCOME STATEMENT

The second basic financial statement we are introducing you to—the income statement—presents the revenues and expenses of the business over a period of time. Thus, it is not a snapshot as of one date, as the balance sheet is, but more of a motion picture. The income statement presents the results of the primary operating activities of the business, which provides services or the production and/or sale of goods. The income statement also computes the net income or profit for the period (if revenues > expenses) or the net loss (if expenses > revenues). It is probably apparent now how the income statement gets its name: It computes income for the period (assuming the company was profitable). If a company has suffered a loss for the period, the statement still is referred to as the income statement. Sometimes, however, this statement is called the profit and loss statement.

Revenues are the resources that flow into the business primarily from the provision of services or the production and/or selling of goods. Examples of revenues include consulting fees earned, commissions earned, rental fees earned, and sales revenue earned. Expenses are the costs associated with generating revenues. Examples of expenses are salaries and wages, rent, utilities, supplies used, cost of goods sold, insurance, interest, and taxes.

Be careful not to equate revenues with cash inflows. The accounting profession requires that revenues presented on the income statement represent amounts that have been "earned" regardless of whether those amounts actually were received in cash during that period. The same concept holds true for expenses in that expenses are not necessarily the same thing as cash outflows. The expenses reported on the income statement represent costs that have been "incurred" regardless of whether those costs actually were paid in cash during that period. We'll cover this concept in more detail in Chapter 2 and again in Chapter 6. For now, we want to show you an example of what the income statement might look like (Figure 1.4).

Figure 1.4   Example of an Income Statement

SDK Consulting
INCOME STATEMENT
For the Year Ended December 31, 20x1

REVENUES		
Consulting Fees Earned		$40,000
EXPENSES		
Wages Expense	$10,000	
Equipment Rental Expense	3,000	
Supplies Expense	4,000	
Interest Expense	120	
Total Expenses		17,120
NET INCOME		$22,880

This income statement is for the same company whose balance sheet we presented earlier. It shows the revenues earned and the expenses incurred during the company's first year of activities. The revenues consist of fees earned from providing consulting services to customers during the year regardless of whether the customers have paid for those services in cash yet. The expenses consist of wages, equipment rental, supplies, and interest. These expenses were incurred while the company performed consulting services even though the expenses may not have been paid in cash during that time period. As a result of providing consulting services, the business earned a profit of $22,880.

THE STATEMENT OF OWNER'S EQUITY

The third financial statement we will introduce you to is called the statement of owner's equity. Since stockholders are the owners of a corporation, it stands to reason that this statement is referred to as the statement of stockholders' equity for a corporation.

The purpose of this statement is to report the changes in each separate component of owner's equity and in total owner's equity for a period of time. Sometimes this statement is called the statement of changes in owner's equity. Equity is increased by additional investments of cash or other assets by the owner or owners. Net income also increases equity. Because additional owner investments or net income increases equity, one can deduce what decreases equity: withdrawals by or a distribution of assets to the owner or a net loss (Figure 1.5).

Figure 1.5   Items That Affect Owner's Equity

OWNER'S EQUITY

Increased by	Decreased by
Net income	Net loss
Owner investment of cash or other assets	Withdrawals by owner or distribution of assets to owner

The statement of owner's equity helps link the owner's equity shown in the balance sheet at the beginning of the period with that shown at the end of the period.

The statement of changes in owner's equity for the business appears next. Notice that it presents the amounts and causes of the change in owner's equity from the beginning to the end of the first year (Figure 1.6).

Figure 1.6 Example of a Statement of Owner's Equity

SDK Consulting
STATEMENT OF CHANGES IN OWNER'S EQUITY
For the Year Ended December 31, 20x1

SDK, Capital, January 1, 20x1	$ 1,200
Add: Net income for the year	22,880
Additional investment of equipment	1,000
Subtotal	25,080
Less: Withdrawals by owner	(18,000)
SDK, Capital, December 31, 20x1	$ 7,080

At the beginning of the year, the owner's residual equity in the business was $1,200. The owner's equity of the business increased during the year because of the net income earned by the business of $22,880 and the contribution of equipment by the owner. The owner's equity decreased by $18,000 during the year as a result of the owner withdrawing $18,000 of business assets (probably cash) for personal use.

THE STATEMENT OF CASH FLOWS

The fourth and last financial statement that we are going to introduce you to is the statement of cash flows. This statement presents a summary of the cash flows of a business during a specific period. It shows the amounts and causes of the change in the cash balance during that time and links last year's balance sheet to this year's balance sheet by reconciling the cash balance at the beginning of the year with the cash balance at the end of the year. We'll show that in more detail in Chapter 6.

How is the statement of cash flows different from the income statement? Remember that the income statement calculates the net income (or loss) by subtracting expenses from revenues. These revenues and expenses are not necessarily equal to the cash inflows and outflows, because revenues are recorded when earned and expenses are recorded when incurred. The statement of cash flows focuses on cash. Thus, for example, some revenue earned by selling goods to a customer who hasn't paid yet would appear on the income statement but not on the statement of cash flows.

Why is this distinction important? A company can be profitable yet still be cash-poor if most of its revenues are earned but not yet received in cash. However, a company needs cash to pay its bills, and so the statement of cash flows gives financial statement readers a good idea of the likelihood that the company will be able to pay its debts as they become due and remain solvent in the near term.

The cash flows are presented in three categories: operating, investing, and financing. Examples of what are included in each category are shown in Figure 1.7.

Figure 1.7 The Three Categories of Cash Flow Activities and Examples of Each One

Examples of cash flows from operating activities:
- Cash collections from customers
- Cash received for dividends or interest earned
- Cash payments to suppliers for inventory purchased for resale to customers
- Cash payments to suppliers for raw materials used to manufacture goods
- Cash payments to employees for salaries and wages
- Cash payments for other operating expenses (e.g., rent, utilities)
- Cash payments for interest
- Cash payments for taxes

Examples of cash flows from investing activities:
- Cash paid to purchase assets used by the business
- Cash paid for investments made by the business
- Cash received from the sale of assets used in the business
- Cash received from the sale of business investments

Examples of cash flows from financing activities:
- Cash received from borrowing
- Cash used to pay back a loan
- Cash invested by the owner
- Cash distributed to the owner

The statement of cash flows for the business that we've used in this chapter, SDK Consulting, is shown in Figure 1.8.

Note that the statement of cash flows shows the cash flows from operating, investing, and financing activities; the change in the cash balance from the beginning to the end of the year, which may be an increase or a decrease; and the noncash investing and financing activities. Why is the last element included? These items may affect cash flows in future years, and so this information helps readers of the financial statement to predict whether cash flows will differ significantly in the future as a result of these items.

How do we interpret SDK Consulting's statement of cash flows for this year? It shows that operating activities—in other words, what the company is in the business of doing—increased cash by a net amount of $20,580, which consisted of cash collected from customers and cash paid for the various expenses during the period. You may have noticed that the amounts of cash received and paid for the various operating activities differ from the amounts of revenues and expenses shown for those items in the income statement. Again, that is the case because the income statement reports revenues earned, regardless of whether the cash has been received, and expenses when incurred, regardless of whether the cash has been paid.

The statement of cash flows also shows that investing activities, in this case the purchase of equipment, used $5,000 of the cash available. Financing activities used a net amount of $14,800 of the cash available, consisting of cash received from

Figure 1.8 Example of a Statement of Cash Flows

SDK Consulting
STATEMENT OF CASH FLOWS
For the Year Ended December 31, 20x1

Cash Flows from Operating Activities			
Cash received from customers		$37,000	
Cash payments for:			
Wages	$9,500		
Equipment rental	3,000		
Supplies	3,800		
Interest	120	16,420	
Net Cash Flows from Operating Activities			$20,580
Cash Flows from Investing Activities			
Cash paid to purchase equipment			(5,000)
Cash Flows from Financing Activities			
Cash received from borrowing on			
notes payable		4,000	
Cash used to repay note payable		(800)	
Cash withdrawn by owner		(18,000)	
Net Cash Flows from Financing Activities			(14,800)
INCREASE IN CASH DURING THE YEAR			780
Cash balance, January 1, 20x1			1,800
Cash balance, December 31, 20x1			$ 2,580
NONCASH INVESTING AND FINANCING ACTIVITIES			
The owner contributed additional equipment to the business, valued at $1,000.			

additional borrowing, repayment of borrowed money, and cash withdrawn by the owner. In addition, other equipment was acquired through a contribution made to the business by the owner, which did not use any of the cash available to the business. Overall, the cash balance increased by $780, from $1,800 at the beginning of the year to $2,580 at the end of the year.

Disclosure of Other Information

Financial statements are more useful to people outside the business when explanations of other relevant information are provided. Examples of the type of additional information commonly disclosed include the methods of accounting used (particularly where there are alternative ways of accounting for certain events), guarantees of the debt of other parties, and explanations of unusual or significant events reported in the statements. This additional information usually is presented in the notes to financial statements, which often are referred to simply as the footnotes. The footnotes may require several pages for a complex business, but they contain a great deal of relevant information.

Relationships Between the Four Basic Statements

As you reviewed each of the financial statements, you may have noticed that each statement presents different information but that the statements are interrelated. We began with the balance sheet presenting the assets, liabilities, and owner's equity of a new business at the time it was formed. During the course of the year, the business engaged in many activities. The operating activities of the business were summarized and presented in the income statement, which showed the revenues earned, the expenses incurred, and the resulting net income. Cash receipts and payments arising from operating activities were summarized and presented in the statement of cash flows.

The business also engaged in other activities, including borrowing and repaying loans, purchasing equipment, the owner's contribution of additional equipment to be used by the business, and a withdrawal of cash by the owner. The cash receipts and payments from these investing and financing activities were presented in the statement of cash flows, along with disclosure of the investing and financing activities that did not affect cash. The relationships among the financial statements are shown in Figure 1.9.

Figure 1.9   How the Four Financial Statements Are Related

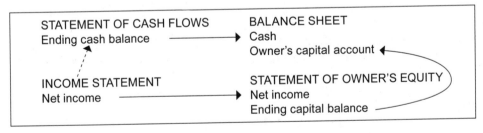

Why is there a dotted line from the income statement's net income to the statement of cash flows? As you'll learn in Chapter 6, there are two different methods of preparing the statement of cash flows. One method begins with the net income reported on the income statement, which is not the method we briefly introduced in this chapter. We'll introduce you to both methods in Chapter 6.

When you review the SDK Consulting balance sheet presented earlier in this chapter, you will notice that the cash balance shown there ($1,800) doesn't equal the ending cash balance shown on the statement of cash flows ($2,580). This apparent discrepancy is not an error because the balance sheet we have presented earlier in Figure 1.3 was for January 1, 20x1, when the business was formed. The statement of cash flows shows the cash balance one year later, on December 31, 20x1. Using the information we have presented for SDK Consulting, the ending balance sheet would look like the one shown in Figure 1.10.

Figure 1.10   Example of a Balance Sheet, End of Year

SDK Consulting
BALANCE SHEET
December 31, 20x1

ASSETS		
Cash	$2,580	
Accounts Receivable	3,000	
Supplies on Hand	–0–	
Equipment	6,000	
Total Assets		$11,580
LIABILITIES		
Wages Payable	$ 500	
Notes Payable	4,000	
Total Liabilities		$ 4,500
OWNER'S EQUITY		
SDK, Capital		7,080
Total Liabilities and Equity		$11,580

If you are feeling adventurous and are wondering where the balances for all the amounts on the December 31, 20x1 balance sheet came from, continue reading this paragraph. Otherwise, be content to note the interrelationships among the four financial statements that we just illustrated and come back to this paragraph later. Here is how we derived the balances:

- Cash of $2,580: See the ending cash balance on the statement of cash flows.
- Accounts receivable of $3,000: This is the amount you should receive in the near future from your customers because they owe you for services you already have provided or goods you already have sold to them. If you look at the income statement, you'll notice that we generated revenues from

consulting of $40,000, but the statement of cash flows indicates that only $37,000 was collected in cash from customers. Thus, our customers must owe us the remaining $3,000.

- Supplies on hand of $0: We began the business with $200 of supplies, but the income statement shows that we expensed $4,000 of supplies. The statement of cash flows indicates that we spent cash of $3,800 on supplies for the year. Thus, we used up (expensed) all the supplies we started with ($200) plus all the supplies we purchased during the year ($3,800).

- Equipment of $6,000: Per our beginning balance sheet, we owned no equipment (which is probably why we show some equipment rental expense on the income statement). The statement of cash flows reports that we purchased equipment costing $5,000 and also that the owner made an additional $1,000 investment of equipment in the business (which is also shown on the statement of changes in owner's equity).

- Wages payable of $500: The beginning balance sheet shows that we owed no wages (which makes sense because we just started business that day). However, the income statement reports that we expensed $10,000 in wages, and the statement of cash flows shows that we paid $9,500 cash for wages. This means we still owe our employees $500 for wages they have earned.

- Notes payable of $4,000: The beginning balance sheet reports that we started with a note payable of $800. The statement of cash flows indicates that we borrowed more money with another note, receiving $4,000. Also, the statement of cash flows indicates that we paid $800 on a note payable that we owed (probably the original note), meaning we still owe $4,000 in total as of the end of the year.

- SDK, Capital, of $7,080: See the ending balance on the statement of owner's equity.

Note, of course, that assets = liabilities + owner's equity on the December 31, 20x1, balance sheet (again, that equality always must hold because the balance sheet must balance).

Information overload? Actually, we think you will be surprised by how much you have learned already. You learned that the business was profitable, its operating activities provided a positive cash flow, it was able to pay its current obligations, it was able to return profits to the owner, and it has grown. By reviewing each of the four financial statements, you have learned important information about the past activities of the business and its financial position at the end of the year. This information would be useful to the owner in planning and controlling the activities and finances of the business and to other parties making investment and credit decisions about the business. Later chapters will present expanded discussions of each of the financial statements and the concepts underlying their preparation and use.

Quiz for Chapter 1

1. The balance sheet equation is:
   a. Cash − liabilities = owner's equity
   b. Assets = liabilities + stockholders' equity
   c. Cash = liabilities + stockholders' equity
   d. Assets = liabilities − owners' equity

2. An example of an asset is:
   a. Salaries payable
   b. Common stock
   c. Supplies on hand
   d. Rental fees earned

3. The balance sheet shows the assets, liabilities, and owners' equity:
   a. For a point in time
   b. For a period of time
   c. For the future
   d. Since the company was established

4. The income statement:
   a. Computes a company's net worth
   b. Presents a company's financial position at a point in time
   c. Shows a company's cash inflows and outflows for a period of time
   d. Presents a company's revenues and expenses for a period of time

5. If a business bills its clients $100,000 for services performed during the year but collects only $80,000 in cash, revenues reported on the income statement will be:
   a. $20,000
   b. $80,000
   c. $100,000
   d. $180,000

6. If a business incurs $40,000 of expenses associated with operating the business during the year, of which only $35,000 was paid in cash, expenses on the income statement will be:
   a. $5,000
   b. $35,000
   c. $40,000
   d. $75,000

7. Decreases in owner's equity are caused by:
   a. Net income
   b. An additional investment of cash during the year
   c. Net income minus net loss
   d. Withdrawals by the owner

8. Which of the following is not one of the categories shown on the statement of cash flows?
   a. Cash flows from business activities
   b. Cash flows from operating activities
   c. Cash flows from investing activities
   d. Cash flows from financing activities

9. If a business reports revenues of $200,000 and expenses of $180,000 and had $170,000 cash received from customers and $145,000 cash payments for expenses, its cash flow from operating activities is:
   a. $10,000
   b. $20,000
   c. $25,000
   d. $55,000

10. Accounts receivable represents:
    a. The amounts of cash received from customers for services or goods provided
    b. The amount owed by customers for goods or services received but not yet paid for
    c. The amount of revenue earned from providing goods or services to customers
    d. An expense of the business as a result of borrowing

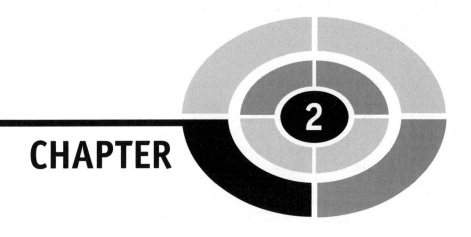

CHAPTER

Basic Concepts

We introduced you to the form and basic content of the four financial statements in Chapter 1, where we also showed you the interrelationships among the financial statements. Before we go into more detail about each financial statement, it's important to understand some of the basic concepts that underlie the preparation of the statements.

Why are any basic concepts necessary? Financial statements may be prepared for use by many different parties, including business owners and managers, investors, creditors, and regulatory bodies such as the Securities and Exchange Commission. Preparing general-purpose financial statements, which is our focus in this book, helps ensure that there is some degree of consistency in the information presented to users outside the business. In other words, anyone comparing the financial statements of ABC Company and DEF Company doesn't have to wonder whether ABC Company prepared its financial statements by using a set of concepts completely different from those used by DEF Company.

In Chapter 1 we introduced you to the objectives of financial reporting (why we prepare financial statements). Understanding how we prepare those statements helps a reader interpret and understand them. To begin, we will introduce you to the qualitative characteristics of accounting information. These characteristics are the bridge between the why and the how (see Figure 2.1).

Figure 2.1   How Qualitative Characteristics of Accounting Connect the Why with the How of Financial Statement Preparation

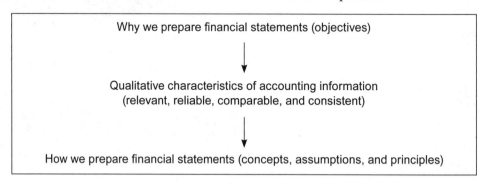

Why we prepare financial statements (objectives)

Qualitative characteristics of accounting information
(relevant, reliable, comparable, and consistent)

How we prepare financial statements (concepts, assumptions, and principles)

Qualitative Characteristics of Financial Statements

Useful financial statements should contain information that is relevant, reliable, comparable, and consistent. What is meant by these terms?

Relevant information helps users make predictions of future company performance on the basis of past information and provides feedback about past predictions. Relevant information is important, useful information to the readers of a financial statement.

Reliable information can be verified, is neutral rather than biased in favor of the business, and represents the substance (true nature) of the underlying events. Reliable information is free from errors.

Information that is presented or reported in a similar manner for different companies is comparable. Comparable information is useful because it allows one to make comparisons among different companies and identify real similarities or differences among those companies.

Consistent financial information is presented in the same manner from one period to the next for a particular company. Consistency helps ensure that the financial statements of one company are comparable from one period to the next. A reader of financial statements should be able to assume that any differences among a company's financial statements between years are due to real economic events, not to a simple change in the accounting treatment.

Basic Concepts, Assumptions, and Principles Used in Financial Statements

General-purpose financial statements are based on several basic concepts, assumptions, and principles. We will introduce you to these topics next, along with the related accounting terminology. In later chapters, you will apply these topics and terms to specific examples. The basic concepts, assumptions, and principles we will introduce you to in this chapter are as follows:

- Business entity assumption
- Monetary unit assumption
- Objectivity
- Going concern assumption
- Historical cost principle
- Time period assumption
- Revenue recognition principle
- Matching principle
- Accrual basis of accounting versus cash basis of accounting
- Full disclosure principle
- Materiality
- Conservatism
- Generally accepted accounting principles (GAAP)

BUSINESS ENTITY ASSUMPTION

The business, whether it is formed as a sole proprietorship, a partnership, or a corporation, is considered a separate and distinct entity from the owner or owners. Because the business is considered a separate entity, the financial statements reflect only the transactions of the business. The owner's personal transactions are not included in the business records. For example, if the owner purchases a vehicle for his or her family's use, the vehicle is not reported in the business's records or financial statements.

MONETARY UNIT ASSUMPTION

Only transactions or events that can be measured in terms of money are reported on financial statements. Because of this assumption, some important events may not be recorded by a business. For example, if a company hires the best employee workforce, it is not possible to assign a dollar value to this event and it therefore will not appear directly on the financial statements. Indirectly, however, the effect of this superior workforce may be reflected on the financial statements through increased profitability over time, but the reader of those statements may not be able to see this cause-and-effect relationship.

In the United States, financial statements are prepared using the dollar as the unit of measure, and it is assumed that the value of the dollar remains relatively stable. Although inflation affects the value of the dollar over time, the effects of inflation are not reflected in financial statements. Some people consider this a limitation of financial statements because the length of the ruler used to measure events continually changes with changes in the purchasing power of the dollar.

OBJECTIVITY

All the transactions entered in the accounting records should be based on objective, verifiable evidence rather than on something subjective, such as one's opinion. For example, assume that a company buys a piece of land for a price far below what the company believes the land is worth. Regardless, the land is recorded in the company's accounting records at the actual price paid (which can be verified or supported by various documents). The land is not recorded at how much the company believes it is worth (an opinion that undoubtedly will vary from individual to individual).

GOING CONCERN ASSUMPTION

Accounting methods are based on the assumption that the business will remain in existence forever unless there is evidence that it will not continue indefinitely. For example, this assumption may be questioned when a business is suffering financially and the liquidation (sale) of its assets is imminent. Among other things, the going concern assumption affects the values of assets on the balance sheet, which we discuss next.

HISTORICAL COST PRINCIPLE

Goods and services purchased are recorded at the cost when they were acquired, which is referred to as the historical cost or original cost. Consistent with the objectivity principle, cost is an objective, verifiable measure. Market values are not used often as a basis for recording. Why? Because of the going concern assumption, we assume that the company's assets will continue to be used in the business and not be sold, making the current market values less relevant.

Using the example above of a company purchasing land for a price far below what the company believes the land is worth, the land will remain on the company's books at the price the company actually paid for it. Even if there is indisputable evidence that the land is worth much more than that, the land will remain on the company's books at its historical cost.

TIME PERIOD ASSUMPTION

Financial statements are more useful if they present information for short periods rather than at the conclusion of a company's existence. The time period assumption (sometimes called the periodicity assumption) implies that a company can divide its business activities and transactions into shorter periods.

The time period covered by the statements is usually one year, although quarterly or monthly financial statements often are prepared. Many businesses use the calendar year, January 1 through December 31, for financial reporting purposes. Other companies may use a fiscal year, which covers the natural cycle of the business and ideally ends on a date when business activity is at a low point. The fiscal year is also 12 months in length. For example, a ski resort's fiscal year might end shortly after the end of the ski season, whereas a retailer's fiscal year may end in January after the holiday shopping season.

If financial statements were not prepared until the conclusion of the business's life, it would be fairly easy to measure the firm's total profit or loss. However, in the meantime it would be difficult to make business decisions without timely financial information. When the business uses short periods to report its activities, the information is more timely, but it is necessary to make judgments about the period in which certain business activities should be reported and when estimates of amounts should be made. The shorter the period is, the more difficult the estimates and judgments can be. For example, if you provide services to a customer in year 1 but do not receive cash from the customer until year 2, you must determine in which period the revenue was earned and will be reported. A similar judgment must be made about expenses incurred in one period but paid in another. The accounting profession has established the revenue recognition principle and the matching principle to provide guidelines.

REVENUE RECOGNITION PRINCIPLE

Revenue generally is considered earned and reported in the income statement in the period in which the business provided the service or sold the goods even though the customer may not pay for the services or goods until a later time. This principle applies even if the customer paid for the services or goods in advance. In this way, the income statement is more useful in assessing the accomplishments of the business during a specific period. In other words, it is easier to determine how successful the company was at generating a profit when the focus is on the earning process, not on the timing of the cash receipts. Figure 2.2 shows a few examples.

Figure 2.2   Revenue Recognition Examples

Example	When to Record the Revenue on the Books
Your company cleans a customer's swimming pool in May and bills the customer. Your company receives the check in the mail in June.	In May
Your company cleans a customer's swimming pool in May, and the customer pays your employee as soon as the work is finished.	In May
In January, a customer pays in advance for your company to clean her swimming pool once a month for a year.	After your employee cleaned the swimming pool in January, your company would record one-twelfth of the advance payment as revenue. Your company would follow this same approach for the remaining 11 months.

MATCHING PRINCIPLE

Costs incurred by the business generally are recorded as expenses on the income statement in the period in which the related revenue is produced. In other words, revenues are matched with the costs and efforts associated with producing those revenues, resulting in the net income or loss during the specific period. Figure 2.3 shows examples of the matching principle.

Figure 2.3   Matching Principle Examples

Example	When to Record the Expense on the Books
Your employees work during the monthly pay period December 1–December 31 and are paid on January 15.	In December
Your company paid for 12 months of warehouse storage space in advance.	At the end of January, your company would record one-twelfth of the advance payment as rent expense. Your company would follow this approach for the remaining 11 months.
Your company purchases inventory at the end of year 1 that is not sold to your customers until year 2.	The cost of the goods sold in year 2 will appear on year 2's income statement.
Your company purchases a delivery vehicle for business use.	The cost of the delivery vehicle will be recorded gradually as an expense over all the years of use (this is called depreciation and is explained more fully in Chapters 4 and 5).

These expenses are all being matched with the revenues they helped produce. For example, the employees who worked for the company in December helped generate revenues in some capacity, such as by performing services for customers or selling goods to customers.

ACCRUAL BASIS OF ACCOUNTING VERSUS CASH BASIS OF ACCOUNTING

When the income statement presents the revenues earned and the expenses incurred during a time period (without regard to when the cash actually was received or paid), the company is using the accrual basis of accounting. The accounting profession views the accrual basis as the most appropriate way to present income statement information. If the income statement merely reports the cash receipts and cash payments during a period, the company is using the cash basis of accounting. Why does the accounting profession prefer the accrual basis? It believes that the accrual basis of accounting better presents the underlying efforts and accomplishments of a business, which are not necessarily reflected in cash flows. Let's use a simplified example to demonstrate this.

Assume that a new company started business operations this year.

- It performed services worth $100,000 for customers, who have paid $40,000 so far.
- The company paid its employees $60,000 for wages and owes its employees another $5,000 for work they have performed, which will be paid on the next payday.

What is the net income generated by the business in its first year (see Figure 2.4)?

Figure 2.4 Net Income Calculation under the Accrual Basis of Accounting versus the Cash Basis of Accounting

	Accrual Basis of Accounting	Cash Basis of Accounting
Services revenue	$100,000	$40,000
Wages expense	65,000	60,000
Net income (loss)	$ 35,000	($20,000)

Notice that under the accrual basis of accounting the company has generated a profit of $35,000 in its first year of operations, whereas under the cash basis of accounting the company appears to be having problems since it suffered a loss of $20,000. The difference is due to the timing of the recognition of the revenues and related expenses. By following the revenue recognition and the matching principles introduced earlier in this chapter, the company is using the accrual basis of accounting. The accounting profession believes that this more fairly reflects the economic reality of the company's operating results. The company earned more revenues than it incurred in expenses, and assuming that this trend continues in the future, the company will continue to be profitable over time.

Cash flow is important, of course. A company needs cash to pay its bills as they come due. The operating activity section of the statement of cash flows can be used to assess cash flows, and this is much like an income statement prepared using the cash basis. By presenting both an income statement using the accrual basis of accounting and a statement of cash flows, the company allows a financial statement reader to assess both profitability and cash flows from operating activities.

FULL DISCLOSURE PRINCIPLE

Financial statements are more useful when significant information is disclosed adequately to the readers. The concept of full disclosure affects whether certain events are shown individually or combined with other items in the financial statements, how and where they are shown, the types of descriptions appearing in the financial statements, and the degree of explanatory material provided in the footnotes to the financial statements. Materiality, which is discussed next, also affects the way information is presented or disclosed.

MATERIALITY

Financial statement information and disclosures are presented for material (significant) items. Information is considered material if it would influence the decision of a reasonable financial statement user. Immaterial or insignificant items might not be disclosed separately. Whether an issue is material is a matter of judgment.

CONSERVATISM

When significant uncertainty surrounds the proper accounting treatment of an item or event, accountants apply the concept of conservatism by selecting the treatment that is least likely to overstate net income or assets. For example, if a business is uncertain about its ability to collect a portion of its accounts receivable (amounts customers owe the company), it may record an estimated loss from uncollectible accounts and report the accounts receivable on the balance sheet at the net amount it expects to collect.

Conservatism does not mean that preparers of financial statements intentionally understate assets or net income. Instead, it is a guideline that is used when there is doubt. If there is no doubt, there is no reason to apply this concept. The logic behind the concept is that once the uncertainty is resolved, if it is determined that net income or net assets are actually a higher amount, the financial statement readers will be pleasantly surprised. In contrast, if the opposite situation occurs and it is determined that net income or net assets are actually a lower amount than initially was reported, the financial statement users are likely to be upset. Good news is better than bad news.

GENERALLY ACCEPTED ACCOUNTING PRINCIPLES

The phrase "generally accepted accounting principles"—often simply stated as GAAP (pronounced "gap")—are the guidelines and standards developed by the accounting profession that must be followed in preparing financial statements. There is no single authoritative source of GAAP, although primarily GAAP is developed by an organization called the Financial Accounting Standards Board (FASB, pronounced "fazz-bee"). GAAP is not carved in stone, and as circumstances change or new business transactions evolve, GAAP will change. We will be explaining GAAP to you throughout this book, for example, in Chapter 3 when we discuss how to compute earnings per share on the income statement. In that instance, you will notice that GAAP can be fairly specific; you also will find that GAAP can provide broad guidelines, such as the revenue recognition principle and the matching principle.

Quiz for Chapter 2

1. Which of the following is one of the qualitative characteristics of financial reporting?
   a. Material
   b. Relevant
   c. Objective
   d. Conservative

2. Reliable information:
   a. Can be verified
   b. Is neutral
   c. Is free from errors
   d. All of the above

3. The business entity assumption requires that the owner's personal assets and liabilities must be included on the business's financial statements.
   a. True
   b. False

4. The monetary unit assumption:
   a. Recognizes that the value of a dollar changes over time
   b. Requires that financial statements be restated to show the effects of inflation
   c. Means that only transactions and events that can be measured in terms of money are reported on financial statements
   d. Requires judgment in assigning dollar values to nonmonetary transactions such as hiring a superior workforce

5. The time period assumption:
   a. Recognizes that a company can divide its business activities and transactions into shorter periods, such as a year or less, and still provide useful financial statements
   b. Requires that financial statements cover a period of at least one year to be useful
   c. Requires that companies use a calendar year (January 1–December 31) for financial statement reporting purposes
   d. Requires that reporting periods must be of sufficient length that no judgments or estimates are built into the financial statements

6. The objectivity concept:
   a. Allows opinions to be used in developing financial statement data
   b. Requires that transactions entered into the accounting records be based on verifiable evidence
   c. Would allow a company to record assets at the values the company believes the assets are worth
   d. Allows opinions to be used in developing financial statement data as long as the company's accountants agree with the opinions

7. The conservatism concept in accounting:
   a. Encourages the overstatement of assets and revenues
   b. Encourages the understatement of liabilities and expenses
   c. Supports the selection of an accounting method that will understate assets or net income when there is doubt about the proper accounting treatment of an item or event
   d. Supports the selection of an accounting method that will overstate liabilities or expenses when there is doubt about the proper accounting treatment of an item or event

8. The assumption that the business will remain in existence forever unless there is evidence to the contrary is called the:
   a. Going concern assumption
   b. Business entity assumption
   c. Monetary unit assumption
   d. Time period assumption

9. The historical cost principle requires that goods and services purchased be recorded at the:
   a. Original cost
   b. Original cost with adjustments to market value at the end of each reporting period
   c. Original cost with adjustments to market value at the end of each reporting period only if there is indisputable proof that the market value is reliable
   d. Original cost adjusted for inflation

10. The matching principle requires that expenses:
    a. Be recorded when the cash revenue is received
    b. Be recorded when the cash is paid
    c. Be recorded as soon as the company knows it will incur those expenses
    d. That are incurred by a business be recorded in the same period in which the related revenue is recognized

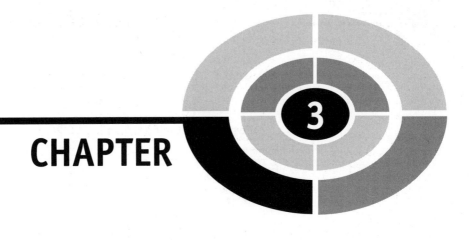

CHAPTER 3

The Income Statement

The material in Chapters 1 and 2 introduced you to the basic form and content of financial statements and the underlying concepts of financial reporting. Each of the types of financial statements will be discussed in more detail in Chapters 3 through 6, along with examples and references to the basic concepts. This chapter covers the income statement in more detail, using financial statements from Example Company to provide illustrations.

Basic Format

The income statement shows the revenues earned, the expenses incurred, and the resulting net income or net loss during a period of time. The basic form and content of the income statement for Example Company are shown in Figure 3.1.

Figure 3.1 Basic Income Statement Format

Example Company
Income Statement
For the Year Ended December 31, 20x1

Revenues	$801,000
Expenses	(701,000)
Net Income	$100,000

An income statement prepared using the accrual basis of accounting reports revenues earned and expenses incurred during a period, based on the revenue recognition and matching principles. In other words, revenues do not necessarily equal the cash receipts, nor do the expenses necessarily equal the cash payments made by the business during that period. The income statement covers a specific period, generally one year, but also may be prepared for shorter periods.

REVENUES

Revenues are resources flowing into the business, primarily from providing services or selling purchased goods to customers. A company also can manufacture its own goods to sell to customers. Revenues generally provide cash or a future claim to cash, for example, with accounts receivable or a note receivable.

Assume you own your own house-cleaning business. You earn revenue every time one of your employees cleans a customer's house. There are three ways a customer might pay you: (1) in advance, (2) as soon as your employee finishes performing the service, or (3) shortly after you bill the customer for the service (see Figure 3.2).

Figure 3.2 Examples of When to Record Revenue

Situation	Effect on Cash	Effect on Accounts Receivable	Effect on Revenue	Effect on Unearned Revenue
1. Customer pays in advance for your company's house-cleaning service.	↑			↑
Shortly after receiving the advance payment, your employee cleans the customer's house.			↑	↓
2. Customer pays as soon as the employee finishes cleaning his house.	↑		↑	
3. Customer asks that your company send her a bill after your employee has cleaned the house.		↑	↑	
Customer pays the bill shortly thereafter.	↑	↓		

In situation 1, if the customer pays you in advance, your company will record the cash when you receive it, but it will be recorded as a liability or a debt (unearned revenue), which appears on the balance sheet. Why is this considered unearned revenue? If your business doesn't fulfill its obligation to clean the house, your company will have to refund the customer's money. However, once your employee has performed the cleaning service, you will remove the liability from your books and record it as earned revenue.

In situation 2, if the customer pays immediately upon the completion of the house cleaning, the cash you receive will also be recorded as revenue.

However, in the third situation, if the customer does not pay you immediately but asks that you send a bill, your company still has earned the revenue. Your business performed the agreed-upon service, and the customer owes your company money. Thus, you will record the revenue as being earned, but you can't record any cash as coming in. Instead, you will record this as an account receivable in your books. An account receivable is an asset, and like all assets, it will appear on the balance sheet. It represents money owed to your business by your customers for goods you already have sold to them or services your business already has performed. In other words, accounts receivable represents a claim to cash that your company has against someone, and you should receive the cash sometime in the future.

Note that in all three situations, revenue is considered to be earned once your company has performed the service, regardless of when the cash is received. This approach is in accordance with the revenue recognition principle introduced in Chapter 2, which is also part of the accrual basis of accounting.

EXPENSES

Expenses are costs associated with providing services or selling goods. Examples include:

- Salaries or wages paid to employees
- Rent paid for office space
- Advertising
- Insurance
- Utilities (e.g., electricity, telephone)
- Office supplies used
- The company's cost of inventory sold to customers
- Interest
- Taxes

According to the matching principle, costs are reported as expenses of the same period in which the revenue was earned or in the period in which the expenses were incurred, regardless of when those costs or expenses were paid in cash. In other words, we try to match the expenses, or costs of doing business, with the revenues that the expenses helped generate. This matching process helps develop a more accurate picture of the company's operating success (or failure) during a period of time.

Let's go back to the example in which you own your own house-cleaning business. Some of your expenses may be paid in advance, whereas others may be paid after you incur them (see Figure 3.3).

Figure 3.3   Examples of When to Record Expense

Situation	Effect on Cash	Effect on Accounts Payable	Effect on Expense	Effect on Prepaid Expense
1. Your business pays its insurance company for 12 months of insurance coverage.	↓			↑
The 12 months covered by the policy pass.			↑	↓
2. Your office consumes electricity daily and receives the bill from the electric company at the end of the month.		↑	↑	
Your company pays the electric bill.	↓	↓		

If your company pays a cost of doing business in advance, such as the insurance in situation 1, you must record the cash payment when you made it or your cash account will not reflect the actual amount of cash you have on hand. However, you have not incurred the expense yet because the time period for which you have paid has not passed. For example, if you decided to change insurance carriers, your old insurance company would have to refund you a prorated amount of the premium you had paid but for which you had not yet received coverage. Therefore, an expense that your company has paid for in advance is called a prepaid expense, which is an asset (and will appear on the balance sheet). However, as time passes, your prepaid expense no longer is prepaid but is actually an incurred expense. The insurance company provided you with insurance coverage during this period, and once the 12 months have passed, you must remove the balance from the prepaid insurance expense account and add it to the insurance expense account (which will appear on the income statement).

However, in the second situation your company did not pay for a cost of doing business in advance but instead paid shortly after receiving the bill for the past month of service. Even though you have not paid your electric bill, you have incurred the expense. Your business used the electricity provided by the electric company, and even though you have not paid the bill yet, your company owes the money to the electric company. To reflect this transaction, you will record the expense, but there will be no cash going out until you actually make the payment. Instead, you will record this as an account payable in your books. An account payable is a liability or a debt (and will appear on the balance sheet). It represents money your business owes for goods or services another party already has provided to you. It is an account you must pay in the future.

Note that in both situations, an expense is recorded as incurred once the cost of doing business has happened, regardless of when the cash is paid. This approach is in accordance with the accrual basis of accounting, which was introduced in Chapter 2.

According to the concepts of materiality and full disclosure, each significant revenue and expense should be shown separately in the income statement, but insignificant or immaterial items may be combined. The footnotes may provide additional information about items reported on the income statement.

NET INCOME (OR LOSS)

Net income or net loss is the difference between revenues and expenses and reflects the results of all the income-producing activities of the business (see Figure 3.4).

Figure 3.4   Net Income (Loss) Formula

> **Revenues – Expenses = Net Income (or Net Loss)**
>
> If revenues > expenses, your company has earned a net income
>
> If expenses > revenues, your company has experienced a net loss

There are other terms for net income, all of which cover the same concept. These other terms include *earnings, profit,* and simply *income.*

Income Statement Format for A Business That Sells Goods

The income statements presented in Chapter 1 and in the earlier part of this chapter were for simple service businesses. If a company purchases goods (products or inventory) for resale to customers or manufactures the goods that it sells to customers, additional items must be reported in the income statement.

An example of an income statement for Example Company appears in Figure 3.5.

Figure 3.5 Income Statement Example

Example Company
Income Statement
For the Year Ended December 31, 20x1

Net Sales Revenue	$800,000
Cost of Goods Sold	(500,000)
Gross Profit	300,000
Operating Expenses	(196,000)
Operating Income	104,000
Other Income and Expenses, net	(4,000)
Net Income	$100,000

Example Company purchases goods from other sources (or manufactures its goods) for resale to its customers. This basic income statement form may be used for both sole proprietorships and partnerships. The income statement for a corporation is similar and is discussed later in this chapter.

NET SALES

As we have discussed, sales revenue represents revenue earned from the sale of goods during the time period, whether the customers paid cash at the time of sale, paid in advance, or will pay in the future. Recall that the cash advances collected from customers, such as customer deposits and gift certificates that were not earned during the period, will be shown on the balance sheet as a liability: unearned revenues. Revenues that were earned during the period but have not been collected in cash (such as sales on credit) will be shown on the balance sheet as an asset: accounts receivable.

More detailed reporting of sales revenue may be necessary when significant or material amounts of merchandise are returned by customers or when cash discounts are taken by customers for early payment on account. For example, the sales revenue for Example Company may appear as it does in Figure 3.6.

Figure 3.6 Net Sales Revenue Detail

Sales Revenue		
Gross Sales Revenue		$900,000
Less: Sales Returns and Allowances	$80,000	
Sales Discounts	20,000	(100,000)
Net Sales Revenue		$800,000

In this example, gross sales revenue represents the total sales of the company for the year. However, some of those sales were returned by customers, and so it would be misleading to report only the gross sales revenue on the income statement. A separate account is created to record the sales returns: sales returns and allowances. Allowances also are recorded in this account, and they represent reductions in the amount owed by the customer. The company might agree to grant an allowance because the customer was not happy with the purchase for some reason (e.g., slightly inferior goods, wrong color). Since the original sale was recorded as part of the gross, or total, sales revenue, it would be misleading not to reduce the gross sales revenue by any allowances granted.

Sales discounts are reductions in the amount owed by the customer in return for prompt payment. For example, a company may offer terms of 2/10, n/30, which is read as "two ten, net thirty." These terms mean that the seller will give the buyer 2 percent off the total sale if the buyer pays within 10 days of the invoice date, typically the date of the bill. Otherwise, the entire amount owed is due within 30 days of the invoice date, with no discount.

Why would a seller offer a sales discount? A company needs cash to pay its own bills. It can't pay its bills with a sale it made on account (an account receivable) even though that is an asset and represents cash the company should be receiving in the near future. Thus, the seller prefers to receive cash as soon as possible.

Why would a buyer take advantage of a sales discount? Discounts are a great deal for the buyer. By paying the bill only 20 days early (since the entire amount is owed within 30 days with no discount), the buyer gets 2 percent off. Interest rates typically are stated on an annual basis, such as the interest rate your bank pays you on your savings account. However, this discount interest rate pertains to a 20-day period only. To see how much interest the buyer would be paying to keep his or her cash for only an extra 20 days, convert the discount interest rate to an annual basis. For ease in computation, assume there are 360 days in a year, which translates to eighteen 20-day periods. Without considering compounding interest, this equals an annual interest rate of approximately 36 percent (18 periods times 2 percent), an astronomically high rate by most standards.

Why are separate accounts kept for sales discounts and sales returns and allowances? It would be possible simply to reduce sales revenue for those items, but if that is done, this information is lost. Keeping separate accounts for these items allows management (and the readers of the financial statements) to determine, for example, if sales returns seem to be excessively high, which may indicate that the company is experiencing a problem with its products.

COST OF GOODS SOLD

Cost of goods sold sometimes is referred to as cost of sales, and the name of the account aptly describes what it represents. This account is an expense and includes the cost of the merchandise sold to customers during the year, not necessarily the amount of cash paid by the company for the merchandise. Some of this merchandise may have been purchased in a prior period, or the company still may owe money to its suppliers for some of the merchandise. Calculating cost of goods sold and reporting it on the income statement is another illustration of the matching principle that was discussed in Chapter 2 and is shown in Figure 3.7.

Figure 3.7 Examples of When to Report Cost of Goods on the Income Statement

Situation	Merchandise Is Purchased	A Company Pays for Merchandise	Merchandise Is Sold by Company to Its Customers	Customers Pay for Merchandise	What Year Should the Company Record Revenue?	What Year Should the Company Record the Cost of Goods Sold?
1	Year 1	Year 1	Year 1	Year 1	Year 1	Year 1
2	Year 1	Years 1 and 2	Year 1	Years 1 and 2	Year 1	Year 1
3	Year 1	Year 1	Years 1 and 2	Years 1, 2 and 3	Years 1 and 2	Years 1 and 2

In situation 1, the accrual basis of accounting will result in the same reporting as the cash basis of accounting since the purchase, sale, and cash flows all occurred during the same period (year 1).

In situation 2, however, the company sold some merchandise that it had not paid for yet and for which it had not collected all the cash from its customers yet. Under the matching principle followed with the accrual basis of accounting, the revenue is to be recorded when it is earned (i.e., sold to the customers) and the expense is to be recorded in the same period as its related revenue (the sales of the merchandise).

Following the matching principle, situation 3 requires that the revenue be recorded when sold to the customers in years 1 and 2 (i.e., when earned) and the related expense be matched against that revenue (i.e., the goods sold in year 1 are expenses of year 1, and the goods sold in year 2 are expenses of year 2).

What happens to goods that are purchased but not yet sold? These goods are not shown on the income statement as part of cost of goods sold but rather are an asset called inventory that is shown on the balance sheet.

More detailed reporting of the cost of goods sold section of the income statement for Example Company appears in Figure 3.8.

Figure 3.8   Cost of Goods Sold Detail

Cost of Goods Sold	
Inventory on hand, January 1, 20x1	$ 40,000
Add: Cost of Goods Purchased during the Year	525,000
Cost of Goods Available for Sale	565,000
Less: Inventory on hand, December 31, 20x1	(65,000)
Cost of Goods Sold	$500,000

The formula shown in the figure makes logical sense. Essentially, what the formula for cost of goods sold states is that the inventory you have on hand at the beginning of the year plus the additional inventory you purchase during the year equals the inventory you have available to sell. Subtracting the inventory you still have on hand at the end of the year (it wasn't sold if it is still on hand) from what was available to sell must equal the amount of inventory sold. Since all the components of the formula are stated in dollars, the end result is not the number of units sold but the cost of the inventory sold. Specifically, it is the cost to your company: what your business paid for the inventory, not what your company is selling it for to your customers.

GROSS PROFIT

Gross profit often is referred to as gross margin and represents the markup on the goods sold. This markup is the difference between what your company paid to purchase the inventory you will sell to your customers and the price you will charge your customers for the inventory they purchase from you. Your company should earn a gross profit. If not, it means you are selling your inventory for less than or exactly what it cost, and your company obviously won't be in business for very long in this case.

OPERATING EXPENSES

The only expense we have placed on the income statement up to this point is the cost of goods sold. Before any income or loss is computed, the other operating expenses must be deducted from the gross profit.

Operating expenses represent expenses arising from the primary business activity, which in this case is the sale of inventory to customers. These expenses are deducted from gross profit to determine operating income (or operating loss). Typical operating expenses may include the ones shown in Figure 3.9.

Figure 3.9   Examples of Operating Expenses

OPERATING EXPENSES
• Salaries and wages
• Employer payroll taxes
• Pension and retirement
• Depreciation
• Rent
• Utilities
• Supplies
• Uncollectible accounts
• Property taxes
• Telephone
• Postage
• Insurance
• Repairs and maintenance
• Advertising

Where do the owner's personal expenses belong? According to the business entity assumption, personal expenses of the owners that were paid by the business are not included in the income statement but instead are shown in the statement of owner's equity as withdrawals. Similarly, salaries withdrawn by the owner or owners of a sole proprietorship or partnership usually are treated as withdrawals rather than expenses of the business because the owner is not considered an employee. Instead, the salary withdrawn by the owner is considered a distribution of the profits of the business to the owner.

Operating expenses often are categorized further as selling expenses and general and administrative expenses. Immaterial expenses may be combined rather than shown separately, particularly in financial statements used by parties other than management.

As with cost of goods sold, the matching principle applies to operating expenses. The salaries and wages expense consists of the salaries and wages earned by employees during the period even though the business may not pay the employees until a later time. For example, assume the income statement was for the calendar year, which ended on Tuesday, December 31, 20x1, and the weekly pay period ends on Friday, January 3, 20x2, which is in the next accounting period. Further, assume the business is closed on weekends. This year's salaries and wages expense includes two days of wages expense incurred (Monday and Tuesday) even though the wages have not been paid (see Figure 3.10).

Figure 3.10   Example of Accrued Wages Expense (Matching Principle)

Sunday	Monday	Tuesday	Wednesday	Thursday	Friday	Saturday
29 Business is closed	30	31 End of fiscal year 20x1	1	2	3 End of pay period	4 Business is closed

Wages earned during these two days belong on the 20x1 income statement.

Wages earned during these three days will be an expense of 20x2, and will not appear on the 20x1 income statement.

What happens with the liability for the two days of wages owed by the company to its employees as of December 31, 20x1? That debt will appear on the balance sheet as salaries and wages payable. When it is paid on Friday, January 3, 20x2, cash will be decreased and the liability will be decreased (since nothing more is owed), but there will be no impact on expense. This is an example of an accrued expense: one that is incurred but not yet paid.

Another example of the matching principle is the treatment of rent expense. Rent expense consists of the cost of renting space for the business that was incurred during the accounting period even though the rent may have been paid in advance. For example, assume the lease requires one year of rent to be paid on December 1, 20x1 and the accounting time period ends on December 31. How much rent expense will appear on the income statement for the year ending December 31, 20x1?

The income statement will include the cost of 1 month (or 1/12) of the lease as rent expense, and the remaining 11 months (11/12) will be shown on the balance sheet as an asset: prepaid rent (see Figure 3.11). This is an example of a prepaid expense: one that is paid but not yet incurred.

Figure 3.11   Example of Prepaid Rent (Matching Principle)

December
End of fiscal year 20x1

Only 1/12th of the total lease cost is expensed in 20x1

January	February	March	April	May	June
20x2	20x2	20x2	20x2	20x2	20x2
July	**August**	**September**	**October**	**November**	
20x2	20x2	20x2	20x2	20x2	

The remaining 11/12ths of the total lease cost is expensed in 20x2

Most other expenses are treated similarly; they are reported as expenses of the period in which they were incurred. As a practical matter, most operating expenses are both incurred and eventually paid in the same accounting period, except for those that fall close to the beginning or end of the accounting period. Consequently, accountants realize the importance of looking for and analyzing prepaid and accrued expenses at the end of the accounting period to make sure they are reported properly.

Although almost all operating expenses require cash payments at or near the time they are incurred, certain types of operating expenses do not require cash payments. Depreciation expense is a common example of an operating expense that does not use any of the business's cash that is based on a different application of the matching principle. When a business purchases an asset that will be used in the company for a long time, such as office equipment, part of the cost of the asset is treated as an operating expense in each of the years in which it is used rather than treating its entire cost as an expense in the year in which it is purchased. The accounting profession considers this the proper treatment of these types of assets because the assets are used in the business for many years, helping the business generate revenues. In other words, it is another application of the matching principle. The annual expense is referred to as depreciation and will be explained in more detail in Chapters 4 and 5, along with other similar expenses, when the related balance sheet accounts are discussed.

The operating expense section of the income statement for Example Company is shown in Figure 3.12.

Figure 3.12   Operating Expense Detail

Operating Expenses	
Salaries and wages	$130,000
Depreciation	10,000
Advertising	20,000
Telephone and utilities	15,000
Supplies and postage	7,000
Insurance	9,000
Property taxes	5,000
Total operating expenses	$196,000

OPERATING INCOME (OR LOSS)

Operating income represents the profit earned by the business as a result of its primary business activity: revenues and expenses arising from the sale of goods. An operating loss is the opposite, representing the loss suffered by the business from its primary business activity. Other items affecting the overall profit of the business for the time period are shown in a separate category: other revenues and expenses.

OTHER REVENUES AND EXPENSES

This category of revenues and expenses sometimes is referred to as other income and expenses. It represents the activities affecting the profit or loss of a particular period which are not the result of the primary business activity (the sale of goods in the Example Company case). If material, the results of these activities should be separated from the normal operating activities, with each material item presented separately. Examples of what might be shown in this section of the income statement are listed in Figure 3.13.

Figure 3.13   Examples of Other Revenues and Other Expenses

Examples of Other Revenues:
- Interest earned on notes receivable
- Interest earned on investments
- Dividends earned on investments
- Rent earned from subleasing unused office space
- Gains on sales of business assets (e.g., an investment or equipment that no longer is needed)

Examples of Other Expenses:
- Interest incurred on borrowed money
- Losses on sales of business assets (e.g., an investment or equipment that no longer is needed)

The gains and losses on sales of business assets which are included in the above list of examples are based on the difference between the selling price of an asset and its cost. If an asset sells for more than it cost, a gain results. Conversely, if an asset sells for less than it cost, the company has suffered a loss.

The other income and expense section of the income statement for Example Company is shown in Figure 3.14.

Figure 3.14   Other Income and Expense Detail

Other Income and Expense	
Interest income	$ 1,000
Interest expense	(5,000)
Other Income and Expense, net	($4,000)

Net income (or net loss) is the last item on the income statement. It represents the net result of all revenues and other income earned during the period minus all costs and expenses incurred during the period, whether from the primary business activity or from other activities. Pulling together all the components of the income statement that we have discussed, Figure 3.15 shows a more detailed version of the income statement of Example Company.

Figure 3.15   Example of Detailed Income Statement

Example Company
Income Statement
For the Year Ended December 31, 20x1

Sales Revenue		
Gross Sales Revenue		$900,000
Less: Sales Returns and Allowances	$80,000	
Sales Discounts	20,000	(100,000)
Net Sales Revenue		800,000
Cost of Goods Sold		
Inventory, January 1, 20x1	40,000	
Add: Cost of Goods Purchased	525,000	
Cost of Goods Available for Sale	565,000	
Less: Inventory, December 31, 20x1	(65,000)	
Cost of Goods Sold		(500,000)
Gross Profit		300,000
Operating Expenses		
Salaries and wages	130,000	
Depreciation	10,000	
Advertising	20,000	
Telephone and utilities	15,000	
Supplies and postage	7,000	
Insurance	9,000	
Property taxes	5,000	
Total Operating Expenses		(196,000)
Operating Income		104,000
Other Income and Expense		
Interest income	1,000	
Interest expense	(5,000)	
Other Income and Expense, net		(4,000)
Net Income		$100,000

By using the Example Company income statement, you can answer several questions, as shown in Figure 3.16.

Figure 3.16 Examples of Questions That Can Be Answered
from the Income Statement

Question	Answer
Did the customers return any goods or receive any price allowances?	Yes (there is a balance of $80,000 in the sales returns and allowances account for the year)
How much of a gross profit was the company able to generate from selling its inventory?	$300,000 (on net sales of $800,000)
What was the amount of total operating expenses incurred during the year?	$196,000
How much of the total net income was generated by the primary business activity (the sale of goods)?	$104,000 (operating income)
What were the types of other revenues and expenses?	Interest income of $1,000 and interest expense of $5,000
Was the business profitable in 20x1?	Yes; the business earned a net income of $100,000 from all of its income-producing activities during the year

However, with the income statement alone there are some questions you cannot answer, such as the ones shown in Figure 3.17.

Figure 3.17 Examples of Questions That Cannot Be Answered from
the Income Statement

Question	To answer this question, the following information is needed
How much of the sales revenue was collected in cash during the year?	The balance sheet and/or the statement of cash flows
Were all of the operating expenses paid in cash during the year?	The balance sheet and/or the statement of cash flows
Is the company solvent (i.e., able to pay its bills as they become due)?	The balance sheet
How much of the business profits did the owner withdraw during the year?	The statement of cash flows and/or the statement of owner's equity
How do I know these income statement numbers are not materially misstated? In other words, can I rely on this information?	The independent auditor's report on the financial statements

Income Statement Format for A Business That Manufactures Its Products

When a business manufactures its goods for resale to its customers, additional information about manufacturing costs incurred may be presented in a separate schedule that is referred to as the manufacturing statement. The manufacturing statement presents a summary of the principal manufacturing costs, as shown in Figure 3.18.

Figure 3.18   Example of a Manufacturing Statement

X Company
Manufacturing Statement
For the Year Ended December 31, 20x1

Goods in process inventory, January 1, 20x1		$ 10,000
Add: Manufacturing costs incurred during the period		
Raw materials used	$270,000	
Direct labor	180,000	
Overhead	80,000	530,000
Total		540,000
Less: Goods in process inventory, December 31, 20x1		(15,000)
Cost of Goods Manufactured		$525,000

What do each of these elements represent?

- Goods in process at the beginning of the period represents the cost of raw materials, direct labor, and overhead incurred on goods in prior periods that have not been completed as of the beginning of the year. Additional materials, labor, and overhead costs are incurred during the year to finish manufacturing those goods as well as other goods started during the period. Goods in process at the end of the year represents the cost of materials, labor, and overhead on incomplete goods.
- Raw materials used represents the cost of materials that become part of the finished product during the year. For example, in an automobile manufacturing plant, raw materials would include steel, glass, tires, and so on.
- Direct labor is the cost of salaries and wages of employees directly involved in manufacturing goods. For example, the wages of employees who work on the assembly line in an automobile manufacturing plant installing windshields in the vehicles would be classified as direct labor. The salary of the company's chief executive officer cannot be traced directly to the manufacture of vehicles, and so that amount would not be classified as direct labor.

- Overhead represents all the indirect costs of production. Indirect costs cannot be traced directly to manufactured goods and include the salaries of supervisors, office supplies, depreciation of equipment or buildings, utilities, maintenance, marketing, advertising, salaries of company accountants and attorneys, and so forth. Each significant type of overhead cost may be disclosed separately.
- Cost of goods manufactured represents the cost of goods completed during the period that are ready for sale, similar to the cost of goods purchased by a business that purchases goods for resale.

The costs associated with manufactured goods would be shown as an expense of the accounting period in which the goods were sold because of the matching principle. The cost of unused raw materials on hand, the costs of partially completed goods, and the costs of unsold finished goods would be shown on the balance sheet as inventories. A manufacturer typically has three types of inventories: (1) raw materials, (2) goods in process or work in process, and (3) finished goods. The cost of these inventories will become part of cost of goods sold in future periods as the goods are completed and sold.

Income Statement for a Corporation

We will discuss corporations again in Chapter 4 when we go over the balance sheet and in more detail in Chapter 5; however, it is useful to see how the income statement for a corporation differs from the income statement for a sole proprietorship (Example Company) discussed earlier in this chapter (see Figure 3.19).

Figure 3.19   Example of a Corporation's Income Statement

Example Company, Inc.
Income Statement
For the Year Ended December 31, 20x1

Net Sales Revenue	$800,000
Cost of Goods Sold	(500,000)
Gross Profit	300,000
Operating Expenses	(196,000)
Operating Income	104,000
Other Income and Expenses, net	(4,000)
Income before Income Taxes	100,000
Income Tax Expense	(22,500)
Net Income	$ 77,500
Basic Earnings per Share	$ 7.75

The basic content of the corporation's income statement in Figure 3.19 is similar to what was presented for Example Company in Figure 3.5, with two basic differences: (1) income taxes and (2) earnings per share.

INCOME TAXES

A corporation is a separate legal entity, and as a separate entity it must pay income taxes on its profits. For a sole proprietorship and a partnership, each owner reports his or her share of the company's profits on his or her personal tax return, but the business itself does not pay taxes.

Note in Figure 3.19 that income before income taxes is $100,000: the same amount that was reported as net income in our earlier example for a sole proprietorship (Figure 3.5). Since this business entity is a corporation, income tax expense is shown as a cost of doing business on the corporation's income statement. Income tax expense represents income taxes incurred by the business entity on its accounting income regardless of whether the taxes have been paid in cash or will be paid in the future. The taxes incurred are calculated in accordance with the Internal Revenue Service's tax code, which is beyond the scope of this book. (Maybe there will be a book called *Taxes Demystified* someday.)

EARNINGS PER SHARE

A corporation is required to disclose the earnings associated with a share of common stock (the unit of ownership of a corporation). In a corporation, the stockholders are the owners of the company. In a sole proprietorship or a partnership, common stock does not exist, and so any kind of earnings per share calculation would be meaningless.

Earnings per share (EPS) is the corporation's net income divided by the number of shares of common stock outstanding, and so it represents a measure of the earnings associated with a single share of stock (the basic unit of ownership). In the above example, it was assumed there were 10,000 shares of common stock outstanding (i.e., out in the hands of the stockholders; in other words, owned by stockholders), so when the corporation earned $77,500 its EPS was $7.75.

EPS is a favorite measure of profitability among investors and Wall Street analysts, and companies pay close attention to their EPS for a specific period and from period to period because reported EPS can affect a corporation's stock price. There are two different types of EPS that can be reported on the income statement, which we will introduce you to next.

Basic or Simple Earnings Per Share

All corporations will report a basic (or simple) EPS. The formula is shown in Figure 3.20.

Figure 3.20   Basic or Simple Earnings per Share Formula

$$\text{Basic EPS} = \frac{\text{Net Income} - \text{Dividends on Preferred Stock}}{\text{Weighted average number of shares outstanding}}$$

Dividends are a distribution of the profits of a corporation to its stockholders. Preferred stock is a type of ownership interest that is different from that represented by common stock, and this concept will be explained more fully in the discussion of the balance sheet in Chapter 5. The numerator in the formula in Figure 3.20 represents the year's net income that is available to the common stockholders. Some corporations may have no preferred stock outstanding, in which case the numerator is simply net income.

The denominator represents the number of shares of common stock outstanding during the year, weighted by the period in which the shares were outstanding. What do we mean by "outstanding"? We mean that the shares are owned by the common stockholders: The shares have been issued to the stockholders, and they hold the shares. (There is some other terminology associated with shares of stock that we will introduce in Chapter 5 when we cover the stockholders' equity in the balance sheet in more detail.)

If a corporation has 10,000 shares of common stock outstanding all year long, the computation of the weighted average number of shares is quite simple: 10,000. But what happens if a corporation issues additional shares of stock during the year or possibly buys back some shares (called treasury stock and introduced in Chapter 5)? In these cases, the number of shares outstanding must be weighted by the fraction of the year during which they are outstanding. This sounds more complicated than it really is. Here is an example:

- Assume that Your Corporation, Inc., has 100,000 shares of common stock outstanding as of January 1, 20x1 (and the corporation has a fiscal year end of December 31).
- On April 1, 20x1, another 30,000 shares were issued for cash.

Question: What is the weighted average number of shares outstanding?

Answer: 122,500, which is calculated as $(100,000 \times 3/12) + (130,000 \times 9/12)$

How do we arrive at that number? The corporation began the year with 100,000 shares of common stock outstanding, and those shares were outstanding for three months. On April 1, another 30,000 shares were issued for cash, and so now a total of 130,000 shares was outstanding for the rest of the year (nine more months).

Note that in this example, the total number of shares outstanding at the end of the year (130,000) is not the denominator in the EPS calculation. That is the case because the additional assets (specifically, cash) received in April when the additional 30,000 shares were sold were not available to help the corporation become more profitable for the entire 12 months. Thus, EPS is computed more accurately by using the weighted average number of shares outstanding rather than the ending number of shares outstanding.

Diluted Earnings Per Share

Many but not all corporations also report diluted earnings per share. Diluted EPS will always be less than basic EPS. Diluted EPS represents the worst-case scenario for what could happen to EPS if additional shares of common stock were issued when a corporation also has issued certain other securities that can be exchanged for shares of common stock on a future date based upon the wishes of the holders of those securities. The actual computation of diluted EPS is more complicated than we describe here, and so, for our purposes, it is important that you understand that diluted EPS is a hypothetical worst-case scenario showing the lower amount of EPS that could result if additional common stock was issued. However, these convertible securities have not actually been exchanged for shares of common stock at this point.

The accounting profession requires that diluted EPS be presented for reasons of full disclosure, a concept that was explained in Chapter 2. If these other securities were actually converted into shares of common stock during the following year, the financial statement reader should not be surprised to see a decrease in EPS because additional shares of common stock are now outstanding.

Figure 3.21 shows the basic EPS and diluted EPS amounts reported by two well-known publicly traded corporations: Target and Kellogg's.

Figure 3.21   Comparison of Basic Earnings per Share and Diluted Earnings per Share for Two Corporations

Target Corp.	Basic EPS	Diluted EPS
2006	$3.23	$3.21
2005	$2.73	$2.71
2004	$2.09	$2.07
2003	$1.78	$1.76
2002	$1.52	$1.51
2001	$1.22	$1.21

Kellogg Co.	Basic EPS	Diluted EPS
2006	$2.53	$2.51
2005	$2.38	$2.36
2004	$2.16	$2.14
2003	$1.93	$1.92
2002	$1.77	$1.75

However, not all companies will report diluted EPS if they have what is called a simple capital structure; in other words, these companies do not have any potentially dilutive securities that if converted into shares of common stock could reduce (dilute) EPS. For example, Tootsie Roll, Inc. reports only basic EPS and explains in its financial statement footnotes that because the company has a simple capital structure with no potentially dilutive securities issued, it does not report a diluted EPS.

WHAT ABOUT DIVIDENDS?

You may have noticed throughout our discussion of the income statement that we did not show dividends declared and/or paid to stockholders as an expense. The reason for this is that dividends are not an expense of the business. Expenses are a cost of doing business and are incurred in providing services or selling goods or performing any other activity associated with the company's primary business activity. Dividends are a distribution of some of a corporation's profits to its owners—the stockholders—usually in the form of cash. As such, dividends do not belong on the income statement; instead, they appear on the statement of changes in stockholders' equity. For a sole proprietorship or a partnership, withdrawals represent a distribution of some of the business profits to the owner or owners, and, similar to dividends, owner withdrawals appear on the statement of changes in owner's equity and not on the income statement.

Variations in Income Statement Format

Income statements may be presented in different formats. Regardless of the format presented, you'll notice that the basic content of the income statement has not changed: it contains the revenues, expenses, and any gains or losses experienced by the company for the period of time being reported.

Multiple-Step Versus Single-Step Income Statement

The most common variations in income statement format are multiple-step versus single-step income statements. Our earlier examples were generally multiple-step income statements with several categories before reaching the bottom-line net income figure. The multiple-step format emphasizes the relationship of sales and cost of goods sold (through the computation of gross profit) and the operating versus nonoperating results.

The income statement presented next is in the single-step format, using the same amounts as before. The single-step format calculates the bottom-line net income figure in one single step by grouping all the revenues and other income

together, and grouping the expenses and losses. The single-step format does not emphasize the distinction between the primary operating and nonoperating status of each item (see Figure 3.22).

Figure 3.22 Example of a Single-Step Income Statement for a Corporation

Example Company, Inc.
Income Statement
For the Year Ended December 31, 20x1

Revenues		
Net Sales Revenue	$800,000	
Other Income	1,000	
Total Revenue		$801,000
Expenses		
Cost of Goods Sold	500,000	
Selling, General, and Administrative Expenses	196,000	
Other Expenses	5,000	
Income Tax Expense	22,500	
Total Costs and Expenses		(723,500)
Net Income		$ 77,500
Basic Earnings per Share		$ 7.75

The full disclosure and materiality concepts affect the amount of detail in the income statement and the number and depth of explanations or detailed schedules needed in the footnotes to the financial statements.

Quiz for Chapter 3

1. Which of the following items belong on the income statement?
    a. Assets and liabilities
    b. Revenues and expenses
    c. Assets and equity
    d. Unearned revenues and prepaid expenses

2. Net income is computed as:
    a. Gross margin minus cost of goods sold
    b. Cost of goods sold minus operating expenses
    c. Revenues minus expenses
    d. Assets minus liabilities

3. Gross profit:
   a. Is the same as net income
   b. Represents the excess of net sales revenue over cost of goods sold
   c. Is the excess of the cash received on sales over the cash paid for goods sold
   d. Equals revenues minus operating expenses

4. When a company provides a service to a customer, the revenue is recorded when:
   a. The cash is received
   b. The company performs the service
   c. The company bills the customer
   d. It is certain the customer is not going to complain about the quality of the service

5. Which of the following is not an example of an expense?
   a. Dividends
   b. Utilities
   c. Rent
   d. Depreciation

6. Which of the following forms of business will report income tax expense on its income statement?
   a. Sole proprietorship
   b. Partnership
   c. Corporation
   d. All of the above

7. Cost of goods sold equals the cost of merchandise:
   a. Purchased this year, whether with cash or by credit
   b. Purchased with cash this year
   c. Sold to the customers this year for which cash payment has been received
   d. Sold to the customers this year

8. An accrued expense:
   a. Is one that has been incurred but not yet paid
   b. Is not recorded unless it has been paid in cash
   c. Is paid in advance but not yet incurred
   d. Occurs only with the cash basis of accounting

9. Which of the following is not one of the inventory classifications that a manufacturing business will have on its manufacturing statement?
   a. Overhead
   b. Raw materials
   c. Work in process
   d. Finished goods

10. Earnings per share:
    a. Is calculated for all forms of business (sole proprietorships, partnerships, and corporations)
    b. Is computed for both common stock and preferred stock
    c. Is always presented in two forms: basic and diluted
    d. Is a profitability measure that shows the earnings associated with a single share of common stock

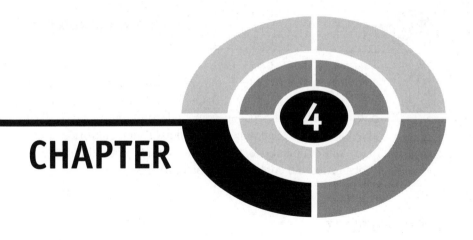

CHAPTER 4

The Balance Sheet:

Classifications and Concepts

Chapters 1 and 2 introduced you to the basic form and content of financial statements and the underlying concepts of financial reporting; that was followed by a more detailed discussion of the income statement and related concepts in Chapter 3. We will take a closer look at the balance sheet and the statement of owners' equity in this chapter and again in Chapter 5.

We begin this chapter with a brief overview of the basic concepts, form, and content of the balance sheet. The next section focuses on the concepts and guidelines used to classify the various assets and liabilities into meaningful and useful categories and provides brief descriptions of the items you are likely to find in each category. The final section of the chapter discusses how owners' equity is presented in the balance sheet and in the statement of owners' equity.

By the end of this chapter, you will have a better understanding of important balance sheet concepts and classifications, but there is still much more to learn in your quest to understand financial statements. We will revisit each of the balance sheet

classifications in Chapter 5 and will discuss the unique characteristics and financial reporting impact of many items in much more detail. The examples and concepts in both chapters will broaden your understanding of not only the balance sheet but also the income statement and financial statement disclosures.

As was stated above, this chapter begins with a brief overview of the basic concepts, form, and content of the balance sheet.

Basic Format

The balance sheet presents the assets, liabilities, and equity of the business owner or owners, representing the financial position of a business at a moment in time. The balance sheet also is referred to as a statement of financial position.

Balance Sheet = Statement of Financial Position

Recall that the income statement presents the results of business transactions that took place during a specific period; this is somewhat like reporting the events as you watch a video unfold. Reading the balance sheet, by contrast, is somewhat like seeing a still frame shot as you hit the pause button; it is a snapshot of the assets, liabilities, and equity at that moment in time. It is important to note that the balance sheet may provide a much different view if you hit pause at a different moment in time.

Income Statement = Events Taking Place During a Period of Time
Balance Sheet = Snapshot Taken at a Moment in Time

A simple balance sheet for Example Company appears in Figure 4.1, followed by a brief overview of some basic terms and concepts.

Figure 4.1 Example Company Balance Sheet December 31, 20x1

Assets	$1,000,000
Liabilities	$ 600,000
Owners' Equity	400,000
Total Liabilities and Equity	$1,000,000

- Assets represent the economic resources of a business.
- Parties with an interest in or a claim to the business assets are referred to as either creditors or owners.
- Liabilities are obligations of the business or creditor claims to the assets.
- Equity represents the residual interest or the owners' claims to the assets of the business.

As was discussed in Chapter 1, the balance sheet is based on a simple equation, presenting the assets, liabilities, and equity of a business at a specific moment in time:

ASSETS = LIABILITIES + EQUITY
$1,000,000 = $600,000 + $400,000
Economic   Creditor   Owner
Resources   Claims   Claims

Sometimes the balance sheet is presented with assets on the left and liabilities and equity on the right, further illustrating the equality of the balance sheet equation, as is shown in Figure 4.2.

Figure 4.2 Example Company Balance Sheet December 31, 20x1

Assets	$1,000,000	Liabilities	$ 600,000
		Owners' Equity	400,000
		Total	$1,000,000

When the balance sheet equation is rearranged, it accentuates the residual nature of the owners' interest in the business and why owners' equity often is referred to as net assets or net worth.

ASSETS − LIABILITIES = EQUITY Net Assets
$1,000,000 − $600,000 = $400,000 Net Worth

The term *net assets* is used more commonly in business conversations, though the term *net worth* is used more commonly in referring to an individual's wealth. Bill Gates is a noteworthy front-runner.

Assets

Assets represent economic resources of the business, which may be tangible (such as cash, supplies, and equipment) or intangible (such as patents and goodwill). Assets also may represent amounts due from other parties, such as accounts and notes receivable, or prepaid expenses. Assets initially are reported on the balance sheet at their cost, which is an objective, verifiable measure of their value at the time they are acquired.

Liabilities

Liabilities represent obligations of the business such as accounts and notes payable or accrued expenses such as salaries, taxes, and interest payable. Liabilities also may include obligations to provide services or goods in the future for which a customer may have paid in advance. Liabilities generally are recorded at cost; this is determined by the cost of the goods or services received for which payment is due. Liabilities may be viewed as creditor claims to the assets of the business.

Equity

As was discussed above, equity represents the owners' interest in or claims to the assets of the business. However, as was discussed earlier, the claims of creditors (suppliers, lenders, and others) come first, before the claims of the owners; thus, owners' equity is a residual interest in the assets owned by a business.

Assets − Liabilities (Creditor Claims) = Equity

A business can be structured using one of many different forms of ownership, each with its own unique advantages and disadvantages. It may be a sole proprietorship owned and operated by a single owner or be structured as a partnership or a corporation with multiple owners (this is discussed further in Chapter 5). In a sole proprietorship or partnership, the equity of each owner is referred to as *capital*, and the term *stockholders' equity* applies to a corporation.

Business Form	Ownership	Terminology
Sole Proprietorship	Single owner	Capital
Partnership	Two or more owners	Capital
Corporation	Multiple owners	Stockholders' Equity

Although you may tend to think of owners as individuals like yourself, other companies, pension and mutual funds, and a variety of other parties may hold ownership positions in a company. Regardless of the business structure or the nature of the parties with ownership, owners' equity in the balance sheet includes amounts the owners originally invested in the business and subsequent profits which were reinvested (retained) by the business rather than returned to the owners.

Owners' Equity = Investments + Profits Retained (Reinvested)

Classified Balance Sheet

The information presented in a balance sheet is much more meaningful and useful if significant items are shown separately and related items are grouped in some sort of classification scheme, just as an income statement is more useful when the results of routine, ongoing operating activities (sales, cost of goods sold, and operating expenses) are presented first and clearly distinguishable from nonrecurring or some-what incidental events. In accordance with the basic concepts of materiality and full disclosure that were discussed in Chapter 2, information is significant and thus material if it would influence the decision of a reasonable financial statement user. Just as each material revenue and expense is reported separately (immaterial items may be combined), each material asset and liability should be shown separately in the balance sheet, and the information is more useful when related items appear together or are reported under descriptive categories.

A condensed version of a classified balance sheet appears in Figure 4.3. As you will notice, the balance sheet has several categories listed under the assets, liability, and equity headings. We will discuss the reasons for this classification scheme below.

Figure 4.3 Example Company Balance Sheet December 31, 20x1

Assets		
Current Assets	$300,000	
Long-term Investments	50,000	
Property, Plant and Equipment	400,000	
Natural Resources	150,000	
Intangible Assets	100,000	
Total Assets		$1,000,000
Liabilities and Owners' Equity		
Liabilities		
Current Liabilities	$200,000	
Long-Term Liabilities	400,000	
Total Liabilities		$ 600,000
Owners' Equity		400,000
Total Liabilities and Owners' Equity		$1,000,000

The discussion which follows first focuses on the current asset and current and long-term liability classifications. Other asset and owners' equity classifications are discussed in the final portion of the chapter.

Current Assets

Current assets include cash, along with other assets that generally will be converted to cash or sold or used within a year and are listed on the balance sheet in order of liquidity, a relative term that indicates how soon or how easily these assets will produce cash the business can use to purchase more assets and/or pay off its short-term obligations when they come due.

The current asset section of the balance sheet typically includes the items in Figure 4.4, listed in order of liquidity. Only brief explanations of each item are provided below; we will focus on the unique characteristics of current assets and other categories of assets in much more detail later in this chapter.

Figure 4.4   Examples of Current Assets

Current Assets		
Cash and Cash Equivalents	$109,280	
Short-term Investments	130,000	
Accounts Receivable	45,000	
Notes Receivable	2,000	
Accrued Receivables	20	
Related Party Receivables	1,000	
Inventories	8,700	
Prepaid Expenses	4,000	
Total Current Assets		$300,000

- **Cash**: currency and coins on hand, amounts on deposit, undeposited cash receipts, and cash register and petty cash funds
- **Cash equivalents**: a special category of investments that can be sold quickly and easily; often combined with cash on the balance sheet
- **Short-term investments**: temporary investments of excess cash to earn interest or dividends
- **Accounts receivable**: amounts owed by customers who purchased goods or services on credit, perhaps due in 30 days; may be referred to as trade receivables
- **Notes receivable**: formal promissory notes with specific maturity dates, interest rates, and repayment terms
- **Accrued receivables** (or **accrued revenues**): amounts a company has earned but not yet collected, such as interest on loans or investments, or rent
- **Related party receivables**: amounts owed to the company by affiliated companies, such as subsidiaries; reported separately from customer receivables

- **Inventories**: merchandise held for resale or, for a manufacturing business, raw materials on hand, work in process, and unsold finished goods
- **Prepaid expenses**: supplies and postage on hand or rent or insurance premiums paid in advance

Current Assets and Liquidity

As was mentioned earlier, current assets are presented in order of liquidity. Cash is listed first as it is immediately available for any purpose. Short-term investments can be sold immediately if the business runs short on cash. If a company extends credit to its customers, it can expect to collect most of its accounts receivable within the credit period (often 30 days) or perhaps earlier if customers take advantage of the cash discount terms discussed in Chapter 3 and to collect the principal and interest when due on short-term notes. In addition, some businesses sell or borrow against their accounts and notes receivable to generate cash more quickly. Cash, short-term investments, and receivables are referred to as *quick current assets* as they are the most liquid and generate cash in a very short time frame.

However, inventory is another matter. For a business that sells merchandise or manufactures and sells goods, it may take a considerable amount of time before the goods actually are sold (if at all) and the customer accounts are collected. Inventory is not as liquid as most other current assets and thus appears near the bottom of the list of current assets.

CURRENT ASSETS: MORE DETAILS

The guideline used to distinguish current assets is actually more specific than was mentioned earlier. Current assets consist of cash or other assets that will be converted to cash, sold, or consumed within a year or within the operating cycle of the business, whichever is longer. Most customers will pay for the goods or services they received at some point, the inventory will be sold, and the company eventually will receive cash from its customers; other receivables, such as interest earned on loans and investments, will be received in cash; and prepaid expenses such as supplies, rent, and insurance will be used or consumed.

CURRENT ASSETS AND THE OPERATING CYCLE

The term *operating cycle* refers to the length of time it takes for an investment in inventory to be converted to cash; this means the length of time it takes for inventory to be sold and for customer accounts to be collected.

Operating Cycle: Inventory → Sale (Accounts Receivable) → Cash

For some businesses, such as a produce store or a meat shop, the operating cycle may be only a few days, whereas the operating cycle for a retail clothing store may be a few months if it sells seasonal apparel. At the other end of the spectrum, the operating cycle for a construction company specializing in large-scale projects that take years to complete or a company producing aged liquor products may span several years. Therefore, within the current asset classification, there can be considerable diversity depending on the nature of the business involved. Along with key financial ratios you will learn about in Chapter 8, the length of time it takes to sell the product and collect the amounts owed by customers is an important consideration in evaluating a company's liquidity.

CURRENT VERSUS LONG-TERM LIABILITIES

From the discussion above, it makes sense that current liabilities are generally obligations that must be fulfilled or debts that must be repaid within a year and that long-term liabilities are not due for at least a year or perhaps will not be settled in full for many years. The distinction between current and long-term assets and liabilities is significant. Such classifications provide valuable information about liquidity, which refers not only to how quickly current assets will generate cash but also to a company's ability to meet its short-term obligations as they become due.

The current liability section of a balance sheet typically includes the items shown in Figure 4.5. Only brief explanations of each item are provided in this chapter; we will focus on the unique characteristics of both current and long-term liabilities in much more detail in Chapter 5.

Figure 4.5   Examples of Current Liabilities

Current Liabilities		
Accounts Payable	$81,000	
Notes Payable	10,000	
Estimated Warranty Obligations	30,000	
Unearned Revenues	8,000	
Accrued Liabilities	600	
Payroll Tax Liabilities	9,400	
Income Taxes Payable	48,000	
Dividends Payable	10,000	
Current Portion of Long-term Debt	3,000	
Total Current Liabilities		$200,000

- **Accounts payable**: amounts the company owes to suppliers and others for goods and services purchased on credit
- **Notes payable**: formal promissory notes with specific maturity dates, interest rates, and repayment terms
- **Estimated warranty obligations**: estimated costs of repairs and replacements for products sold under warranty
- **Unearned revenues**: amounts a company received from customers in advance, including sales of gift certificates, subscriptions, future rent, and customer deposits for special orders
- **Accrued liabilities** (or **accrued expenses**): expenses for which the company has not yet paid, such as salaries and wages, interest on notes payable, and utilities
- **Payroll tax liabilities**: payroll taxes withheld from employees and employer payroll taxes which have not yet been paid to the taxing authorities
- **Income taxes payable**: income taxes the company owes on the basis of its estimated or completed income tax return for the year
- **Dividends payable**: cash dividends declared by a corporation's board of directors to distribute a portion of corporate earnings to the stockholders
- **Current portion of long-term debt**: the amount due and payable in the coming year on a long-term loan, such as the next year's monthly payments on a 30-year mortgage note payable

CURRENT LIABILITIES AND LIQUIDITY

If current assets consist of cash and other assets that will generate cash soon and current liabilities are obligations that must be settled or debts that must be repaid soon, the relationship between current assets and current liabilities seems quite important. In fact, much attention is focused on this in evaluating a company's liquidity: its ability to meet its currently maturing obligations.

For example, have you ever worried about making your monthly mortgage payment on time because your next payday falls a couple days after the due date? Or maybe you just changed jobs, and although you will be paid a higher salary, your first paycheck will be delayed. Your house is worth $300,000 and your loan balance is $160,000, and so you could pay off the loan in full easily if you sold your house. Your net worth is $140,000 and you are solvent, meaning that you have more assets than liabilities. But you plan to live in your house, not sell it; you will have your paycheck soon, but you need a few more days to make this month's mortgage payment.

But what if you have been laid off and can't find a new job? At first, it might seem like a temporary cash crunch, but when you still haven't landed a new job after several months, it is a much bigger problem. You aren't very liquid, and if this goes on for too long, you no longer will be solvent.

Similarly, a business may face a temporary cash crunch, but over the long run, if it continues to have problems coming up with enough cash from its normal operations to pay its bills on time (or in your case, a regular paycheck), it (you) cannot survive indefinitely. Suppliers may discontinue extending credit and demand to be paid in cash at the time of purchase or service. Banks may become unwilling to make even a short-term loan when the borrower's ability to repay it on time, if at all, is in question. Even if the bank approves a loan, it may be at a high interest rate to compensate for this additional risk.

WORKING CAPITAL AND THE CURRENT RATIO

Working capital is a term used commonly to describe the relationship between current assets and current liabilities; it provides an indication of a company's short-term liquidity: its ability to pay its current obligations when due using cash it generates from its routine operations. Working capital is the excess of current assets (which generate cash) over current liabilities (which use cash). For example, a company with $300,000 of current assets and $200,000 of current liabilities has $100,000 of working capital.

$$\begin{array}{ccccc} \textbf{Current Assets} & - & \textbf{Current Liabilities} & = & \textbf{Working Capital} \\ \$300,000 & - & \$200,000 & = & \$100,000 \end{array}$$

It would seem that this company is in a better position to be able to repay its short-term obligations on time and has a fairly good cushion in case something unexpected arises than is a company that also has $300,000 of current assets but has $295,000 of current liabilities and only $5,000 of working capital.

The relationship between current assets and current liabilities also can be expressed as a ratio that indicates the amount of current assets for every dollar of current liabilities, also indicating whether there is an acceptable cushion. In this case, one would say the company has 1.5 times as many current assets as current liabilities, or $1.50 of current assets for every $1.00 of current liabilities.

$$\frac{\text{Current Assets}}{\text{Current Liabilities}} = \frac{\$300,000}{\$200,000} = 1.5 \text{ to } 1$$

We will discuss several key benchmarks commonly used to analyze a business, including working capital and other measures used to assess a company's liquidity, in Chapter 8.

CURRENT LIABILITIES: MORE DETAILS

As with current assets, the guideline used to distinguish current liabilities is more specific than was mentioned earlier. Current liabilities are obligations that are due within a year or within the operating cycle of the business, whichever is longer, and are settled by using current assets or through the creation of other current liabilities.

We discussed the concept of the operating cycle earlier and defined it as the length of time required to convert an investment in inventory back into cash. You already understand that a produce store or a meat shop may have an operating cycle of a few days, whereas a clothing retailer may have four operating cycles within a year if it stocks seasonal apparel and a construction contractor or liquor producer may have an operating cycle that spans several years.

But along with the operating cycle, there are other factors that must be considered in deciding under which category some liabilities should be reported. Sometimes certain liabilities are reported in both the current and long-term liability classifications of the balance sheet. For example, if a business has a 30-year mortgage note payable which it used to finance the purchase of land and its office building, one most likely would classify the mortgage note payable as a long-term liability. However, if the business is required to make monthly installment payments on the loan, the monthly principal payments for the coming year should be classified as a current liability, whereas the remaining principal balance of the loan should be classified as long-term.

Thus, you might find the *current portion of long-term debt* included among the current liabilities, which represents the portion of the loan principal balance that must be repaid within the coming year. The remaining loan balance will be reported as a long-term liability as this amount is not payable for at least one year in the future. The current versus long-term classification depends on when obligations are due and what resources will be used to settle those obligations.

To complicate matters, the second part of the definition of a current liability also requires a bit more explanation. Current liabilities are obligations which will be settled by using current assets or through the creation of other current liabilities. Let's assume your business sells gift certificates or gift cards that the recipient can present to receive products you sell in your store. Is this a current liability? Yes: The obligation will be settled by using a current asset: the merchandise inventory chosen when the gift certificate is redeemed.

Perhaps your business has a 90-day note payable to the bank, but rather than requiring you to pay it off and negotiate another new loan, the bank permits you to replace it with another 90-day loan. Is this a current liability? Yes: The obligation will be settled through the creation of another current liability: another 90-day note payable.

Another example pertains to dividends, a way corporations return part of the business's profits to their owners (stockholders). A corporation can declare a cash dividend to be paid to the stockholders at a specified future date; this sounds like, and is, a current liability. But if it is a *stock dividend*, meaning that the corporation plans to give the owners more shares of stock in the corporation, it is not a current liability because it will not be settled by using cash but rather with equity: more shares of stock.

Let's turn to another example that requires a bit more thought. Corporations often borrow substantial amounts of money for long periods by issuing bonds payable (discussed in more detail in Chapter 5). The corporation generally is required to pay the interest owed each year (usually every six months) but does not have to pay back the amount borrowed for many years, maybe not for 100 years, as in the case of the Walt Disney Company bonds issued a few years ago. For the first 99 years, the bonds payable would appear as a long-term liability on Disney's balance sheet. But where is this liability reported at the end of year 99?

If Disney must repay the bonds within the coming year, it seems that it should be classified as a current liability. In most cases, bonds payable maturing within the coming year would be a current liability, but what if Disney created a fund, setting money aside each year to pay off the bonds when due, and the fund could not be used for any other purpose? Should the bonds payable within the coming year be reported as a current liability in this case? Probably not; Disney has a fund set aside for this purpose and will not use its current assets to pay the obligation.

The system of classifying liabilities into current and long-term categories provides valuable information even though one has to think carefully about the sources of money that are available to settle some types of obligations.

LONG-TERM LIABILITIES

Although it might have been more logical to discuss all the asset classifications first and then discuss liability and equity categories, we hope you can appreciate the importance of the current versus noncurrent asset and liability distinctions as they are covered in this sequence. As was mentioned earlier, we will provide a much more detailed discussion of liabilities and equity in Chapter 5, but it is important to give you a preliminary idea of what you might see under the long-term liability classification of a balance sheet. That section of a balance sheet typically includes the items in Figure 4.6.

Figure 4.6   Examples of Long-Term Liabilities

Long-Term Liabilities		
Notes Payable	$10,000	
Mortgage Notes Payable	97,000	
Capital Lease Obligations	137,000	
Pension Obligations	60,000	
Bonds Payable	92,000	
Deferred Income Tax Liabilities	4,000	
Total Long-Term Liabilities		$400,000

- **Notes payable**: formal promissory notes with specific maturity dates, interest rates, and repayment terms; generally not due for at least one year
- **Mortgage notes payable**: the principal balance of a note payable used to finance the purchase of plant assets, with the assets pledged as collateral for the loan
- **Capital lease obligations**: the obligation to make future lease payments under the terms of a long-term capital lease agreement which is, in substance, similar to financing the acquisition of an asset with long-term debt
- **Pension and postretirement obligations**: obligations to provide pension and other benefits that employees have earned and are entitled to receive in the future
- **Bonds payable**: a common form of long-term borrowing used by corporations to raise substantial amounts of money for long periods; interest payments generally are paid semiannually, but the principal amount borrowed may not be due for many years in the future
- **Deferred income tax liabilities**: income taxes that may be due in future years, arising from differences in accounting and taxable income

A Quick Review

Let's take a moment to review the key concepts discussed so far in this chapter. The balance sheet presents assets, liabilities, and equity, providing a snapshot of a company's financial position at a moment in time, and sometimes is referred to as a statement of financial position. The way individual items are classified and the order in which they are listed provide useful information.

Current assets include cash, short-term investments, receivables, inventory, and prepaid expenses. Along with cash, the other current assets are expected to generate cash in the near term, generally within a year, and are listed in order of liquidity, a relative term indicating how soon or how easily these assets will produce cash. Liabilities are obligations that must be settled or debts that must be repaid and are classified as either current or long-term.

Current liabilities are generally due within a year and will be settled by using current assets. The relationship between current assets and current liabilities is useful in evaluating a company's liquidity. Working capital—the excess of current assets over current liabilities—and the current ratio and other measures provide information about a company's ability to meet its current obligations.

The next section will take a closer look at other asset categories, and then the chapter will conclude by discussing the owners' equity portion of the balance sheet.

Noncurrent Assets

A balance sheet presents several other types of asset categories that appear below the current asset heading, typically including those being used in business operations or investments held to achieve a particular long-term business objective. They may be tangible physical assets the business owns or has the right to use, intangible assets which convey specific legal rights to the business and have value even though one cannot touch or feel them, funds set aside to repay long-term debt, or perhaps investments in other companies to maintain a beneficial business relationship.

These assets generally are not held for sale and thus are not a ready source of cash, in contrast to short-term investments, inventory, and other items presented in the current asset classification. The terms *noncurrent* and *long-term, long-lived,* or *fixed* assets are all broad references commonly used to describe this group of assets.

The asset section of the balance sheet for Example Company introduced earlier in this chapter appears in Figure 4.7, followed by a discussion of each major category.

Figure 4.7   Example Company Balance Sheet (partial) December 31, 20x1

Assets		
Current Assets	$300,000	
Long-term Investments	50,000	
Property, Plant, and Equipment	400,000	
Natural Resources	150,000	
Intangible Assets	100,000	
Total Assets		$1,000,000

LONG-TERM INVESTMENTS

Investments appearing in this category often are made to achieve a long-term business objective or as a result of a contractual requirement. The investments are expected to be held for more than a year, perhaps for many years, unlike investments classified as current assets, which are viewed as a ready source of cash to cover short-term needs.

Long-term investments in equity and debt securities (such as stocks and bonds) of other companies may be held to generate dividend and interest income and gains from market value appreciation. Investments also may be made to establish and maintain a beneficial long-term business relationship or may represent a substantial ownership position in another company or in a joint venture arrangement. Land or other assets held for investment or future expansion purposes and funds set aside and invested to provide for the eventual payment of long-term debt or pension obligations also are included in long-term investments. Figure 4.8 shows the types of investments that may be classified as long-term.

Figure 4.8 Examples of Long-Term Investments

Long-Term Investments:		
Available for Sale Securities	$5,000	
Held to Maturity Securities	15,600	
Bond Sinking Fund	8,000	
Pension Fund Assets	6,080	
Investments in Affiliated Companies	4,320	
Joint Venture Investments	1,000	
Land Held for Investment Purposes	10,000	
Total Long-Term Investments		$50,000

- **Available for sale securities**: investments in equity or debt securities (stocks and bonds) of other companies which are expected to generate income from cash dividends and interest and/or market price appreciation. Such investments also may be referred to as *marketable securities* as they can be purchased and sold readily in the financial markets and can be classified as either current or long-term, based on the company's intent.
- **Held to maturity debt securities**: investments in debt securities, such as corporate or government bonds, which the investor intends to hold until they mature, perhaps many years from now.
- **Bond sinking fund**: a fund established to repay bonds payable or other long-term debt at maturity. The fund may consist of investments in stocks and bonds, but unlike other long-term investments, the earnings and proceeds from the sale of these investments can be used only to repay a specific obligation at maturity; thus, it is reported separately from other long-term investments.
- **Pension fund assets**: funds set aside and invested for the purpose of meeting future obligations for employee pension plans and similar obligations.

- **Investments in affiliated companies**: stock investments made for the purpose of establishing and maintaining a beneficial long-term business relationship, perhaps with an important supplier or distributor. These investments represent substantial ownership positions in other companies, typically between 20 and 50 percent.
- **Joint venture investments**: companies may join forces, with each party contributing unique expertise and/or resources, to take on a large-scale or risky endeavor which none could finance or conduct alone. The venture parties may establish and invest in a separate entity or invest resources to be used in joint venture activities which are governed by a legal agreement.
- **Land held for investment purposes**: land purchased for future expansion or for speculative purposes with the expectation that it will appreciate in value. Land currently being used in business operations would be reported under property, plant, and equipment.

PROPERTY, PLANT, AND EQUIPMENT

Property, plant, and equipment, sometimes referred to as *plant assets* or *fixed assets*, includes tangible physical assets currently being used in business operations. Although these assets can be sold or exchanged, they generally are not held for sale in the normal course of business. Along with land, buildings, equipment, furniture, and fixtures, a building under construction for a company's own use may be reported in this classification, and even assets the company is leasing may be included if the lease terms are in substance similar to ownership. The property, plant, and equipment section of a balance sheet typically includes the items in Figure 4.9.

Figure 4.9   Examples of Property, Plant, and Equipment

Property, Plant, and Equipment		
Land	$ 95,000	
Buildings	196,000	
Machinery and Equipment	72,000	
Furniture and Fixtures	30,000	
Construction in Progress	7,000	
Total Property, Plant, and Equipment		$400,000

As was discussed earlier, these assets initially are valued at their cost when acquired and a portion of the cost is reported in the income statement as *depreciation expense* during each year of use, in accordance with the matching principle. Most plant assets depreciate; they wear out or become less efficient or obsolete and eventually must be replaced, with the exception of land, which is permanent in nature and is not depreciated. A depreciable asset such as equipment is reported in the balance sheet as shown in Figure 4.10.

Figure 4.10   Balance Sheet Reporting for a Depreciable Asset

Equipment	$100,000	
Less: Accumulated Depreciation	(28,000)	
Equipment (net)		$72,000

The original (historical) cost of the equipment was $100,000. Accumulated depreciation of $28,000 represents the total amount of depreciation expense to this point. Equipment (net) is the undepreciated cost, which often is referred to as *book value*. Equipment also may be presented in the manner shown in Figure 4.11.

Figure 4.11   Balance Sheet Reporting for a Depreciable Asset, Net

Equipment (net of accumulated depreciation of $28,000)	$72,000

In Chapter 5, we will discuss factors used to determine the cost of a plant asset and the concepts and methods used to calculate depreciation expense.

NATURAL RESOURCES

Natural resources on the balance sheet include ownership or legal rights to minerals, petroleum, timber, and other creations of nature that can be extracted or harvested from the land and then sold in an unprocessed state or processed and sold. A lumber or paper products company may own its forestland or purchase the rights to harvest trees from the owner of the land or the government. An oil producer may lease the land from the property owner and make royalty payments in exchange for the drilling and production rights.

A company engaging in removing natural resources is quite similar to a manufacturing business except that the raw materials are acquired from nature rather than purchased from suppliers. As was discussed in Chapter 3, the inventory reported for a manufacturing company consists of the raw materials, direct labor, and overhead costs incurred to manufacture its product. These costs are not reported as operating expenses during manufacturing; instead, they are expenses when the inventory is sold and will be reflected in the amount reported as cost of goods sold in the income statement.

$$\left.\begin{array}{l}\text{Raw Materials} \\ \text{Direct Labor} \\ \text{Overhead}\end{array}\right\} \rightarrow \text{Inventory} \rightarrow \text{Cost of Goods Sold}$$

However, the natural resource producer does not purchase its raw materials; it acquires them from nature. The accounting concept of *depletion* is similar to the concept of depreciation that was discussed earlier. A part of the cost of the natural resource is allocated to each period of production, and the depletion cost in each period is treated in the same manner as the raw material cost for a manufacturer. A mining company may report its natural resources on the balance sheet as is shown in Figure 4.12, identical to the manner used to report equipment in the earlier example.

Figure 4.12   Balance Sheet Reporting for a Natural Resource

Palladium Mine	$200,000,000	
Less: Accumulated Depletion	(50,000,000)	
Palladium Mine (net)		$150,000,000
OR		
Palladium Mine (net of accumulated depletion of $50,000,000)		$150,000,000

The cost of the natural resource was $200,000,000. Accumulated depletion of $50,000,000 represents the total amount of depletion expense to this point. However, as will be discussed further in Chapter 5, there are several unique costs associated with acquiring and developing a natural resource, with some costs capitalized and others expensed. We also will discuss how the amount of depletion may be determined.

INTANGIBLE ASSETS

Intangible assets represent the cost of assets acquired by a business that lack physical substance, often consisting of legal or contractual rights such as copyrights, patents, franchises, licenses, and trademarks or trade names. If a company negotiates the purchase of an existing business, the acquired company's customer mailing list may be treated as an intangible asset even though it may be difficult to pinpoint its precise value.

Goodwill is also an intangible asset, something unidentifiable associated with the ability of the business to generate favorable earnings from the quality of management, the reputation of the business, the loyalty of customers, or other factors. As a result, one might be willing to acquire the business at a price higher than the value of the specific assets it owns, which is the accounting concept of goodwill. Brief explanations of some common intangible assets appear in Figure 4.13.

Figure 4.13 Examples of Intangible Assets

Patents	A patent provides the holder a legal right to use a particular process or manufacture or sell a product for a period of 20 years
Copyrights	A copyright protects literary, musical, and artistic creations and gives the holder the right to reproduce or sell the work for the life of the creator plus 70 years
Trademarks and Trade Names	A legal right to exclusive use of a word, phrase or logo; if registered, it can be renewed indefinitely every 10 years
Licenses and Franchises	Contractual arrangements granting rights to sell products or services, such as operating a fast-food restaurant or hotel chain
Goodwill	The excess cost of acquiring a company over the fair value of the specifically identifiable assets acquired and liabilities assumed

Although intangible assets will be discussed further in Chapter 5, there are a couple of important things that should be mentioned now. First, the intangible assets presented on the balance sheet are only those which have been purchased or acquired. For example, a company may have developed its own valuable customer mailing list, but that would not appear on its balance sheet as an intangible asset because it was internally developed. However, if it was sold to another company, the purchaser would include the cost of the mailing list as an intangible asset. The same is true with goodwill; it may exist but is not recorded as an intangible asset unless it is purchased.

Another example is a company which spent $5 million on research and development (R&D) activities and ultimately acquired a new patent for which it paid $10,000 in legal and registration fees. Only the $10,000 legal and registration fees would appear as the cost of the patent on its balance sheet; the $5 million R&D costs were expensed. Maybe the patent has a value of $20 million because of the exclusive right and competitive advantage it provides, but it appears on the balance sheet at its direct cost of $10,000. However, if it is sold to another party for its value, the purchaser will show the patent on its balance sheet at $20 million, which is the purchaser's acquisition cost.

These examples illustrate a key concept pertaining to intangible assets. Internal development costs, including R&D costs, are expensed; only the direct costs of acquiring intangible assets are included on the balance sheet.

Just as with other long-lived assets, for most intangible assets, a portion of the cost is treated as an expense of each period of use. The term used for intangible assets is *amortization expense,* but the concept is similar to that of depreciation of plant assets and depletion of natural resources discussed earlier.

Owners' Equity

This chapter concludes with a discussion of the owners' equity portion of the balance sheet and the related statement of owners' equity. Recall that the balance sheet is based on a simple equation, presenting the assets, liabilities, and equity of a business at a specific moment in time, as shown below.

$$\textbf{ASSETS} \; = \; \textbf{LIABILITIES} \; + \; \textbf{EQUITY}$$

ASSETS	LIABILITIES	EQUITY
Economic	Creditor	Owner
Resources	Claims	Claims

Or, rearranged:

$$\textbf{ASSETS} \; - \; \textbf{LIABILITIES} \; = \; \textbf{EQUITY}$$

Net Assets or Net Worth

In the rearranged form, this equation emphasizes that creditor claims (liabilities) to the assets come before those of the owners and the residual nature of the owners' interest in the business, often referred to as *net assets* or *net worth* for this reason.

Most businesses finance their formation and growth with some combination of funds provided by owners and borrowed funds. It is unlikely that banks would make loans or suppliers would extend credit to a company unless the owners also had invested their own resources in the business. It is expected that the company will repay creditors when due and repay the principal and interest on loans when they mature, before the owners withdraw cash or other assets from the business for their own use, again emphasizing the residual nature of their interest in the business.

A business can be structured as a sole proprietorship, owned and operated by a single owner, or have two or more owners and be structured as a partnership, a corporation, or variations of these two forms. Individuals, other companies, pension funds, mutual funds, and many other parties can hold an ownership interest in a company.

Regardless of the business structure or the nature of the parties with ownership, owners' equity in the balance sheet has two components: (1) the amounts owners invested in the business and (2) the profits earned by the business which were reinvested (retained) rather than being distributed to or withdrawn by the owners. We will provide two examples based on the information shown in Figure 4.14, which shows total owners' equity of $400,000 at the end of the first year, 20x1.

In sole proprietorships and partnerships, owners' equity is referred to as *capital*, which is presented as a single amount for each owner and includes both investments made by the owners and profits retained by the business.

Figure 4.15 shows how owners' equity will appear in the balance sheet if the business is a partnership. Swithin's capital balance of $100,000 represents her initial investment of $20,000 and an $80,000 share of the company's profit during its

Figure 4.14   Information Used to Illustrate Reporting Owners' Equity
December 31, 20x1

	Swithin	Patrick	Total
Owners' Investments	$ 20,000	$ 60,000	$ 80,000
Business Profit	80,000	240,000	320,000
Total	$100,000	$300,000	$400,000

first year of business. Patrick's capital balance of $300,000 represents his invest-
ment of $60,000 and his $240,000 share of the profit. We assume that profits are
allocated in the proportion of capital invested, although partners can allocate profits
in any manner to which they agree.

Figure 4.15   Balance Sheet Reporting for a Partnership
December 31, 20x1

Partnership Equity		
Swithin, Capital	$100,000	
Patrick, Capital	300,000	
Total Partnership Equity		$400,000

In the case of a corporation, owners' equity is referred to as *stockholders' equity.*
Owners receive shares of stock as evidence of their ownership of and investment in
the corporation, typically common stock, although there are other types. Figure 4.16
shows how owners' equity is presented if the business is structured as a corporation.

Figure 4.16   Balance Sheet Reporting for a Corporation
December 31, 20x1

Stockholders' Equity		
Common Stock, 40,000 shares	$ 80,000	
Retained Earnings	320,000	
Total Stockholders' Equity		$400,000

In the examples in Figures 4.15 and 4.16, note that total owners' equity is $400,000
in both cases; however, there are two primary differences. First, the amounts
invested by the stockholders and the profits retained by the corporation are shown
separately rather than as a single amount. Second, the total equity of an individual
stockholder is not shown; this makes sense when you realize that ownership in a

public corporation can change frequently as shares of stock are traded on a daily basis in the financial markets.

Building on this example, Figure 4.17 illustrates how owners' equity events in the second year of operations would be presented in the statement of changes in owners' equity. During 20x2, the second year, Swithin and Patrick each invested additional capital, earned a share of the profits, and withdrew a portion of the profits for personal use.

Figure 4.17 Statement of Changes in Partnership Equity
For the Year Ended December 31, 20x2

	Swithin	Patrick	Total
Capital, January 1, 20x2	$100,000	$300,000	$400,000
Add: Additional Capital Investments	5,000	15,000	20,000
Net Income for 20x2	20,000	60,000	80,000
Total	125,000	375,000	500,000
Less: Withdrawals	(10,000)	(30,000)	(40,000)
Capital, December 31, 20x2	$115,000	$345,000	$460,000

If the company is structured as a corporation, Figure 4.18 shows the same events, but as changes in common stock and retained earnings rather than as changes in the individual capital accounts of each owner.

Figure 4.18 Statement of Changes in Stockholders' Equity
For the Year Ended December 31, 20x2

	Common Stock	Retained Earnings	Total
Balances, January 1, 20x2	$ 80,000	$320,000	$400,000
Add: Common Stock Issued	20,000		20,000
Net Income for Year 20x2		80,000	80,000
Less: Dividends Declared		(40,000)	(40,000)
Balances, December 31, 20x2	$100,000	$360,000	$460,000

Of the $80,000 net income earned during the year, $40,000 was distributed to the stockholders in the form of cash dividends and the remainder was retained by the corporation. By the end of 20x2, the second year, retained earnings of $360,000 represents the cumulative amount of profits earned to date that was retained or reinvested in the business.

Summary

This chapter discussed the concepts and guidelines used to classify the various assets and liabilities into meaningful and useful categories and provided brief descriptions of each of the items you probably would find in each category. We also introduced you to some basic owners' equity concepts and illustrated how owner transactions are reported in the financial statements, using simple examples for both partnerships and corporations.

Building on this foundation, Chapter 5 will focus on specific and unique characteristics of many of the balance sheet items discussed here. We feel these additional concepts are important so that you understand not only the balance sheet but also how they pertain to certain revenues or expenses reported in the income statement. We hope you find Chapter 5 to be a useful reference when you run across a particular financial statement item and need a refresher.

Quiz for Chapter 4

1. A company has $300,000 of liabilities and total assets of $700,000. What is the dollar amount of its owner equity?
   a. $ 300,000
   b. $ 400,000
   c. $ 700,000
   d. $1,000,000

2. Current assets include cash and other assets, such as:
   a. Receivables that will be collected in cash
   b. Merchandise inventory that will be sold
   c. Supplies on hand that will be used
   d. All of the above if each occurs within a year or within the operating cycle of the business, whichever is longer
   e. None of the above

3. Current liabilities include:
   a. Unearned revenues
   b. Payroll tax liabilities
   c. Accounts payable to suppliers
   d. Interest payable
   e. All of the above

4. Which of the following is true?
   a. Current assets are presented in the balance sheet in order of liquidity.
   b. Working capital is the dollar amount of excess of current assets over current liabilities.
   c. The ratio of current assets to current liabilities can be used to evaluate a company's liquidity.
   d. A company is liquid if it is able to meet its current obligations as they become due.
   e. All of the above

5. Investments in marketable securities such as stocks and bonds can be classified as either current assets or long-term investments, depending on the intent and expected holding period.
   a. True
   b. False

6. Equipment purchased at an original cost of $7,000 has a book value of $3,200. A total of $3,800 depreciation expense has been taken on the equipment in the past.
   a. True
   b. False

7. Which of the following pertaining to intangible assets is true?
   a. Patents, copyrights, and trademarks represent legal rights conveyed to the holder for a specific period of time.
   b. Contractual arrangements such as franchise and licensing agreements are classified as intangible assets.
   c. Goodwill is the amount paid to buy another company in excess of the fair value of the assets that can be specifically identified.
   d. All of the above are true.
   e. None of the above are true.

8. Capital is the term used to describe the equity of an individual owner if the company is a sole proprietorship or partnership.
   a. True
   b. False

9. The amount of profit a company distributes to its owner(s) is referred to as:
   a. Dividends if the company is a corporation
   b. Withdrawals if the company is a sole proprietorship or partnership
   c. Both of the above are true.
   d. Neither of the above is true.

10. At the beginning of the year, a corporation had $300,000 of common stock and $700,000 of retained earnings. During the year, the corporation issued $200,000 of additional common stock, earned net income of $500,000, and paid cash dividends of $100,000. Total stockholders' equity at year end is:
   a. $1,200,000
   b. $1,500,000
   c. $1,700,000
   d. $1,600,000
   e. Some other amount

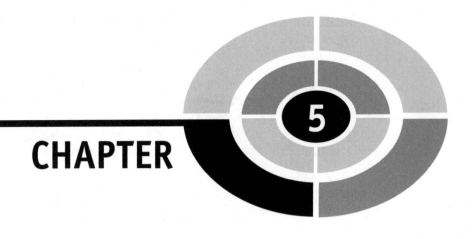

CHAPTER 5

The Balance Sheet:

A Closer Examination

In Chapter 4, we discussed the form and content of the balance sheet, along with the guidelines that are used to classify the different assets, liabilities, and types of equity. These categories are useful in gaining a better understanding of the financial position of a company at a specific point in time. Much of the discussion focused on the current asset and current liability distinctions. Those are important factors in evaluating a company's liquidity: its ability to meet its current obligations when due, using cash generated from its ongoing operating activities. Chapter 4 also provided examples and brief discussions of the other major asset, liability, and owners' equity categories typically presented in the balance sheet.

Building on this foundation, we will now focus on specific and unique characteristics of many balance sheet items that were discussed only briefly in Chapter 4. These important concepts affect not only the information reported in the balance sheet but also the income statement, and so we will discuss and illustrate how these relate to and affect certain revenues and expenses. You can return to this chapter as a useful reference source when you run across a particular financial statement item and need a quick refresher. The classified balance sheet in Figure 5.1 shows the balance sheet format and the major categories of assets, liabilities, and stockholders' equity that were discussed in Chapter 4. The business presented in this example is legally structured as a corporation and its owners are referred to as stockholders.

Figure 5.1   Balance Sheet Format and Categories for a Corporation Example Company Balance Sheet December 31, 20x1

Assets		
Current Assets	$300,000	
Long-Term Investments	50,000	
Property, Plant and Equipment	400,000	
Natural Resources	150,000	
Intangible Assets	100,000	
Total Assets		$1,000,000
Liabilities and Stockholders' Equity		
Liabilities		
Current Liabilities	$200,000	
Long-Term Liabilities	400,000	
Total Liabilities		$ 600,000
Stockholders' Equity		
Common Stock	80,000	
Retained Earnings	320,000	
Total Stockholders' Equity		400,000
Total Liabilities and Stockholders' Equity		$1,000,000

Current Assets

Current assets generally consist of cash or other assets which will be converted to cash or sold or used within a year or during the operating cycle of the business, whichever is longer. For a company that sells merchandise, the operating cycle is the length of time it takes for inventory to be sold and for customer accounts to be collected:

Operating Cycle: Inventory → Sale (Accounts Receivable) → Cash

Most businesses complete one or more operating cycles within a year and use the one-year benchmark when classifying assets as current, although the cycle is longer for some businesses, as was discussed in Chapter 4.

Current assets are presented in order of *liquidity,* a relative term indicating how soon or how easily those assets will produce cash the business can use to purchase more assets and/or pay its obligations when due. Working capital—the excess of current assets over current liabilities—and the ratio of current assets to current liabilities are measures that are used to evaluate a company's liquidity.

Figure 5.2 shows the items typically found in the current asset classification, presented in order of liquidity. We described each item briefly in Chapter 4 and will discuss some of them in more detail later in this chapter.

Figure 5.2   Balance Sheet Reporting: Current Assets

Current Assets		
Cash and Cash Equivalents	$109,280	
Short-Term Investments	130,000	
Accounts Receivable	45,000	
Notes Receivable	2,000	
Accrued Receivables	20	
Related Party Receivables	1,000	
Inventories	8,700	
Prepaid Expenses	4,000	
Total Current Assets		$300,000

VALUATION OF CURRENT ASSETS

The initial balance sheet value of a current asset generally is based on the historical cost concept; the cost when acquired for items such as short-term investments, inventory, and prepaid expenses; or the amount of cash the company is entitled to collect on accounts, notes, and other receivables. However, the accounting concept of conservatism applies to all assets, including current assets. If a receivable is unlikely to be collected or if inventory is obsolete or can be sold only at a substantially reduced price, balance sheet values should be reduced. Current assets appear on the balance sheet at a conservative value—the lower of the initial amount or the current value—with one exception. Investments in marketable securities are based on current market values, whether below or above the initial cost, as these investments can be sold and converted to cash immediately at the current market price.

CASH

Cash includes amounts on deposit with banks or other financial institutions, currency and coins on hand, cash and checks which have not been deposited, and cash

register and petty cash funds (cash on hand that can be used to pay for small or unexpected expenditures without writing a business check). Postdated checks and IOUs from employees are receivables, not cash. Postage stamps are supplies or prepaid expenses, not cash. A bank overdraft is a current liability and represents amounts owed for checks written which exceed the amount on deposit.

Cash balances that appear in the current asset classification are presumed to be immediately available for any purpose. Separate account balances are combined into a single amount; however, an overdraft in one account should be reported as a current liability unless the overdraft can be legally offset against another account balance. Sometimes there are restrictions on the use or availability of amounts on deposit. Depending on the nature and significance of those restrictions, the restrictions may be described in a financial statement footnote, the balance on deposit may be classified elsewhere on the balance sheet and excluded from current assets, or both.

CASH EQUIVALENTS

Cash equivalents are actually a special category of short-term investments that are almost like cash and typically are combined with actual cash amounts on the balance sheet. For an investment to be considered a cash equivalent, it must be highly liquid and readily marketable (it can be converted to cash quickly and easily via financial market mechanisms), and if the investment had to be sold, the amount of cash received would not be substantially different from the amount invested (meaning that the value of the investment is not likely to change substantially during this short period). In light of these parameters, cash equivalents are viewed as a relatively risk-free investment of excess cash; they are investments that can be sold quickly and easily with little risk of changes in value if an urgent cash need arises.

SHORT-TERM INVESTMENTS

Short-term investments and *marketable securities* are generic terms used to describe a variety of investments a company may hold. An investment generally is considered marketable if it can be purchased or sold in the public financial markets, but a company may hold other types of investments too. This general category may include investments in stocks and bonds of other companies, U.S. Treasury bills and bonds, mutual funds, money market funds, certificates of deposit, and commercial paper. Many of these types of investments can be classified as either short-term or long-term, some may be classified as cash equivalents and combined with cash on the balance sheet, and others may be underlying investments held in a fund to repay long-term debt or pension obligations. *Equity securities* and *debt securities* are other terms used to describe some investments.

Equity Securities

An *equity security* generally represents some form of ownership in another company, such as owning the common stock of a corporation:

Equity Security = Ownership = Common Stock

You are not guaranteed to make money on a common stock investment. In theory, the market price of that investment should rise if the company does well, although there are many other factors which influence stock prices, not all of which are based on a company's performance. At its discretion, the board of directors may declare a cash dividend to be paid to the stockholders, distributing a portion of the corporation's profits to its owners, with the remaining earnings retained or reinvested in the company. A more complete discussion of corporations, stock, and dividends appears in the material on stockholders' equity later in this chapter.

Debt Securities

A *debt security* represents a borrower-lender relationship:

Debt Security = Borrowing = Bonds Payable

If you purchase a debt security such as a corporate bond, you are directly or indirectly making a loan to the company for which it has promised to pay a stated amount of interest, usually semiannually, and to repay the amount loaned on a specific maturity date, often many years in the future.

In the meantime, the market value of the bond investment may change over time with changes in interest rates caused by general economic conditions and changes in investor perceptions of risk for a particular company. A more complete discussion of corporate bonds appears in the material on long-term liabilities later in this chapter.

Equity, debt, and other forms of securities are publicly traded on a daily basis in the financial markets, with regulated mechanisms bringing together parties with money to invest and companies that need to raise capital via stockholder investments or borrowings. When you (or a company) purchase a marketable debt or equity security, you can hang on to it for years, sell it later the same day, or sell it at any other time of your choosing, based on its current market value.

Balance Sheet Classification: Investments in Equity and Debt Securities

It is important to note that most of these investments could be classified as either current assets or long-term investments. In part, the distinction between the two classifications is based on the company's judgment regarding the nature of these investments. If the investments are included among the current assets, you generally would conclude that these are investments of idle cash, with the expectation that the investments will generate dividends or interest income and/or increase in value and be sold at a profit when the idle cash later is needed to finance ongoing business activities.

However, if these investments are classified as long-term, the company may be taking a longer-term view and hoping to maintain an ongoing business relationship with another company (perhaps a supplier) or to support a joint venture with another company when neither company can provide adequate financing or assume the full risk of a particular business venture, whether a domestic or a foreign endeavor.

Although specific types of investments may be classified as either short-term or long-term, the purpose and intent of such investments is a key factor in deciding under which classification the investments will be reported. The purpose and nature are revealed further by specific financial statement terms; investments in market-able securities may be presented in the balance sheet as *trading, available for sale*, or *held to maturity* securities.

Trading Securities

The term *trading securities* typically is applied to companies which invest in and actively manage a portfolio of equity and debt security investments, with frequent purchase and sales transactions (trading), taking advantage of short-term changes in market price to produce earnings, along with the earnings from dividends and interest. These investments are classified as current assets and appear immedi-ately below cash and cash equivalents because they can be sold readily to generate cash if needed. The dividends and interest earned, along with the gains or losses from the sale of these investments, are reported as other income or expense in the income statement.

Trading securities initially are valued at their cost but later are presented on the balance sheet on the basis of the current market price of the portfolio of invest-ments, even if that price is higher than cost. This treatment is a rare exception to the concept of conservatism; most assets are reported at cost, or at less than cost if their value has declined, but are not adjusted above cost if their value has increased. However, this practice may be justified because the investments can be sold readily.

Let's assume that the investments a company owns at year end were purchased for $100,000 but the current market value is $130,000. If the investments were sold at this current market price, the company would report a *gain* on the sale of its investments of $30,000. But it still owns the investments, and the balance sheet value reported is $130,000. Where is the $30,000 increase in market value reported? In the income statement, almost as though the investments had been sold.

Assume that the company also earned $10,000 in dividends and interest on its trading securities portfolio during the year, sold some investments at a $2,000 loss, and adjusted its year-end investment portfolio to market value. The financial statements would present the information shown in Figure 5.3.

Figure 5.3 Trading Securities: Financial Statement Reporting

BALANCE SHEET	
Current Assets	
Investments in Trading Securities ($130,000 market value; $100,000 cost)	$130,000
INCOME STATEMENT	
Other Income and Expense	
Dividends and Interest Earned	$ 10,000
Loss on Sale of Investments	(2,000)
Unrealized Gain on Trading Securities	$ 30,000

The increase in market value is considered an *unrealized gain* (or unrealized holding gain) because the investments were not sold. Similarly, if the market price of the investments had declined, an unrealized holding loss would be reported in the income statement. Even though the gain or loss is unrealized, it was largely a matter of discretion whether to sell or hold the investments at this time; they could have been sold readily if the company desired.

Available for Sale Securities

Although some companies hold trading security portfolio investments, a more common purpose for investments in marketable securities is to generate dividend or interest income or to gain from market price appreciation rather than carrying excessive cash balances during low points in the business cycle. If necessary, such investments can be sold, but they also can be held for months or even years and are referred to logically as *available for sale securities*. The current versus the long-term classification of these investments provides an indication of the company's purpose and intent.

Just as with trading securities, available for sale securities are valued and presented on the balance sheet on the basis of current market prices, and the dividends and interest earned and gains and losses from sales are reported in the income statement. However, in the case of available for sale securities, an unrealized (holding) gain resulting from the increase in the market price of the investments is not included in the income statement; instead, it is reported as *accumulated other comprehensive income*, which is a unique and separate component of stockholders' equity. When gains and losses are reported in the income statement and included in net income for the period, they ultimately are reflected in the year-end retained earnings included in total stockholders' equity. However, the unrealized gain in our example was excluded from net income and from year-end retained earnings; as a result, the unrealized gain must be reported as a separate component of year-end stockholders' equity. We will discuss these concepts again in the last section of this chapter on stockholders' equity.

If the company classified the investments in the example above as available for sale securities, the financial statements would appear as shown in Figure 5.4.

Figure 5.4   Available for Sale Securities: Financial Statement Reporting

BALANCE SHEET	
Current Assets	
Investments in Available for Sale Securities ($130,000 market value; $100,000 cost)	$130,000
Stockholders' Equity	
Accumulated Other Comprehensive Income	
Unrealized Holding Gain: Available for Sale Securities	$ 30,000
INCOME STATEMENT	
Other Income and Expense	
Dividends and Interest Earned	$ 10,000
Loss on Sale of Investments	(2,000)

Held to Maturity Securities

A bond investor (bondholder) is directly or indirectly making a loan to the corporation in return for a stated amount of interest that typically is paid semiannually and a stated amount that will be paid back on a specified future date. As is discussed in more detail in the section on long-term liabilities in this chapter, the bondholder is guaranteed to receive a stated amount of interest, but if the stated interest is too low, an investor pays less for the bond; likewise, if the stated interest rate is higher than current conditions indicate, the bond must be purchased at a higher price.

Bond prices fluctuate over time, influenced by current market conditions, the state of the economy, and the perceived risk of a particular corporation. However, at the time of the initial investment, the price paid by the bondholder locks in a long-term rate of return if the bond is held to maturity. The investor can either hold the bond until it matures to earn that rate or sell the bond to another investor at its current market price, again based on the market conditions existing at the time.

When bond investments are classified as trading or available for sale securities, the stated interest payments the investor receives will be reported as income in the income statement for the year, the bond investment on the balance sheet will be based on its current market value, and the change in the value of the bond investment will be reported either in the income statement or in stockholders' equity, as was discussed above.

However, if the investor intends to hold the bond investment until it matures, it generally will be classified as a long-term investment, specifically as a *held to maturity* security. Unlike trading and available for sale securities, a held to maturity investment is not adjusted to market value at year end because the company does not expect to sell the investment in the near term; the current market price of the bond is less relevant than it is for other investments the company can or intends to sell in the near term.

The purpose and form of some other types of investments will be discussed later in this chapter in the material on long-term investments.

ACCOUNTS RECEIVABLE

Accounts receivable represents the amounts due from customers for services rendered or goods sold in the past. Receivables from customers also are referred to as *trade receivables*; they are the result of routine business transactions in which goods and services are traded for the right to collect cash immediately or not long afterward. A company may increase its sales volume by allowing customers to buy on credit, but in that case there is a risk that some customers will not pay their balances when due. Accounts receivable initially are recorded on the basis of the amount of sales or services revenue to be received, but when the accounting concept of conservatism is applied, the balance sheet value should reflect the amount the company expects to realize or actually collect in cash.

Estimated Bad Debts Expense and the Allowance for Doubtful Accounts

Estimated *bad debts expense* (or uncollectible accounts expense) should be included in the operating expenses in the income statement, matching sales earned in the current period with the associated expense of uncollectible accounts. Estimates generally are based on past experience, current credit policies, and economic conditions. Companies may estimate uncollectible accounts by using a percentage of sales revenue or examine the age of year-end receivables based on the due date, paying close attention to past due accounts, knowing that the likelihood of collection diminishes the longer an account has been past due.

For example, in 20x1, a company's first year of operations, it made credit sales of $500,000, collected $450,000 on account, and has $50,000 in year-end receivables. It estimates that $5,000 of its year-end receivables will be uncollectible. The balance sheet at year end reports the amounts legally due from customers less an allowance for estimated uncollectible accounts, as shown in Figure 5.5.

Figure 5.5   Balance Sheet Reporting: Accounts Receivable

Current Assets		
Accounts Receivable	$50,000	
Less: Allowance for Uncollectible Accounts	(5,000)	
Accounts Receivable (net)		$45,000

Accounts receivable (net) of $45,000 represents the amount of cash the company expects to collect; this often is referred to as *net realizable value*. Alternatively, the company may report only the net amount of receivables, with the amount of the allowance shown parenthetically, as in Figure 5.6.

Figure 5.6   Balance Sheet Reporting: Accounts Receivable—Net

Current Assets	
Accounts Receivable (net of allowance for uncollectible accounts of $5,000)	$45,000

Although the company expects that it will collect only $45,000 of its current accounts receivable, let's assume it still continues to pursue collection in the next year, 20x2, but to no avail, and finally writes the $5,000 of accounts receivable off its books in 20x2. Should the $5,000 of bad debts expense appear in the 20x1 or the 20x2 income statement? According to the matching principle, it is an expense of 20x1, matched with the sales revenue earned in that period, not an expense of some future year when the decision is made to write the specific accounts off the books. The financial statement results for 20x1 and 20x2 would be as shown in Figure 5.7. The example highlights the proper matching of the bad debts expense associated with sales revenue earned in 20x1, and ignores any additional sales revenue the company earned in 20x2.

Figure 5.7 Matching Bad Debts Expense with Sales Revenue

	20x1	20x2
Income Statement		
Sales Revenue	$500,000	$0
Operating Expenses		
Bad Debts Expense	$ (5,000)	$0

Contrary to the accounting concept of matching, some companies may use the *direct write-off method* and report bad debts expense in the income statement in the year in which the specific accounts are written off. Although this method is used for income tax purposes, it is contrary to the matching principle and should be used in financial statements only if the amounts are immaterial (insignificant).

If the company's estimate was accurate, the net amount of receivables both before and after the write-off is $45,000, which is the amount the company expected to collect from its year-end receivables, as shown in Figure 5.8.

Figure 5.8 Balance Sheet Effects: Writing Off a Specific Customer Receivable

	Before	After
Balance Sheet		
Accounts Receivable	$50,000	$45,000
Less: Allowance for Uncollectible Accounts	(5,000)	0
Accounts Receivable (net)	$45,000	$45,000

Is it easy to estimate uncollectible accounts accurately? Even companies which have been in business for years and have used consistent credit policies may be affected by unexpected events. For example, Hurricane Katrina probably had an impact on the likelihood of collecting receivables from customers in New Orleans. Easy credit, declining real estate values, and rising homeowner defaults on mortgage loans in recent years have had far-reaching effects on lenders, investors and the economy. At the time of this writing, many financial institutions have failed, credit has dried up, and the United States is in the midst of an unprecedented financial and economic crisis.

Allowances for Cash Discounts, Sales Returns, and Collection Expenses

As was discussed in Chapter 3, many companies offer cash discounts to credit customers as an incentive for early payment. For example, if the credit terms are 2/10 net/30 on

a $10,000 account balance, the customer is offered a 2 percent cash discount of $200 if the account balance is paid within 10 days (2/10), but the customer must pay the full amount due of $10,000 in 30 days (net/30). Although the company would receive less than it billed, if receivables are collected soon, it may be able to take advantage of cash discounts on amounts it owes to its own suppliers.

Customers often are permitted to return items purchased on credit or may be granted a price allowance on damaged goods they otherwise might return. A company may engage the services of another company to process its receivables or pursue past-due accounts. As with cash discounts, sales returns and allowances and collection expenses reduce the amount of cash the company expects to generate from its receivables. Depending on the nature and significance of these amounts, the company may review its year-end receivables and establish additional allowances, somewhat like the allowance for uncollectible accounts. In that case, it will report a more conservative value for its receivables, reflecting the amount of cash it expects to generate, and the estimated discounts, returns, and collection expenses will be matched with the revenue earned in the year of the sales, not in a later time period when they are taken.

NOTES RECEIVABLE

A company may offer relatively informal credit terms to its customers, but if credit is extended for a longer time or if a customer's account is past due, the company may require the customer to sign a formal promissory note specifying the maturity date, the repayment terms, and any assets pledged as collateral for the loan. Although a business may make a cash loan to an individual or another company, this would not be a common practice unless lending activities are a significant part of ongoing and routine business operations.

Formal promissory notes offer two advantages over the somewhat informal credit terms associated with accounts receivable. First, the note is a legal document which offers the company better protection in the event of default; second, the note typically specifies that it be repaid with interest.

Let's assume a company sold merchandise to a customer and accepted a $2,000 promissory note on December 1, 20x1. The stated annual interest rate on the note is 12 percent, and the $2,000 principal and interest owed on the note are due when the note matures in six months, on June 1, 20x2. The total amount of interest that will be received when the note matures is calculated as follows:

Principal	$\times$	Interest Rate	$\times$	Time	=	Interest
$2,000	$\times$	12%	$\times$	6/12 months	=	$120

The 12 percent interest rate on the note is an annual interest rate, but the note term is only six months, and so only $120 in interest will be received. How should these events be reported in the December 31, 20x1, financial statements? The company has earned one month of interest even though it will not collect the note or the interest until 20x2.

According to the revenue recognition principle, a portion of the total interest that will be received is to be reported in the income statement each year: one month in 20x1 and the other five months in 20x2. On the December 31, 20x1, balance sheet, notes receivable of $2,000 is the principal amount of the note, and the $20 of interest earned but not yet collected is an accrued receivable, as shown in Figure 5.9.

Figure 5.9   Income Statement and Balance Sheet Reporting: Notes Receivable and Interest

	20x1	20x2	Total
Income Statement			
Other Income			
Interest Earned	$ 20	$100	$120
Balance Sheet, December 31, Year 1			
Current Assets			
Notes Receivable	$2,000		
Accrued Interest Receivable	20		

In some industries, companies borrow against or sell their notes and accounts receivable to generate cash more quickly. In secured borrowing arrangements, the company pledges its receivables as collateral for the loan and then describes the arrangements in the footnotes to the financial statements.

In other cases, it may sell its receivables either *with recourse* or on a *without recourse* basis. If a customer defaults and does not pay the balance when due, if the receivable was sold without recourse, the party purchasing the receivable bears the risk of loss and must estimate the bad debts expense, as was discussed above.

However, if a customer defaults on a receivable sold with recourse, the party selling the receivables must reimburse the purchaser for the loss. In this case, the seller must estimate the amount of uncollectible receivables it sold with recourse, and the *recourse obligation*, which is the estimated amount the seller may owe the buyer, will be reported as a liability on the seller's balance sheet. Additional information about these arrangements must be provided in the footnote disclosures.

ACCRUED RECEIVABLES (ACCRUED REVENUES)

According to the matching principle, the income statement should include revenues earned during the time period even though the cash may not be received until a future date. *Accrued receivables* (accrued revenues) represent amounts yet to be collected for revenues a company has earned, such as interest earned on investments and notes receivable, or revenues unrelated to routine business operations such as amounts billed for rent or other incidental services provided. An illustration of accrued interest was presented in the earlier section on notes receivable, and other examples and concepts pertaining to accrued receivables were discussed in Chapters 2 and 3.

RELATED PARTY RECEIVABLES

Related party receivables may include amounts owed to the company by affiliated companies, such as advances or loans to subsidiaries. It also may include receivables from company executives or employees. As these receivables are very different from the trade receivables from company customers, they should be disclosed separately on the balance sheet, and additional information may be included in the financial statement's footnotes. Recent business scandals have heightened the public's awareness of such matters as unscrupulous executives have gained personally by taking advantage of their companies' resources.

INVENTORIES

Merchandise inventory is the term applied to companies which acquire products for resale. The cost of any unsold goods on hand is included in the current asset classification of the balance sheet as it will generate cash when it is sold and customer accounts are collected. As was discussed in Chapter 3, according to the matching principle, the cost of inventory appears as an expense in the income statement in the period in which it is sold, referred to as *cost of goods sold*.

Balance Sheet − Current Assets Inventory	→	Income Statement − Expenses Cost of Goods Sold

Inventory Cost

Inventory generally is valued at its historical cost on the balance sheet, which includes the invoice price and transportation charges on goods purchased less any returns, price allowances and cash discounts taken for early payment. Transportation costs paid for the delivery of purchased inventory are referred to as *transportation-in* or *freight-in;* these costs are included in the total cost of the inventory rather than as operating expenses. A detailed schedule showing how cost of goods sold is determined, which also might be presented in the income statement, appears in Figure 5.10.

Figure 5.10 Detailed Schedule of Cost of Goods Sold

Cost of Goods Sold			
Inventory, January 1		$ 3,000	
Purchases	$18,000		
Transportation-In	100		
Purchase Discounts	(300)		
Purchase Returns and Allowances	(700)		
Net Purchases		17,100	
Cost of Goods Available for Sale		20,100	
Inventory, December 31		(8,700)	
Cost of Goods Sold			$11,400

Manufacturing Inventories

A manufacturer presents three categories of inventory as current assets on its balance sheet: raw materials and supplies inventory, goods in process inventory, and finished goods inventory. *Raw materials and supplies inventory* are items that will be used to manufacture products. *Goods in process inventory*, as the name implies, are products which are not complete, and the inventory amount consists of the manufacturing costs incurred to date. *Finished goods inventory* is similar to merchandise inventory, the term used to describe inventory purchased for resale and are completed goods on hand that are ready for sale.

The cost to manufacture a product consists of direct (raw) materials, direct labor, and manufacturing overhead costs. *Direct materials* are the raw materials which become part of the finished product. *Direct labor* is the cost of the salaries and wages of those directly involved in manufacturing or assembling the product. *Manufacturing (or factory) overhead* consists of all the indirect costs associated with the manufacturing process, such as supervisory wages, building and equipment depreciation, insurance, utilities, and supplies. The three components of manufacturing costs are shown in Figure 5.11.

Figure 5.11 Manufacturing Costs

Direct Materials	Raw materials and components used to manufacture the finished product
Direct Labor	Labor cost for employees directly involved in manufacturing and assembling the product
Manufacturing Overhead	Indirect manufacturing costs such as supplies, supervision, depreciation, utilities, and insurance

Unlike selling and administrative expenses, which are reported as operating expenses in the time period incurred, these manufacturing costs are referred to as *product costs* and are reflected in the cost of inventory on the balance sheet until the products are sold, as shown in Figure 5.12.

Figure 5.12   Manufacturing Costs: Inventories and Cost of Goods Sold

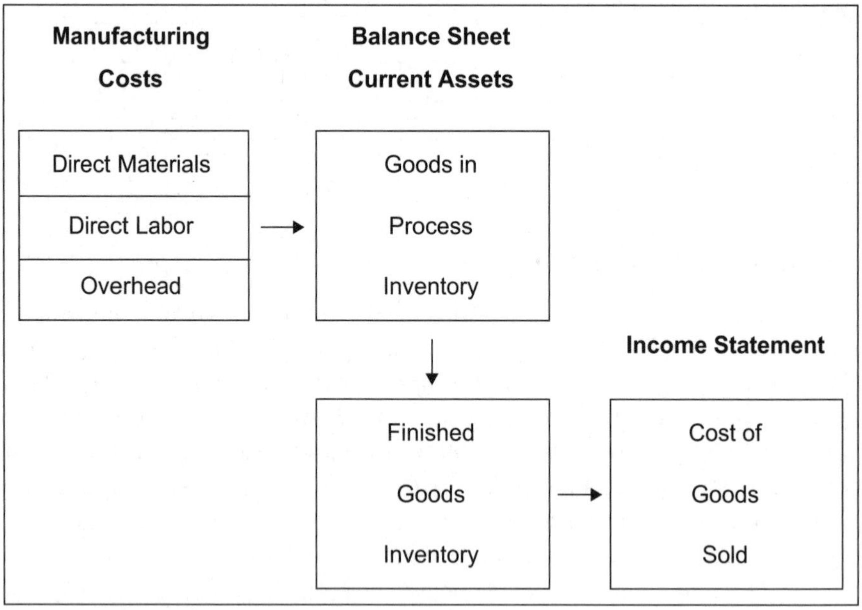

Gross Profit

The difference between the selling price and the cost of the inventory (cost to purchase or manufacture) is referred to as *gross profit* or *gross margin*. For example, if an item of inventory was purchased for $100 and sold for $125, the gross profit is $25:

Sales	−	**Cost of Goods Sold**	=	**Gross Profit**
$125	−	**$100**	=	**$25**

For the company to be profitable, whether the inventory consists of goods purchased for resale or manufactured goods, individual selling prices and the total sales volume must generate a sufficient amount of gross profit to cover operating and other ongoing expenses. The length of time it takes to manufacture and sell the inventory and collect receivables—in other words, the operating cycle—is an important aspect of a company's liquidity.

Inventory Systems and Controls

Inventory quantities may be determined by using a *periodic inventory system* where a physical count is conducted at least once a year, or by using a *perpetual inventory system* which keeps a running balance of inventory purchased, sold, and on hand. If a perpetual inventory system is used, the recorded inventory quantity also should be verified periodically by a physical count. In preparing monthly or quarterly financial statements, it may be necessary to estimate inventory balances unless a perpetual inventory system is used. Although more complex and costly, a perpetual inventory system provides much better inventory control and makes it easier to identify errors and losses from theft. Technological advances such as bar code scanners and point of sale registers make the use of a perpetual system much more feasible than it was in the past.

Inventory Cost-Flow Assumptions

Let's consider the case of a campus bookstore which sells clothing and other items imprinted with the university name or logo. It makes frequent purchases and sales of its most popular logo items, but the cost varies a bit each time an item is reordered, perhaps because of quantity price breaks, transportation costs, and/or cash discounts for early payment; all these factors are considered in determining inventory cost. If the items it sells always could be purchased at exactly the same price, it would be simple to determine the cost of ending inventory and the cost of the goods sold. However, if the cost to purchase (or manufacture) a particular item varies, what is the right dollar amount for ending inventory and cost of goods sold? It depends.

As an example, let's take a closer look at a particular style of sweatshirt the bookstore always keeps in stock. As shown in Figure 5.13, the bookstore started the year with 300 of these sweatshirts, which were purchased last year at a cost of $10 each. It placed two reorders during the year, first purchasing 800 sweatshirts for $12 each and later purchasing another 500 at $15 each. A total of 1,600 sweatshirts were available for sale during the year, which were purchased at a total cost of $20,100.

At year end, a physical inventory count was taken; 600 sweatshirts were still on hand, and the other 1,000 were sold during the year. How much of the $20,100 total

Figure 5.13   Cost of Inventory Available for Sale

	Quantity	Unit Price	Total
Beginning Inventory	300	$10	$ 3,000
Purchase 1	800	$12	9,600
Purchase 2	500	$15	7,500
Total	1,600		$20,100

cost should be assigned to the 600 sweatshirts in year-end inventory? How much to the 1,000 sweatshirts that were sold? It depends.

Figure 5.14 is a visual representation of the inventory purchased at different prices and the quantities sold and on hand at year end, along with the questions we will answer. As we will explain in the discussion below, the bookstore might use a specific identification system and keep track of each individual sweatshirt, or it might take an easier approach and use a cost-flow assumption to determine the cost of the inventory sold during the year and the cost of the inventory on hand at year end.

Figure 5.14   Cost of Inventory Available for Sale

Purchase #2		
500 units x $15 = $7,500		600 units are on hand
		Which ones?
		What cost?
Purchase #1	Inventory Available for Sale	
800 units x $12 = $9,600	1,600 units	1,000 units were sold
	$20,100 Total Cost	Which ones?
		What cost?
Beginning Inventory		
300 units x $10 = $3,000		

Specific Identification

It is logical to assume that a car dealer knows specifically which cars were sold, which are still on the lot, and the specific cost of each one. Dealers of rare and collectible art and jewelers who sell expensive one-of-a-kind items are also likely to keep very specific records for each item purchased and sold. Each would use a *specific identification system* to keep track of individual inventory items and could readily determine the cost of the goods sold and the cost of inventory on hand.

However, our campus bookstore and many other companies make frequent purchases and sales of identical low-cost items, and manufacturers produce large quantities of those items. Keeping track of each individual item would be tedious and time-consuming, and the cost could exceed the potential benefits of such an elaborate system (the cost-benefit concept that was introduced earlier in Chapter 2). Instead, the bookstore might base its cost of goods sold and inventory values on an assumption about which items were sold, which remain in inventory, and their cost. In fact, most companies employ a *cost-flow assumption* for items which are similar or low-cost and are not nearly as easily or readily identified as are vehicles, original art, or one-of-a-kind jewelry items. It might adopt a FIFO, LIFO, or weighted average cost-flow assumption.

It is very important to understand these concepts because the assumption a particular company employs may have a significant impact on the amounts reported in its financial statements. Companies that might be otherwise identical could present very different financial statement results as a result of choosing from one of several acceptable accounting methods.

First-in, First-out (FIFO)

The *first-in, first-out (FIFO)* assumption is based on the notion that the first goods purchased (first-in) are the first that will be sold (first-out) and that the last goods purchased will remain in inventory. To visualize this concept, think about buying milk or other perishable items from a grocery store. The grocery store attempts to sell milk and other perishable items on a FIFO basis by placing the "old" milk at the front of the shelf and the "new" milk at the back. This plan works if the customer buys a carton of old milk from the front of the shelf and the new milk is still on hand. You also might think about a jelly bean dispenser, a jar that is filled from the top but whose contents are dispensed from a spout at the bottom. The old jelly beans are dispensed first, and the new ones are still in the jar.

From a physical-flow standpoint, most companies sell their inventory on a FIFO basis, trying to sell the old stock of a specific inventory item first, with the new stock of that item still on hand. If the bookstore uses a FIFO assumption for this style of sweatshirt that it always keeps in stock, the dollar amount for cost of goods sold and for ending inventory would be determined as shown in Figure 5.15.

Figure 5.15   FIFO: Cost of Goods Sold and Ending Inventory Calculations

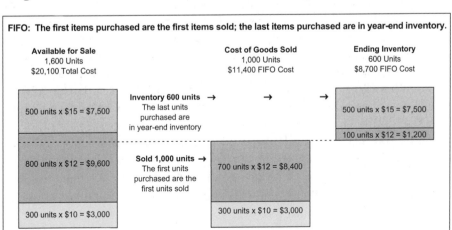

As noted in Figure 5.15, the first items purchased were the first items sold and the last items purchased remain in inventory at year end. The bookstore sold all 300 of the sweatshirts purchased for $10 each and 700 of those purchased for $12. Ending inventory is assumed to consist of the sweatshirts most recently purchased, which includes the remaining 100 sweatshirts purchased for $12 and the 500 that were purchased for $15. A bit earlier, we mentioned that a company might determine the cost of inventory on hand and sold using a *cost-flow* assumption (such as the FIFO example above), which is not necessarily the same as the *physical flow* (how the actual physical inventory changes as in the jelly bean jar example). Cost-flow assumptions and financial statement results will be discussed again as we conclude our inventory section.

Last-in, First-out (LIFO)

The *last-in, first-out (LIFO)* concept is based on the assumption that the last goods purchased (last-in) will be the first sold (first-out) and that the first goods purchased will remain in inventory. To visualize this concept, you might think about the time you went to the hardware store and purchased nails from a large wooden keg or metal bin. You most likely grabbed a handful of nails from the top, as did each customer who came after you. When the keg ran low, the hardware store dumped the new shipment of nails into the keg, but the old nails remained at the bottom. Lumber, firewood, crushed rock, and landscaping bark also may be sold in this manner. In the case of the jelly bean jar, instead of using the dispenser at the bottom of the jar, you might decide to grab a big handful from the top of the jar and eat the new jelly beans, with the old ones still left in the jar. Or you might reach to the back of the milk shelf and buy the freshest milk, not the milk that has been on the shelf for a few days that the grocery store wants you to buy first.

If the bookstore uses a LIFO assumption for this particular style of sweatshirt that it always keeps in stock, the dollar amount for cost of goods sold and for ending inventory will be determined as shown in Figure 5.16.

As noted in Figure 5.16, the last items purchased were assumed to be the first items sold and the earliest items purchased remain in inventory at year end. The bookstore sold all 500 of the sweatshirts purchased for $15 each and 500 of those purchased for $12. Ending inventory consists of the 300 earliest purchased sweatshirts that were on hand at the start of the year and were purchased for $10 apiece and 300 of the ones purchased for $12.

By now, you might be wondering if the bookstore actually would sell this particular sweatshirt in this way, selling the new shipment first and keeping the ones it purchased months or maybe even years ago on hand. Probably not, but it still might use a LIFO cost-flow assumption for reasons that will be discussed later.

Figure 5.16 LIFO: Cost of Goods Sold and Ending Inventory Calculation

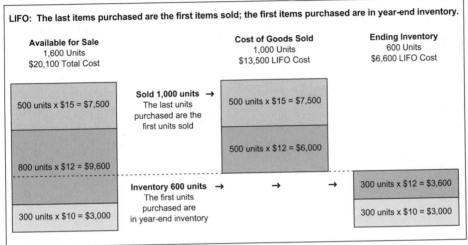

Weighted Average

This cost-flow assumption is based on the use of a *weighted average* unit cost for all inventory items available for sale during the year rather than on an examination of the individual prices associated with items purchased at a particular time. When you pull into a gas station to fill up your car, you pump gas from a large reservoir that usually is stored in an underground tank. You might visualize the weighted average assumption by thinking about how the old gas becomes mixed with the new gas when the distributor arrives and replenishes the storage tank. Or you could go back to the example of the jelly bean jar; if you shook up the jar and then grabbed a handful of jelly beans, the old and new jelly beans would be mixed; you would be eating jelly beans from this mixture, and the ones remaining in the jar also would be a mixture of old and new jelly beans.

If the bookstore uses a weighted average cost-flow assumption for this particular style of sweatshirt that it always keeps in stock, the dollar amounts for cost of goods sold and ending inventory would be determined as shown in Figure 5.17.

Note that the unit cost of $12.56 was determined by using the total cost and the total quantity of all items available for sale—$20,100 total cost ÷ 1,600 units = $12.56—rather than a simple average of the unit costs of $12.33 [($10 + $12 + $15) ÷ 3]. The weighted average calculation considers that half of the units were purchased for $12 and fewer were purchased at the $10 and $15 prices.

Figure 5.17 WEIGHTED AVERAGE: Cost of Goods Sold and Ending
Inventory Calculations

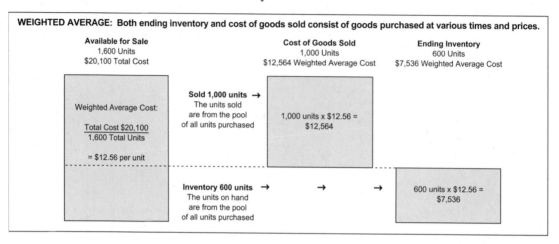

Physical Flow versus Cost-Flow Assumptions

Most companies attempt to sell each particular item on a FIFO basis by selling the old stock and keeping the new stock of that item on hand. However, a company may adopt any one of the three cost-flow assumptions illustrated and described above regardless of the physical flow of its inventory purchases and sales. In theory, the cost-flow assumption a company uses should achieve a better matching of the sales revenue earned and the associated cost. However, companies that are otherwise identical might present substantially different results for cost of goods sold and ending inventory in their respective financial statements, depending on the cost-flow assumption adopted.

A Comparison of Inventory Cost-Flow Assumptions

From our discussion and examples illustrating the different cost-flow assumptions above, you learned that each method produces different values for inventory and for cost of goods sold. A comparison of the three methods discussed above is presented in Figure 5.18, assuming the business is legally structured as a corporation and is subject to income taxation.

As you review the financial statement results, you should note that inventory prices were rising in our example; each new purchase was made at a higher cost than the one before it. If prices are in an upward trend, FIFO will produce the highest balance sheet value for inventory because the most recent, highest-priced goods are assumed to be on hand; it also will produce the highest profit because cost of goods sold is based on the assumption that the earliest, lower-cost goods are the first ones sold. LIFO, by contrast, reports the lowest inventory value based on the

Figure 5.18 Inventory Cost-Flow Assumptions—Comparison of Financial Statement Effects

Selling price - $25 per unit; Operating Expenses - $10,000; Income Tax Rate - 40%.						
INCOME STATEMENT				**FIFO**	**LIFO**	**Weighted Average**
Sales Revenue (1,000 units @ $25)				$25,000	$25,000	$25,000
Cost of Goods Sold:	Units	Cost				
Beginning Inventory	300	$10		3,000	3,000	3,000
Purchase #1	800	$12		9,600	9,600	9,600
Purchase #2	500	$15		7,500	7,500	7,500
Cost of Goods Available for Sale	1,600			20,100	20,100	20,100
Ending Inventory	*(600)*			*(8,700)*	*(6,600)*	*(7,536)*
Cost of Goods Sold	*1,000*			*11,400*	*13,500*	*12,564*
Gross Profit				**13,600**	**11,500**	**12,436**
Operating Expenses				(10,000)	(10,000)	(10,000)
Income before Tax				3,600	1,500	2,436
Income Tax Expense				(1,440)	(600)	(974)
Net Income				$ 2,160	$ 900	$ 1,462
BALANCE SHEET						
Inventory				$ 8,700	$ 6,600	$ 7,536

assumption that the earliest goods purchased at the lowest prices remain in inventory, and the lower profit is based on the assumption that the most recently purchased goods, those purchased at higher prices, were the first ones sold. As you would expect, the weighted average amounts fall somewhere in between.

Because there could be such different financial statement results between otherwise identical companies, it is important to find out which assumption a particular company is using, but how would one know? The full-disclosure concept introduced earlier in Chapter 2 requires a company to explain the policies and assumptions it is using in the footnotes to the financial statements.

Why LIFO?

In the discussion above, you learned that when prices are rising, the FIFO assumption produces the highest value for inventory on the balance sheet (based on the most recent purchases at higher prices) and cost of goods sold is lower (based on previous

purchases at lower prices), and so a FIFO company is likely to report a higher profit than would a similar company using LIFO. Also recall that for most businesses, the FIFO assumption more closely resembles the actual physical flow of merchandise; the old stock is sold first, and the new stock is on hand. Therefore, you might wonder why a company would use a LIFO assumption in such circumstances.

One might conclude that companies prefer to use the FIFO assumption over LIFO in periods when prices are rising. In that case, why do over one-third of public companies use the LIFO assumption? LIFO is an acceptable method for tax return purposes; if prices are rising, LIFO results in lower taxable income and a lower tax bill. As a result, a company identical to others in all other respects might receive a hefty tax break by using a LIFO assumption.

Although there are many circumstances in which a company can use different methods to determine accounting income versus taxable income, LIFO is an exception. Tax law requires a company using LIFO for tax purposes to employ this method in its financial statements as well; many refer to this as the *LIFO conformity rule*. Companies using LIFO must feel that the potential tax savings outweigh reporting lower profit and inventory values in their financial statements. Figure 5.19 presents a comparison of the income tax effects for each method and highlights the LIFO method income tax savings, during a period of rising inventory prices and an assumed income tax rate of 40 percent.

Figure 5.19   Income Tax Savings: LIFO Inventory Cost-Flow Assumptions

INCOME STATEMENT	FIFO	LIFO	Weighted Average
Income before Tax	$3,600	$1,500	$2,436
Income Tax Expense	*(1,440)*	*(600)*	*(974)*
Net Income	$2,160	$ 900	$1,462

Lower of Cost or Market

There is one final inventory valuation concept that should be mentioned here: the *lower of cost or market (LCM)* concept. Assume that the bookstore's year-end inventory consists of sweatshirts it purchased for $15 each. Maybe some of the sweatshirts in the window display were faded by the sun and can be sold for only $13 in that condition. Or maybe the price of cotton has declined and to compete with off-campus shops which purchased the same sweatshirts more recently at a cost of $14 and are selling them for $24, the bookstore may have to lower its selling price from $25 to $24 regardless of its cost.

When the value of inventory on hand has declined because the inventory is shop-worn or obsolete or when future selling prices must be reduced to pass on cost savings or to stay competitive, according to the concept of conservatism, the inventory should be written down to the *lower of cost or market*. Inventory valued on a FIFO basis is more likely to be affected by such price declines than is a LIFO inventory value based on previous, lower prices. Footnote disclosures indicate whether the company is valuing inventory at the lower of cost or market. If a substantial write-down in value occurs, the footnotes also may indicate the amount and in what income statement classification the loss is included.

PREPAID EXPENSES

We conclude our discussion of current assets with examples of prepaid expenses, the final category under this heading. Prepaid expenses typically consist of the cost of supplies and postage on hand and rent or insurance premiums paid in advance. As the supplies and postage are used or the rental or insurance period lapses, these costs will be shown as operating expenses in the income statement in accordance with the matching principle discussed and illustrated in Chapters 2 and 3.

Long-Term Investments

Investments appearing in this category often are made to achieve a long-term business objective or as a result of a contractual requirement; they are expected to be held at least a year but can be held for years or decades. Long-term investments may include equity and debt securities (such as stocks and bonds) of other companies and land or other assets held for investment rather than operating purposes and funds set aside and invested to provide for the eventual repayment of certain kinds of long-term debt or pension obligations. Substantial investments in affiliated or other companies may be made to build and maintain a beneficial long-term business relationship or may represent a company's share of a separate joint venture with other companies or parties. The long-term investment section of a classified balance sheet may include the items shown in Figure 5.20.

In the discussion of short-term investments near the beginning of this chapter, we discussed the concepts and characteristics of stock and bond investments in detail as well as the specific terminology used in the financial statements. You learned that many of these investments could be classified as either current or long-term, and rather than repeating that discussion, we will review the basic concepts and then focus on the unique characteristics of some other forms of long-term investments.

Figure 5.20   Examples of Long-term Investments

Long-Term Investments		
Available for Sale Securities	$ 5,000	
Held to Maturity Securities	15,600	
Bond Sinking Fund	8,000	
Pension Fund Assets	6,080	
Investments in Affiliated Companies	4,320	
Investments in Joint Ventures	1,000	
Land Held for Investment Purposes	10,000	
Total Long-Term Investments		$50,000

EQUITY AND DEBT SECURITIES

The term *marketable securities* is used to describe investments in equity and debt securities of other companies that can be sold readily in the financial markets. An investment in common stock consists of the purchase of ownership in another corporation and is referred to as an *equity security*. The investor may receive cash dividends on the investment if the corporation distributes a portion of its profits to the stockholders or benefit from an increase in the market price of the stock if the corporation reinvests its profits wisely and prospers but can suffer a loss if the stock price declines.

An investment in a corporate bond is a *debt security* as bonds are actually a form of long-term borrowing that corporations and others use to raise substantial amounts of capital. The investor is entitled to receive a stated amount of interest each year and the principal amount owed when the bonds mature, which may be many years in the future. However, the investor also can choose to sell the bond to another party rather than hold it to maturity, and the value of the bond may change over time as a result of changing market conditions and perceptions of risk.

CLASSIFICATION

Investments in marketable securities are classified on the balance sheet as *trading, available for sale*, or *held to maturity* securities. Actively managed trading security portfolios are considered current assets. However, stock and bond investments classified as available for sale may appear under either the current or the long-term classification. Held to maturity securities, as the term implies, are investments in bonds or other debt securities that the investor intends to hold until they mature on a specified future date (equity securities—stock—do not have a maturity date).

COST, MARKET VALUE, AND EARNINGS

Long-term investments initially are recorded at their cost; dividends and interest received and gains and losses from sales are classified as other income. Recall that trading and available for sale securities are presented on the balance sheet at current market values. *Unrealized holding gains* occur if the market value is greater than the cost of the investment; *unrealized holding losses* occur when the market value falls below cost. Unrealized holding gains and losses are included in net income if the investments are classified as trading securities, but if the investments are classified as available for sale, the unrealized gains or losses are excluded from net income and instead reported as *accumulated other comprehensive income* in stockholders' equity. Accumulated other comprehensive income is explained later in this chapter.

Held to maturity securities are not adjusted to market value because they are not expected to be sold but instead held until the maturity date; thus, the current market value is less relevant than it is for other categories of investments. We will discuss corporate bonds in more detail in the section on long-term liabilities later in this chapter.

BOND SINKING FUND

The terms and conditions for long-term borrowing arrangements can be very complex, and the borrowing agreement may specify that a *sinking fund* be established to repay the debt at maturity. The funds set aside for this purpose are invested, perhaps in stocks and bonds, as was discussed earlier. The earnings from the investments in the fund are reported as other income; the earnings are reinvested, and eventually the investments are sold and the funds are used to retire the debt. However, because the investments and proceeds from this fund can be used only for a designated purpose, the sinking fund is reported separately from other long-term investments.

PENSION FUND ASSETS

A company may elect or be required to establish a fund to cover its future pension obligations. Unfortunately, companies with unfunded or underfunded pension plans are often in the news these days, as is the Social Security system. The concepts pertaining to a pension fund are similar to those for the bond sinking fund discussed above.

INVESTMENTS IN AFFILIATED COMPANIES

A company also may purchase stock investments to establish and maintain a long-term business relationship with another company. For example, if a company wishes to ensure the availability and quality of a key component of its manufactured product, it may make a substantial investment in one of its suppliers to gain influence over its operations or even wish to gain control of the company. The financial reporting for these types of investments differs from those discussed earlier, primarily based on the level of ownership acquired.

20 TO 50 PERCENT OWNERSHIP: EQUITY METHOD

The *equity method* is used when the investor owns 20 to 50 percent of another company and has significant influence over its operating and/or financial policies and decisions. In this case, the investor's income statement includes its share of the net income of the company it owns, not the cash dividends it receives. For example, assume that Manufacturing Company purchases 40 percent of Supplier Corporation's common stock on January 1, 20x8. Supplier Corporation's statement of stockholders' equity for 20x8 appears in Figure 5.21.

Figure 5.21   Supplier Corporation Statement of Stockholders' Equity For the Year Ended December 31, 20x8

	Common Stock	Retained Earnings	Total
January 1, 20x8	$4,000,000	$6,000,000	$10,000,000
Net Income		1,000,000	1,000,000
Dividends Declared		(200,000)	(200,000)
December 31, 20x8	$4,000,000	$6,800,000	$10,800,000

On January 1, 20x8, Supplier Corporation's stockholders' equity (net assets) was $10,000,000, and Manufacturing Company purchased a 40 percent ownership stake, or 40 percent of the net assets, for $4,000,000. During 20x8, Supplier Corporation earned a $1,000,000 profit, distributed $200,000 of that profit to the stockholders as cash dividends, and retained the remaining $800,000 of its net income for the year. How much did Manufacturing Company earn from this investment? How much of this actually was received in cash?

Using the equity method for this investment, Manufacturing Company would include the information presented in Figure 5.22 in its financial statements.

According to the equity method, Manufacturing Company earned $400,000— its 40 percent share of Supplier Corporation's $1,000,000 net income—and received $80,000 in cash—its 40 percent share of the $200,000 income distributed as cash dividends. Supplier Corporation retained $800,000 of its 20x8 net income, of which Manufacturing Company's share is 40 percent, or $320,000, which is added to the amount reported for its investment in the year-end balance sheet. By year

Figure 5.22   Equity Method Investment: Manufacturing Company Financial
Statements (Partial)
For the Year Ended December 31, 20x8

Income Statement	
Earnings from Investment in Supplier Corporation (Equity Method)	$ 400,000
Balance Sheet	
Current Assets	
Cash	$ 80,000
Long-Term Investments	
Investment in Supplier Corporation	$4,320,000

end, Supplier Corporation's net assets are $10,800,000, and Manufacturing Company has a 40 percent interest, or $4,320,000, which is the amount Manufacturing Company reports as its investment in its year-end balance sheet when using the equity method.

When an investor owns 20 to 50 percent of another company and has significant influence over that company's operating and/or financial decisions, under the equity method, the investor recognizes income as it is earned rather than when the income is distributed later (if at all) as cash dividends. Its share of the reinvested earnings is reflected as an increase in the balance sheet value of the investment.

JOINT VENTURES

Joint ventures are formed to combine resources and unique expertise for a particular undertaking. A company may establish or invest in a joint venture to complete a large-scale project, conduct research, or finance and/or share the risk for activities it might be unable or unwilling to accomplish on its own. A separate entity may be established in which each party invests, participates, and/or helps finance, and many joint ventures are structured as partnerships (discussed later in this chapter). Other joint ventures may be based on legal agreements without the formation of a separate entity. The venture parties commonly use the equity method described above to report their investments in joint ventures.

GREATER THAN 50 PERCENT OWNERSHIP AND CONTROL: CONSOLIDATION

When a company owns more than 50 percent of another corporation's common stock, it essentially controls that corporation as its majority owner, although effective control can be achieved by other means. The term *parent* is used to describe a company which owns a controlling interest in another company, and the term *subsidiary* is used for the company it controls. In these circumstances, the investor generally must prepare *consolidated financial statements* that present the combined results as though it were a single entity with branches or divisions. Transactions between the separate companies—for example, when a manufacturer purchases raw materials from its subsidiary supplier—are eliminated, as are receivables and payables between the two companies. If the parent company has 100 percent ownership, the subsidiary is *wholly owned*. However, a parent company can control another company if it owns the majority of its outstanding voting stock, and the subsidiary in this case would be referred to as *majority-owned*. Even with less than 100 percent ownership, the parent company's consolidated financial statements will present the combined results as a single economic entity, but the income and net assets of the subsidiary are allocated between the *controlling interest* (parent) and the *noncontrolling interest*, and these amounts will be identified separately in the consolidated income statement and in consolidated stockholders' equity. For example, the consolidated financial statements might appear as shown in Figure 5.23.

Figure 5.23   Financial Statement Reporting:
Consolidated Financial Statements (Partial)

Consolidated Income Statement		
Revenues		$5,000,000
Expenses		(3,000,000)
Net Income		2,000,000
Less: Income Attributable to the Noncontrolling Interest		(500,000)
Net Income Attributable to the Controlling Interest (or *Consolidated Net Income*)		$1,500,000
Consolidated Stockholders' Equity		
Common Stock	$3,000,000	
Retained Earnings	4,000,000	
Controlling Interest		$7,000,000
Noncontrolling Interest		1,000,000
Consolidated Stockholders' Equity		$8,000,000

We are now ready to take a closer look at the major categories of assets a company acquires and uses in its business operations. We will discuss the characteristics and concepts pertaining to plant assets, natural resources, and intangible assets in the next three sections of this chapter.

Property, Plant, and Equipment

The property, plant, and equipment asset classification includes tangible physical assets currently being used in business operations. The terms *plant assets, fixed assets*, and *long-lived assets* also are used to describe assets in this category. Along with land, buildings, equipment, vehicles, and furniture and fixtures, a building currently under construction for a company's own use may be reported in this classification. Even assets the company is leasing may be included if the lease terms are in substance similar to ownership which is discussed later in this chapter.

Although these assets could be sold or exchanged, they are held for use and not generally held for sale in the normal course of business. New or used equipment, if held for resale by a dealer, would be presented as inventory under current assets. Land purchased for speculative purposes or as a possible site for future expansion would be classified as a long-term investment. A real estate developer would classify the land and its office building as a plant asset, while a land or real estate development held for sale would be classified elsewhere.

The property, plant, and equipment classification of the balance sheet probably would include the items shown in Figure 5.24.

Figure 5.24   Balance Sheet Reporting: Property, Plant, and Equipment

Property, Plant, and Equipment		
Land	$ 95,000	
Buildings (net)	196,000	
Machinery and Equipment (net)	72,000	
Furniture and Fixtures (net)	30,000	
Construction in Progress	7,000	
Total Property, Plant, and Equipment		$400,000

COST OF PROPERTY, PLANT, AND EQUIPMENT

According to the historical cost concept, the balance sheet value for plant assets initially is based on the cost when acquired, which is presumed to be the current market value at that time. Acquisition cost includes reasonable costs necessary to acquire the asset and prepare it for use. For example, the cost of equipment might include not only the invoice price but also the costs of shipping, installation, and trial runs to make sure the equipment is working properly. The cost of a building might include the construction permit, architectural fees, and excavation of the building foundation, along with the more obvious costs associated with the materials, labor, and overhead costs required for constructing the new building. The cost of land purchased as a building site might include the cost to remove an unwanted structure, the cost to clear or drain the site, and any other necessary costs to prepare the land for construction of the new building.

CAPITAL VERSUS REVENUE EXPENDITURES

The amounts spent to acquire a plant asset and prepare it for use, as well as the cost of later additions or significant improvements which extend its useful life, are referred to as *capital expenditures*. One might say that a particular amount should be capitalized; that means that those expenditures are included in the cost of a particular plant asset and eventually depreciated.

By contrast, the costs of routine repairs and maintenance of plant assets are operating expenses, while abnormal repair costs, perhaps arising from vandalism or damages caused by fire or natural disasters, are more likely to be presented in the income statement as losses rather than as operating expenses. The term *revenue expenditures* is used to describe these types of costs as they are matched with the current period's revenues in the income statement and are not included in the asset cost.

CAPITALIZED INTEREST

When a company finances the purchase of a plant asset with borrowed funds, the interest on the loan is reported as interest expense in the income statement. However, if specific conditions are met, for example, when a company constructs a building or another specific plant asset for its own use, the interest incurred during the construction period may be capitalized and included in the cost of the building rather than expensed immediately. As a result, once the asset under construction has been completed and placed in use, the interest that was capitalized during the construction period is reflected in the asset cost and will be included in the depreciation expense during the period of use.

CAPITAL LEASES

In specific cases, assets the company does not own but leases under the terms of a long-term contract are included in plant assets on the balance sheet. If the substance of the lease agreement more closely resembles that of financing the purchase of a long-lived asset with a long-term borrowing arrangement, the leased asset will be capitalized and included on the balance sheet, much like the purchase of a plant asset that was financed by issuing long-term debt. The "cost" of the leased asset will be based on the present value of the future lease payments, and the lease obligation will be reported as a long-term liability in a manner similar to that used for a long-term mortgage note payable. Lease obligations and some related concepts are discussed further in the section on long-term liabilities later in this chapter.

MATERIALITY

Two final accounting concepts, materiality and cost-benefits, often are applied when one is attempting to differentiate between capital and revenue expenditures. For example, a metal wastebasket purchased for $20 may last for decades (or centuries) and theoretically should be included in plant assets, but it may be expensed immediately as an insignificant amount; the benefit of keeping detailed records for wastebaskets and other immaterial items probably is not worth the additional cost.

DEPRECIATION

Just as supplies are treated as an expense when they are used and not when they are purchased, the cost of plant assets are considered to be expenses during the periods of use in accordance with the matching principle. Although plant assets are not used up the way supplies are, the amount invested in plant assets represents a significant cost of doing business. When assets are used in revenue-producing activities, the matching principle requires that a portion of the cost of plant assets be recorded as an expense during each of the periods in which they are used rather than as an expense in the period in which they were acquired. This concept of cost allocation is referred to as *depreciation*.

Your personal experience with depreciation probably differs from the accounting concept. For example, after you purchase a car and drive it for a couple of years, you probably would say it has depreciated, and you might then look online to find its book value in case you want to trade it in or sell it. However, for financial statement purposes, depreciation is considered to be cost allocation, treating a portion of the original cost as an expense during each year in which the asset is used. Accounting depreciation does not necessarily measure the actual decline in value, nor does the accounting book value of an asset necessarily indicate its current value if it were sold or traded in. In fact, some assets actually appreciate or increase in value.

While land is a permanent asset, most other plant assets wear out, lose their value, become obsolete, and/or eventually must be replaced. As was discussed in Chapter 4, a depreciable asset is presented on the balance sheet as shown in Figure 5.25.

In this example, the total acquisition cost of the equipment was $100,000. It is customary to show both the original cost and the *accumulated depreciation* amount, which is the total amount of past depreciation expense: $28,000 in this example. The $72,000 difference is reported as equipment (net), which is referred to as the *book value* of the equipment. Alternatively, this information may be presented in the balance sheet in the manner shown in Figure 5.26.

Figure 5.25 Balance Sheet Reporting: Depreciable Asset

Equipment	$100,000	
Less: Accumulated Depreciation	(28,000)	
Equipment (net)		$72,000

Figure 5.26 Balance Sheet Reporting: Depreciable Asset Net

Equipment (net of accumulated depreciation of $28,000)	$72,000

BOOK VALUE

The term *book value*, as it is used in accounting, is simply the cost of a plant asset that has not been depreciated yet, not an indication of its current value, which could be substantially different for reasons that will be discussed below. Since the company is using the equipment and does not intend to sell it, its current market value is less relevant than would be the market value of an investment the company can or does plan to sell.

Even though the book value is not a measure of an asset's current value, knowing the original cost and accumulated depreciation can be useful in judging how soon an asset may need to be replaced and providing at least a notion of the magnitude of the replacement cost. For example, assume Company A and Company B each report equipment with a net book value of $72,000 on their respective balance sheets as shown in Figure 5.27.

Figure 5.27 Book Value: A Comparison

	Company A	Company B
Equipment	$100,000	$300,000
Less: Accumulated Depreciation	(28,000)	(228,000)
Book Value	$ 72,000	$ 72,000

Although the equipment book value for both companies is $72,000, you should notice that Company B paid $300,000 to purchase its equipment and has taken $228,000 in depreciation. You might then conclude that Company B may need to replace its equipment sooner and perhaps at a much higher cost than Company A. You might wonder if Company B has the cash or the ability to borrow the money it will soon need to replace the equipment.

DEPRECIATION METHODS

The accounting concept of depreciation allocates a portion of the cost of an asset to expense during each period of use in accordance with the matching principle. Different methods and assumptions can be used in determining annual depreciation expense, just as there are different methods for determining inventory and cost of goods sold. Although the total depreciation expense taken on a particular asset would be the same regardless of the depreciation method used, the amount of the expense taken in individual years may be significantly different.

Depreciation expense concepts and some common alternative methods in the context of plant assets will be discussed in detail below, and you will find that similar concepts also apply to the depletion of natural resources and the amortization of intangible assets, which are discussed in later sections of this chapter.

DEPRECIATION BASE

All depreciation methods are based on the cost of the asset, an estimate of its salvage or residual value, and its estimated life or output. The *salvage or residual value* is an estimate of the sale, trade-in, or scrap value of the asset at the end of its useful life. The depreciation base, or the total amount of depreciation expense to be taken, is based on the original cost less its estimated salvage value. In all the examples below, it is assumed that the amount capitalized as the cost of equipment is $100,000, the estimated salvage value is $30,000, and the depreciation base—the total amount of depreciation expense—is $70,000 for all methods.

Cost $100,000 − Salvage Value $30,000 = Depreciation Base $70,000

USEFUL LIFE OR PRODUCTIVE OUTPUT

A company estimates the useful life or productive output of a particular asset on the basis of expected wear and tear, obsolescence, and the company's normal replacement policies. If it is company policy to replace its delivery vans every five years, even though a van may have a serviceable life of 20 years, it will be depreciated using a five-year life or the expected mileage for the five years it will be used by the business.

STRAIGHT-LINE DEPRECIATION

Straight-line (SL) depreciation is a simple and widely used method. An equal amount of depreciation expense is taken during each year of use, as shown in Figure 5.28. If one plotted the amount the annual depreciation expense on a line graph, there would be a straight line, hence the name of this method. The $14,000 of annual depreciation generally will be reported as an operating expense in the income statement, but if the equipment is used to manufacture or assemble products, the depreciation will be included in the manufacturing overhead costs discussed earlier. On the balance sheet, the book value of the equipment will decrease steadily by $14,000 each year, and the book value will be $30,000 at the end of its useful life which is the original estimate of its salvage value, as shown in Figure 5.28.

Figure 5.28   Straight-Line Depreciation

$$\frac{\text{Cost - Salvage Value}}{\text{Estimated Useful Life (Years)}} = \text{Annual Depreciation Expense}$$

$$\frac{\$100,000 - \$30,000}{5 \text{ years}} = \frac{\$70,000}{5 \text{ years}} = \$14,000/\text{yr}$$

Year	Equipment	Accumulated Depreciation	Book Value
0	$100,000	$ 0	$100,000
1	$100,000	(14,000)	$ 86,000
2	$100,000	(28,000)	$ 72,000
3	$100,000	(42,000)	$ 58,000
4	$100,000	(56,000)	$ 44,000
5	$100,000	(70,000)	$ 30,000

The book value of this equipment is simply the cost that has not been depreciated yet and is not meant to be an indication of its value if it was sold; also, accounting depreciation is a matter of allocating a portion of the equipment cost to expense during each year of use and is not meant to measure the decline in the value of the equipment that year.

Recall that the $30,000 salvage value was simply an estimate made when the equipment was purchased. If the equipment in this example was sold at the end of year 5, the company would not necessarily receive $30,000. If the equipment was sold for $25,000, a *loss on sale of equipment* of $5,000 would be reported in the income statement. If it was sold for $32,000, a *gain on sale of equipment* of $2,000 would be reported. The loss or gain would be reported below normal operating results as other income or expense.

UNITS OF PRODUCTION DEPRECIATION

The *units of production (UP)* or similar output- or activity-based depreciation methods use some measure of productivity or actual use. For example, a vehicle may be depreciated on the basis of mileage, heavy construction equipment on the basis of engine hours, or a photocopier on the basis of the number of copies made. Let's assume that the equipment in the example above is used in mining operations and is depreciated on the basis of tons of mineral ore extracted and that an estimated 350,000 tons will be mined using this equipment. The calculation of the depreciation rate per ton of ore and the amounts of depreciation expense for each year are shown in Figure 5.29.

Figure 5.29 Units of Production Depreciation

$$\frac{\text{Cost - Salvage Value}}{\text{Estimated Units of Production}} = \text{Depreciation Rate per Unit}$$

$$\frac{\$100,000 - \$30,000}{350,000 \text{ Tons}} = \$0.20 \text{ per unit}$$

Year	Actual Tons Produced	x $0.20	Depreciation Expense
1	40,000		$ 8,000
2	120,000		24,000
3	90,000		18,000
4	70,000		14,000
5	30,000		6,000
	350,000		$70,000

When the units of production method is used, depreciation expense varies each year; however, this method matches the cost of the equipment with its actual productivity or use, unlike the straight-line method, which simply uses an equal amount of depreciation expense each year. The units of production method makes good sense for certain types of assets, but in most cases it would be hard to justify using this method in depreciating a building.

DECLINING BALANCE DEPRECIATION

Compared with straight-line depreciation, the *declining balance (DB)* method results in higher amounts of depreciation expense in the early years and lower amounts in the later years of use and is referred to as an *accelerated method* of depreciation for that reason. If an asset is more productive and efficient when it is relatively new and requires more repairs and maintenance expenditures and is less efficient as it ages, this concept of matching the cost of an asset to the periods of benefit makes sense for certain types of assets. It is also important to have a basic understanding of the declining balance method because income tax depreciation for many assets is based on some form of this method.

With declining balance methods, a fixed percentage of book value is used as the depreciation expense each year; as the book value declines each year, so does the amount of depreciation expense; this explains the name of these methods. If a company used the straight-line method for equipment with a five-year life, it would depreciate one-fifth of the cost, or 20 percent, each year. A *double declining balance method* involves using twice the straight-line rate: 40 percent in this case. The calculations of the rate and the annual depreciation expense for the double declining balance method are shown in Figure 5.30.

Figure 5.30   Double Declining Balance Depreciation Method

(1) Cost - Accumulated Depreciation = Book Value
(2) Double Declining Balance uses twice the Straight-Line Rate
    Straight-Line Rate = 20% (1/5 per year or 20%) x 2 = 40%
(3) Book Value x Rate = Depreciation Expense

Year	Cost	Accumulated Depreciation	(1) Book Value	Rate (2)	(3) Depreciation Expense
1	$100,000	$ 0	$100,000	40%	$40,000
2	100,000	(40,000)	60,000		24,000
3	100,000	(64,000)	36,000	(4)	6,000
4	100,000	(70,000)	36,000		0
5	100,000	(70,000)	36,000		0
					$70,000

(4) The amount calculated for Year 3 is actually $14,400 ($36,000 BV x 40%). However, the asset cannot be depreciated below salvage value, so only $70,000 of total depreciation expense can be recorded. Only $6,000 depreciation is taken in Year 3, and none in Years 4 and 5

Just as in the previous examples, a total of $70,000 depreciation expense is taken ($100,000 cost − $30,000 salvage). However, salvage value is omitted from the initial calculation of depreciation expense even though the company cannot depreciate the equipment below its estimated salvage value. As a result, only $6,000 of depreciation expense can be taken in year 3 and none in years 4 and 5 because the asset is fully depreciated.

A COMPARISON OF DEPRECIATION METHODS

In the discussion and examples illustrating the different depreciation methods above, you learned that total depreciation expense is the same with each financial statement method; however, the depreciation expense and resulting book value differ each year. A comparison of the three methods discussed is presented in Figure 5.31.

Figure 5.31   Comparison of Depreciation Methods

INCOME STATEMENT - DEPRECIATION EXPENSE			
Year	Straight-Line	Units of Production	Declining Balance
1	$14,000	$ 8,000	$40,000
2	14,000	24,000	24,000
3	14,000	18,000	6,000
4	14,000	14,000	0
5	14,000	6,000	0
Total	$70,000	$70,000	$70,000
BALANCE SHEET - BOOK VALUE			
Year	Straight-Line	Units of Production	Declining Balance
0	$100,000	$100,000	$100,000
1	86,000	92,000	60,000
2	72,000	68,000	36,000
3	58,000	50,000	30,000
4	44,000	36,000	30,000
5	30,000	30,000	30,000

A total of $70,000 of depreciation expense was taken for all three methods; however, the straight-line version was based on an even amount each year, the units of production version was based on the actual use of the asset, and the declining balance version accelerated the amount of depreciation to be taken, with higher expense in the early years. The book value of the equipment at the end of its five-year life was $30,000 in all three methods; however, the balance sheet value for each year differed considerably. Just as with inventory cost-flow assumptions, the choice of a depreciation method can have a significant impact on the financial statement results and should be taken into consideration in evaluating a company's performance. The methods used and other information must be disclosed in the footnotes to the financial statements.

OTHER DEPRECIATION METHODS

Companies may use several other methods to depreciate plant assets, depending on the nature of the assets involved, materiality, the pattern of use, and other factors. The *sum-of-the-years-digits* method is another type of accelerated depreciation, although it is not illustrated here as it is not as widely used as it was in the past. Rather than depreciating individual assets, some companies base annual depreciation expense on a group of similar assets, for example, a leasing company's fleet of vehicles or a utility company's power poles.

INCOME TAX DEPRECIATION METHODS

Companies must use the methods specified in the tax law to prepare their income tax returns. Financial statement and income tax depreciation methods are similar in some respects but differ in others. Currently, tax law is based on the Modified Accelerated Cost Recovery System (MACRS), and many assets are depreciated using a declining balance concept, although optional straight-line methods are permitted in particular cases.

Tax law provides incentives which encourage companies to invest in productive assets. Salvage value is ignored in many cases, and that produces higher depreciation expense deductions; also, the useful lives that are specified in the tax law are often shorter than those which would be used for financial statement depreciation. When a company prepares its income tax return, it uses a specified tax life for the asset and the percentage of cost it can deduct each year can be found in a table that is based on a variation of the declining balance method discussed above. Figure 5.32 shows the annual depreciation deduction that can be taken in the tax return for the asset in the examples cited above.

Higher and earlier tax depreciation deductions reduce tax obligations that otherwise are payable in the early years after the purchase of a depreciable asset. As a result, there may be differences between income as reported in a corporation's income statement and the taxable income based on the corporation's tax return, leading to deferred income taxes, which is briefly discussed later under long-term liabilities. Figure 5.33 illustrates the difference between depreciation expense in the corporation's income statement and the depreciation expense deducted each year on its income tax return.

Figure 5.32   Income Tax Depreciation—MACRS

Tax law specifies the life and method
Similar to financial statement declining balance method, except:
Salvage value is ignored, 1/2 year depreciation in the first and last year
Percentage of cost to be depreciated each year is specified in a table

Year	Cost	Percent from tax table	Tax Depreciation	
1	$100,000	20.00%	$ 20,000	1/2 year
2		32.00%	32,000	
3		19.20%	19,200	
4		11.52%	11,520	
5		11.52%	11,520	
6		5.76%	5,760	1/2 year
		100.00%	$100,000	

Figure 5.33   Comparison of Financial Statement and Income Tax Depreciation

Salvage value is ignored for income tax purposes
The entire $100,000 cost is deductible
Higher tax deductions in early years based on accelerated method

Year	Financial Statements Straight Line	Tax Return MACRS	Higher Tax Depreciation Deduction
1	$14,000	$ 20,000	$ 6,000
2	14,000	32,000	$18,000
3	14,000	19,200	$ 5,200
4	14,000	11,520	($ 2,480)
5	14,000	11,520	($ 2,480)
6		5,760	$ 5,760
Total	$70,000	$100,000	$30,000

IMPAIRMENT LOSSES

You probably noticed that the concept of conservatism came up often in our discussion of the various asset categories. If the market value of investments declined, they were reported on the balance sheet at the lower market value. When it seemed doubtful that customer receivable balances would be collected in full, an allowance for estimated uncollectible accounts was established, and receivables were reported at the lower net realizable value. If inventory on hand was damaged, became obsolete, or could be sold only at significantly reduced prices, if at all, the inventory was written down to the lower of cost or market.

In the face of uncertainty, by taking a conservative approach, a company is less likely to overstate its income or its assets. The concept of conservatism also applies to long-lived assets—not just plant assets but also natural resources and intangible assets, as will be discussed later. Long-lived assets are reported at a conservative value on the balance sheet. They initially are valued at their cost, but only certain costs can be capitalized. Plant assets other than land are depreciated, and the balance sheet values decline over time, yet any appreciation or increase in the actual economic value of a plant asset in use is ignored completely in the financial statements unless that asset is sold to another party for a higher value. Book value is simply the cost that has not been depreciated yet, not the current market value, and the book value of a particular asset can vary with the depreciation method used. For all these reasons, the balance sheet values are already pretty conservative, but what if even this conservative value is too high?

Impairment Indicators

Assume a company constructs an office building using high-quality materials and craftsmanship. All the offices have huge windows with views of the nearby hills and forests and the magnificent mountain ranges in the distance, and there are beautifully landscaped outdoor areas surrounding the building with running paths and a trout pond. Despite the high rent, the owner has leased all the offices and has a long waiting list of prospective tenants in case a vacancy arises.

Business was great for the first five years, until the county opened a 24-hour gravel pit operation on the property adjacent to the office building. Gravel pits, dirt and dust, noisy machinery, heavy truck traffic, and obstructed views caused many tenants to move out as soon as their lease terms expired. Those who remained agreed to do so at a fraction of the rent they had been paying. No one on the waiting list seemed interested anymore.

Regardless of its book value, the office building is certainly worth far less than it was before the gravel pit operations began. The future rent the owner expects to earn may be enough to cover the operating costs but not enough to recover all the costs originally invested in the building. Even though the owner plans to keep leasing the offices in the building, it is certainly worth less than before if the owner decides to sell out.

These events may require the company to report an *impairment loss* in its income statement. An impairment loss occurs when the value of a long-lived asset has declined below its book value, if future earnings are not sufficient to recover the cost, or the asset could be sold only for less than its book value. Although you might not hear the term *impairment loss* in a news broadcast, huge write-downs, sometimes as much as a 50 percent reduction in book value of a company's long-lived assets, are definitely newsworthy items.

Natural Resoruces

Natural resources include ownership of or rights to minerals, petroleum, timber, and other creations of nature that can be extracted or harvested from the land and then sold in an unprocessed state or processed further and sold. For example, a logging company may harvest trees and sell them to a lumber mill, but it also may have its own lumber mill which produces heartwood for furniture and construction-grade lumber such as two-by-fours but then sell other timber by-products to companies which produce plywood, paper, or landscape products made from tree bark.

COST OF NATURAL RESOURCES

There are unique costs associated with acquiring and developing a natural resource; some are capitalized as part of the cost of the natural resource, others may be capitalized as buildings or equipment, and some will be expensed. Costs to purchase land containing a natural resource or to acquire the legal rights to natural resources generally are capitalized as the cost of those resources.

Exploration costs to determine if a natural resource exists or if it exists in a sufficient quantity to be economically feasible to develop and extract generally are expensed in most industries, with one major exception. Oil and gas exploration companies are permitted to capitalize their exploration costs as part of the natural resource, using either the full-cost or the successful-efforts approach.

In the *full-cost approach*, all exploration costs are capitalized, even costs associated with dry holes, whereas with the *successful-efforts approach*, only the costs associated with producing wells are capitalized and the other exploration costs are expensed. The approach used has an impact not only on the balance sheet value of the natural resource but also on the amount of depletion that will be taken each year, and so it is important to determine which method a company is using by reading the footnotes to the financial statements.

The costs to develop a natural resource can be *intangible* in nature, such as drilling, blasting, and tunneling or building roads, and these costs generally are capitalized as part of the cost of the natural resource. *Tangible costs* such as trucks to haul mineral ore and an office trailer generally are capitalized as plant assets and depreciated if those items can be used in other ways or at other locations. By contrast, the

costs of tangible equipment that cannot be moved or has no other use, such as a permanent drilling rig or underground pumps, probably will be capitalized as part of the natural resource.

Many companies are legally obligated to restore the property at the conclusion of extractive operations. Future *restoration costs* can be substantial and are a component of the overall cost of operations even though some restoration costs may not be incurred until operations cease many years later. The company must estimate the future costs it will incur to satisfy any legal requirements and report that restoration (or retirement) obligation in the balance sheet as a long-term liability; the costs will be reflected as an additional component of the depletion cost recorded as the resource is extracted.

DEPLETION OF NATURAL RESOURCES

Depletion is similar to the concept of depreciation used for plant assets, matching the cost of a long-lived asset to the periods of use or benefit. As the natural resource is removed or depleted, a portion of the capitalized natural resource cost will be allocated to each period, using a units of production approach. The depletion rate is calculated on the basis of the cost of the resource less any residual value and the estimated quantity of the resource that will be extracted. The depletion taken each year is based on the actual quantity produced.

As was discussed above, there are costs unique to natural resource assets, some of which become part of the depletion base, while others are capitalized as plant assets, and other costs are expensed. If the company owns the land containing the resource, depletion will be based on the cost of the resource less the estimated residual value of the land. It is often difficult to make a reliable estimate of the quantity or output of some natural resources, particularly mineral deposits and offshore petroleum reserves, and the company may seek the opinion of outside experts. Estimating the board-feet of lumber that could be produced from a tract of standing timber would be less difficult.

Natural Resource Cost − Residual Value = Depletion Base
Depletion Base ÷ Estimated Units = Depletion Rate per Unit

Natural resource producers are similar to manufacturers, except that the raw materials for their products are derived from nature rather than purchased from suppliers. The depletion cost each period is treated in the same manner as the direct material cost for a manufacturing company. Thus, the depletion cost for a particular year is not an operating expense; it is included in the cost of inventory on the balance sheet and later in the cost of goods sold in the income statement, as shown in Figure 5.34.

Figure 5.34   Depletion Cost: Inventory and Cost of Goods Sold

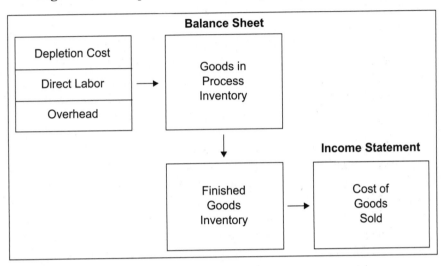

Thus, depletion becomes part of the total cost of the natural resource product produced, along with the labor and overhead costs when determining the cost of the inventories on hand and the cost of the products sold. Depletion rules for income tax purposes may be significantly different from those described above.

NATURAL RESOURCES ON THE BALANCE SHEET

Natural resources are shown in the balance sheet at cost less the amount of depletion taken in previous periods (see Figure 5.35), similar to plant assets, and often appear in the property, plant, and equipment classification. Additional information about natural resources and restoration obligations is provided in the footnotes to the financial statements, and oil and gas producers have other specific disclosure requirements.

Figure 5.35   Balance Sheet Reporting: Natural Resources

Forestlands	$200,000,000	
Less: Accumulated Depletion	(50,000,000)	
Forestlands (net)		$150,000,000
OR		
Forestlands (net of accumulated depletion of $50,000,000)		$150,000,000

Intangible Assets

Intangible assets are quite different from the other asset categories discussed in this chapter, and so we begin with a scenario to get you to think about some of their unique characteristics. Your grandparents married young and moved to a new town to start a family and a business. You are now running a prosperous business that has been in your family for three generations, and out of the blue, you are approached by someone who wants to buy your family business. What is it worth?

As a starting point, you could have the land and building appraised, find trade-in values for your vehicles and equipment, and look up how much it would cost to buy the inventory in your store at today's prices and the market price of your short-term investments.

However, are there some things you can't quite pinpoint, in addition to those you can touch or identify, that make your business more valuable? We think so. It is an established and very profitable business with loyal customers and a sterling reputation spanning three generations. Your employees are knowledgeable and have worked in this business for years, as did their parents and grandparents. People in surrounding states recognize your business name; everywhere you go, you see people wearing T-shirts and hats printed with the unique logo you designed for your store, including people who are not regular customers.

We think your business has some *intangible assets*, and we're sure you think so, too. If you decide to sell the company, we hope the buyer thinks like the rest of us and offers you a higher price as a result! These intangible characteristics have become increasingly significant; in some cases 80 to 90 percent of the price paid to acquire an existing company is for such intangible things, in stark contrast to the past, when the value of manufacturing facilities or other tangible assets acquired was a primary component of the price offered.

Even though financial accounting guidelines for intangible assets have evolved in recent years, you should have at least a basic understanding of these guidelines and their limitations and inconsistencies, which are even more important in light of the importance of intangible assets in the current business era.

CATEGORIES OF INTANGIBLE ASSETS

The term *intangible assets* can refer to a diverse and broad range of items. Some can be identified readily and separately, particularly those which represent legal or contractual rights, whereas others arise from research or good business practices and are associated with the business as a whole. Intangible assets may be developed internally or purchased from others.

Separately Identifiable Intangible Assets

You are probably familiar with some common intangible assets, such as patents, copyrights, and franchises, but accounting guidelines include examples of many others, which are described briefly below:

- **Marketing-related**: trademarks and trade names, certification marks, trade dress (such as a unique product color or shape), a distinctive newspaper masthead, internet domain names, and noncompetition agreements
- **Customer-related**: customer lists, confirmed customer orders, and contracts
- **Artistic-related**: literary works, operas and plays, musical works, photographs and art, movies and television programs
- **Contract-based**: franchise, licensing, royalty, and lease agreements; broadcast rights; advertising, construction, management, and service contracts; and use rights for drilling, water, air, timber, and routes
- **Technology-based**: patented technology, computer software, databases, and trade secrets (such as a secret recipe)

Goodwill

In thinking about what your business might be worth in the example above, there seem to be some very intangible qualities, such as its long-standing reputation, loyal employees and customers, and sustained profitability. These characteristics make your business more valuable than the sum of its parts but cannot be separated from the business as a whole. You might say your business has *goodwill*, another category of intangible assets. The prospective buyer may offer you a higher price to purchase the business because of the goodwill it has developed over time.

Is this goodwill reported as an intangible asset on your balance sheet? No, but it would appear on the balance sheet if the company was purchased by the prospective buyer because there would be an objective measure of its value: the excess amount paid over the tangible and intangible assets that could be identified specifically. For example, if you sold the business for $800,000 and the specific assets were worth $600,000, goodwill of $200,000 would appear on the buyer's balance sheet. Tremendous amounts of goodwill often are recorded by large public corporations which have purchased other large corporations recently.

COST OF INTANGIBLE ASSETS

As implied by the example involving goodwill, there seems to be a difference in whether an intangible asset will appear on the balance sheet, depending on if it was internally developed or it was purchased. The same is true with other types of intangible assets.

Research and development costs may produce intangible benefits to the business but generally are expensed rather than recorded as assets because uncertainty exists about the future benefits provided by those expenditures. As was discussed in Chapter 4, a company that spent $5 million on research and development activities, ultimately leading to a patent registered at a cost of $10,000, would capitalize only the $10,000 direct patent cost, while the $5 million of R&D would be expensed. This conservative approach is used because it is difficult to determine how much of the R&D costs produced a direct benefit.

However, if another party paid $20 million to purchase the patent for the competitive edge it would gain, the patent would appear on the purchaser's balance sheet at $20 million, an objective measure of its cost. In summary, only the direct costs to acquire or maintain an intangible asset are capitalized; internal development costs are expensed.

AMORTIZATION OF INTANGIBLE ASSETS

The matching principle requires that the cost of an intangible asset be expensed over its useful life to the business. The term *amortization* is used to describe the cost allocation for an intangible asset, just like the concepts of depreciation for plant assets and depletion for natural resources.

Many intangible assets have a definite legal life or a limited economic life, such as patents, copyrights, and franchises. An intangible asset with a definite, finite life should be amortized over the shorter of its legal life or its estimated economic or useful life to the business.

However, there are a few intangible assets that are not amortized. Certain types of intangible assets with a short legal life can be renewed, such as a trademark which can be renewed every 10 years and is considered to have an indefinite life. If the company intends to and is able to renew this type of intangible asset indefinitely, it is not amortized. Goodwill is another example of an intangible asset that is not amortized. However, if an intangible asset is not amortized, the company must evaluate the balance sheet value every year. If its value has declined, an *impairment loss* will be reported in the income statement and the intangible asset will be reported in the balance sheet at this more conservative value as we discussed earlier in the plant asset section.

As with plant assets and natural resources, amortization of intangible assets is based on the cost, residual value (if any), and estimated useful life, but with a couple of differences. For most intangible assets, it is assumed that the residual or salvage value is zero unless there is some type of commitment to sell the intangible at the end of its useful life. The useful life should be based on the shorter of the legal life or the economic life. For example, a patent may provide legal protection for 20 years, but if the product patented probably will become obsolete after 5 years, the shorter period should be used.

The method used to amortize an intangible asset should reflect its pattern of use or benefit. For example, a product patent might be amortized using the units of production method rather than the straight-line method. The calculation of amortization expense would be much like the depreciation methods illustrated earlier in this chapter.

Intangible assets are presented on the balance sheet in the same manner as plant assets and natural resources, showing the cost and accumulated amortization separately, or the net amount. Additional information about the types of intangible assets, their manner of acquisition, and accounting policies can be found in the footnotes to the financial statements.

Current Liabilities

Current liabilities are obligations arising from past events which must be paid or settled within a year or within the operating cycle of the business, whichever is longer. These obligations are settled by using current assets (such as cash or merchandise inventory) or by the creation of other current liabilities (such as renewing a 90-day note).

As was discussed in Chapter 4, the distinction between current assets and current liabilities is very important in evaluating a company's ability to meet its short-term obligations as they come due, as is the proper classification of liabilities as either current or long-term. Current assets are expected to generate the cash resources needed to sustain ongoing business activities, cover routine expenses, and pay suppliers and lenders on time to maintain a healthy credit standing. Liquidity depends not only on how quickly a company's current assets generate cash but also on whether the amounts will be sufficient to cover its short-term obligations and provide an adequate cushion if something unexpected arises.

DETERMINING AND VALUING CURRENT LIABILITIES

The amounts reported for current liabilities generally are based on the amounts payable in cash or in goods and services. If an obligation arises from a bank loan, purchasing goods from a supplier on credit, monthly utility bills, or employee salaries and payroll tax liabilities, it is easy to determine that the obligation exists and identify the party to be paid and the amount owed.

However, not all potential obligations are that straightforward. Sometimes it is difficult to determine if a liability actually exists, and if it does exist, it may be difficult to determine the precise amount, the specified party involved, or both. As one would expect, the accounting concept of conservatism also applies to liabilities. As a result, some liabilities are based on estimated amounts, whereas other potential

obligations may be omitted from the balance sheet and described only in the foot-notes to the financial statements.

CONTINGENT LIABILITIES

A *contingent liability* is a potential obligation arising from a past transaction, but whether an actual liability exists depends on or is contingent upon a future outcome. For example, assume your company sells goods to a customer and accepts a one-year note receivable. Rather than waiting a year to collect the note and interest, you sell the note to the bank with recourse. If the customer defaults and does not pay the bank when the note matures, your company is obligated to pay the bank. Does a liability exist? At this moment, the existence of this liability is contingent on a future out-come: whether the customer pays the bank at maturity or defaults on the loan.

Accounting guidelines for contingent liabilities are based on the likelihood that a liability exists and the ability to estimate the amount. If the liability is probable and one can make a reasonable estimate of the amount, it will be included as a liability on the balance sheet and often described in the financial statement footnotes. How-ever, if it is only reasonably possible that there will be an unfavorable outcome, it will be described in the footnotes and not appear on the balance sheet. It is common to see a caption for contingent liabilities on the balance sheet, but with no dollar amount. This form of disclosure is meant to call the reader's attention to informa-tion discussed in the footnotes.

Returning to the example of selling a note receivable with recourse, if you think it is probable that the customer will default and that you will have to pay the bank, you will report the amount you expect to pay as a liability in your balance sheet and the loss in your income statement. If it is reasonably possible but not probable that the customer will default, footnote disclosures will describe the sale with recourse and state that it is reasonably possible the customer will default and also will pro-vide an estimate of the amount of the recourse liability.

As one would imagine, contingent liabilities are challenging and controversial issues, and considerable judgment is involved in determining how they should be treated in financial statements, particularly those arising from pending litigation and environmental obligations.

ESTIMATED LIABILITIES

An estimated liability may involve uncertainty about the amount owed or the spe-cific party to whom there is an obligation. To illustrate an estimated liability, con-sider the case of a manufacturer that provides warranty coverage on its products and that approximately 5 percent of the products it sold in past years were returned for replacement under the warranty. Does a liability exist? Probably.

The obligation under the warranty may be viewed as a contingent liability, but on the basis of past experience it is probable that the company will incur warranty replacement costs on some of the products sold this year, too. Even though it is not known precisely how many products will be returned for replacement or the specific customers involved, drawing upon past experience it is possible to make a reasonable estimate of the overall warranty costs that will be incurred. The estimated warranty costs for products sold should be treated as expenses and thus matched with the sales revenue earned during the current year, and the *estimated warranty obligation* for products that are still under warranty coverage but have not yet been returned for replacement should be reported as liabilities in the year-end balance sheet. The accounting treatment for warranties will be discussed again later in this section of the chapter.

Chapter 4 discussed common types of current liabilities, and we will discuss a few of them in more detail below or refer you to other sections of this chapter where a similar example can be found. Current liabilities typically include the items in Figure 5.36.

Figure 5.36   Balance Sheet Reporting: Current Liabilities

Current Liabilities		
Accounts Payable	$81,000	
Notes Payable	10,000	
Estimated Warranty Obligations	30,000	
Unearned Revenues	8,000	
Accrued Liabilities	600	
Payroll Tax Liabilities	9,400	
Income Taxes Payable	48,000	
Dividends Payable	10,000	
Current Portion of Long-Term Debt	3,000	
Total Current Liabilities		$200,000

ACCOUNTS PAYABLE

Accounts payable also are referred to as *trade payables*; they arise from normal business trade transactions and typically represent amounts owed to suppliers for goods and services purchased on credit. The normal credit period may be 30 days, but it can be longer in certain industries. If the credit terms are n/10 EOM, the amount billed is due within 10 days after the end of the month. As was discussed earlier in the material on accounts receivable, cash discount terms may be offered

as an incentive for early payment. For example, if the credit terms are 1/10 net/30 on a $10,000 account balance, if the balance is paid within 10 days of the invoice, a 1 percent cash discount of $100 can be taken, otherwise one must pay the full $10,000 within 30 days (net/30).

If a company's current assets are not generating cash quickly enough for the company to take advantage of the discounts offered by its suppliers, it might consider a short-term borrowing arrangement in order to do so; the 1 percent discount, if annualized, is an 18 percent effective annual interest rate. For example, assume the company will have the money to pay the full invoice price of $10,000 when it is due in 30 days, but would need to borrow money to be able to pay the invoice 20 days earlier and receive the cash discount of $100. If it borrowed $10,000 at 18% interest for 20 days, it would pay $100 of interest ($10,000 × 18% × 20/360 days = $100). It would pay $100 interest to receive a $100 cash discount and break even. But if it could borrow the money for less than 18%, it would come out ahead.

When cash discounts are offered, a company might record its purchase of merchandise at the full invoice price of $10,000 and deduct the cash discount taken to arrive at an inventory cost of $9,900. Another company might record the purchase at $9,900 if it plans to take the discount and instead monitor the amount of the discounts it missed as this can be costly.

NOTES PAYABLE

Notes payable are formal promissory notes with specific maturity dates, interest rates, and repayment terms. Rather than repeating examples here, we refer you to the discussions of notes receivable in an earlier section and the notes payable and bonds payable sections in later sections of this chapter.

ESTIMATED WARRANTY OBLIGATIONS

Concepts pertaining to contingent and estimated liabilities were discussed in the introduction to current liabilities in this chapter. Obligations and/or unearned revenues arising from warranties and similar arrangements pose some interesting and challenging accounting issues due to the uncertainties involved.

When a company provides warranty coverage for the products it sells, the warranty coverage provided can be viewed from at least two different perspectives. In the case of the manufacturing company that was discussed earlier in this section, the estimated warranty costs were considered to be an additional expense associated with the product sales, even though the precise number of products that would be returned under the warranty and the specific customers involved were unknown at that time.

In that case, drawing upon its past experience, the manufacturer estimated the warranty costs it expected it would incur and treated those costs as expenses of the current year which were matched with the sales revenue earned that year. The obligation for estimated warranty costs on products that were still under warranty coverage but had not yet been returned for replacement was reported as a liability in the year-end balance sheet. This treatment is referred to as an *expensed warranty approach*. You should note that given the uncertainty involved, considerable judgment is used when estimating the costs and the remaining unsettled warranty obligation, which can provide unethical managers an opportunity to paint a more favorable picture of the company than may actually exist.

Another perspective to warranty coverage can be taken which is referred to as a *sales warranty approach*. In this approach, the warranty coverage is viewed as a separate sales component, much like a service contract, which is discussed further in the unearned revenue section below.

UNEARNED REVENUES

Unearned revenues represent obligations that must be fulfilled in the future for which the company has been paid in advance. Common examples of unearned revenues include customer deposits for special orders, amounts received from sales of gift cards and certificates, online and print subscriptions, health club memberships, and future rental payments. You may find potentially returnable deposits, such as a lease security deposit, included in unearned revenues.

The revenues associated with these advance collections will be reported in the income statement in the period in which the goods or services are provided, or the customer's rights to a returnable deposit have expired or the customer has not met the conditions specified in the arrangement. Gift cards are increasingly popular, and many merchants have found that they provide substantial amounts of income and no cost when gift recipients fail to use the cards or have a few unused dollars remaining.

Referring back to the warranty example discussed earlier, a company may treat a portion of the selling price of its product as a separate warranty component, much like a service contract, or separately sell extended warranty coverage. The amount assigned to the warranty is unearned revenue that later will be earned over the period covered by the warranty. Rebates, coupons, premiums, frequent flyer miles and other award programs pose unique issues in determining the amount of revenue to be recognized at the time of sale versus at some future date.

ACCRUED LIABILITIES (ACCRUED EXPENSES)

Accrued liabilities (or accrued expenses) represent expenses which have been incurred but are unpaid, such as salaries and wages, interest on notes payable (even if the note is long-term), and utilities. If employees earn vacation, sick pay, or personal leave days, according to the matching principle, the amounts earned each period should be included in the operating expenses in the income statement, and the estimated liability for days earned but not yet taken will be a current liability on the balance sheet.

PAYROLL TAX LIABILITIES

Payroll tax liabilities include the income tax and FICA (Social Security and medicare) taxes the employer withheld from employee paychecks and additional payroll taxes imposed on the employer that have not been deposited or paid to the taxing authorities. The amount reported as salaries and wages expense in the income statement represents employees' gross pay, and salaries and wages payable on the year-end balance sheet represents the net amount owed to employees after withholdings. However, the employer must remit not only the payroll taxes withheld from employees, but also the additional employer payroll taxes it owes. The amount reported as payroll tax expense in the income statement includes the employer's matching amount of FICA taxes and state and federal unemployment taxes.

INCOME TAXES PAYABLE

Corporations are taxable entities and so any unpaid federal and state income taxes based on quarterly estimates or the completed income tax return are reported as current liabilities. However, income taxes on profits earned by sole proprietorships and partnerships are personal liabilities of the owner or owners, not liabilities of the business entity. Differences between accounting income and taxable income may result in deferred income taxes, which are discussed in the section on long-term liabilities later in this chapter.

DIVIDENDS PAYABLE

A corporation may distribute a portion of its earnings to the stockholders by declaring a cash dividend. There is no guarantee that common stockholders will receive cash dividends even if the corporation has paid regular cash dividends in the past; dividends are declared at the discretion of the board of directors. There are usually several days between the date a dividend is declared and the time it actually is paid. If a cash dividend has been declared but not been paid yet, current liabilities will include the amount of the dividend payable. As will be discussed in a later section, corporations may also issue preferred stock, which does carry a stated dividend rate, and preferred stock dividends must be paid before the common stockholders may receive cash dividend distributions. However, even the stated amount of the preferred stock dividend is not a liability until the board of directors formally declares that the dividend will be paid. The board of directors instead may declare a stock dividend that will be paid in additional shares of stock rather than in cash. This is not a current liability as it will not be settled with current assets or current liabilities; the dividend declared will be reported in stockholders' equity.

CURRENT PORTION OF LONG-TERM DEBT

As will be discussed below in the section on long-term liabilities, some borrowing arrangements require that a portion of the debt be repaid each year, such as an installment loan or serial bonds payable. If this is the case, the principal amount due and payable in the coming year is included in current liabilities and the remaining principal balance is reported as a long-term liability and presented on the balance sheet as shown in Figure 5.37, along with additional footnote disclosures.

Figure 5.37   Balance Sheet Reporting: Long-Term Installment Loans

Current Liabilities		
Current Portion of Long-Term Note Payable		$1,000
Long-Term Liabilities		
Long-Term Installment Note Payable	$10,000	
Less: Current Portion	(1,000)	
Total Long-Term Liabilities		$9,000

Long-Term Liabilities

While current liabilities are obligations which are generally due within a year and are settled by using current assets such as cash or merchandise inventory, long-term liabilities are borrowings or other obligations which are not due or payable for at least one year and perhaps will not be settled in full until many years in the future.

In Chapter 4, we briefly discussed examples of obligations one might find in the long-term liability classification. We now will discuss examples of several of the long-term liabilities shown in Figure 5.38.

Figure 5.38   Balance Sheet Reporting: Long-Term Liabilities

Long-Term Liabilities		
Notes Payable	$ 10,000	
Mortgage Notes Payable	97,000	
Capital Lease Obligations	137,000	
Pension Obligations	60,000	
Bonds Payable	92,000	
Deferred Income Tax Liabilities	4,000	
Total Long-Term Liabilities		$400,000

NOTES PAYABLE

A company may negotiate a loan from a financial institution or another lender to cover its short-term or long-term cash needs and sign a promissory note which specifies the interest rate, maturity date, and repayment terms. It may be an unsecured loan; if the borrower defaults and does not repay the note when due, no specific assets are pledged as collateral for the loan. The lender may require monthly payments which include principal and interest (see Mortgage Note Payable example below), require that only period interest payments be made, or allow the borrower to wait until the loan matures to repay both the principal and the interest that has accumulated.

As an example, assume a company signed a $10,000, 12 percent, five-year promissory note on January 1, 20x1. It was required to make semiannual interest payments only on July 1 and January 1 of each year, but wait to repay the principal amount due when the loan matures. The semiannual interest payment would be calculated as follows:

Principal × **Interest rate** × **Time** = **Interest**
$10,000 × 12% × 6/12 months = $600

Assume the company made the first interest payment on July 1, 20x1, but will not make the second interest payment until January 1, 20x2, the interest payment due date. When the December 31, 20x1, balance sheet is prepared, interest payable of $600 will be classified as a current liability, and the $10,000 note payable will be classified as a long-term liability, as shown in Figure 5.39.

Figure 5.39 Balance Sheet Reporting: Notes and Interest Payable
December 31, 20x1

Current Liabilities	
Interest Payable	$ 600
Long-Term Liabilities	
Note Payable	$10,000

In the final year before the loan matures, in most cases the note payable will be classified as a current liability as it is due within a year and will be repaid (settled by using current assets). But what if the company renegotiates the loan, and rather than repaying when it matures, it signs a new five-year note? In this case, the note may continue to be reported as a long-term liability as it will not be settled in cash but instead replaced with another long-term note.

MORTGAGE NOTES PAYABLE

A *mortgage note payable* is another form of long-term borrowing that typically is used to finance the purchase of land and/or buildings. A mortgage is a *secured* loan; the property financed by the loan is pledged as collateral and can be sold to cover the amount owed to the lender if the borrower defaults. Mortgage loans typically require monthly installment payments of principal and interest. Assume the principal balance of a 15-year mortgage loan is $100,000, and $3,000 of this balance is due within the coming year. The mortgage loan will appear in both the current liability and long-term liability classifications, as shown in Figure 5.40.

Figure 5.40 Balance Sheet Reporting: Mortgage Loan Repaid in Installments
December 31, 20x1

Current Liabilities		
Current Portion of Long-Term Debt		$ 3,000
Long-Term Liabilities		
Mortgage Note Payable	$100,000	
Less: Current Portion	(3,000)	
Total Long-Term Liabilities		97,000
Total Liabilities		$100,000

DISCOUNTED NOTES PAYABLE

Before we discuss what we mean by a *discounted note payable*, let's start with a more straightforward example. Assume that Company A purchases an acre of land in a business park for $10,000 and signs a promissory note payable to the bank. The principal amount of the note is $10,000, it has a 10 percent stated interest rate, and it matures in two years. However, the 10 percent interest will be compounded and added to the amount owed and will be paid when the note matures in two years rather than being paid each year. Figure 5.41 shows how the interest is calculated

Figure 5.41 Calculation of Compound Interest and
Maturity Value of a Note Payable

Year	Beginning Balance	+ 10% Interest	= Ending Balance
20x1	$10,000	$1,000	$11,000
20x2	11,000	1,100	12,100

and shows that a total of $12,100 will be repaid in two years: the $10,000 principal balance of the loan and the $2,100 compound interest. Note that no interest was paid in 20x1 and so the 20x2 interest is calculated on the total amount owed; in other words, the interest was compounded.

Assume Company B purchases an adjacent acre of land in the same business park and signs a note payable, promising to pay $12,100 in two years with zero interest. Does it seem realistic that Company B could borrow for two years and pay no interest? Probably not. There is an implied component of interest in this transaction even though none was stated specifically. If the market value of the land is $10,000, the additional $2,100 paid when the note matures is the implied interest or imputed interest that has accumulated during the two years.

The substance of Company B's loan is identical to that of Company A, although the forms of the two notes differ. In Company B's case, we would say that we are *discounting* the note to reflect the implied interest and that the *present value* of the note is $10,000. Both companies would record the land at its cost of $10,000, and both would pay $12,100 when the notes mature, which includes $2,100 of compound interest. However, on the date the note was signed, Company B would report the note on its balance sheet as shown in Figure 5.42.

Figure 5.42   Balance Sheet Reporting: Discounted Note Payable—Company B
January 1, 20x1

Long-Term Liabilities		
Note Payable	$12,100	
Less: Discount on Note Payable	(2,100)	
Total Long-Term Liabilities		$10,000

Company B's 20x1 income statement would include $1,000 of interest expense ($10,000 × 10 percent), and the December 31, 20x1, balance sheet would present the new ending balance of the loan as shown in Figure 5.43.

Figure 5.43   Balance Sheet Reporting: Discounted Note Payable—Company B
December 31, 20x1

Note Payable	$12,100	
Less: Discount on Note Payable	(1,100)	
Total Long-Term Liabilities		$11,000

Company B's 20x2 income statement would include $1,100 of interest expense ($11,000 × 10 percent), and the December 31, 20x2, balance sheet would present the new ending balance of the loan, the total amount that will be repaid, as shown in Figure 5.44.

Figure 5.44   Balance Sheet Reporting: Discounted Note Payable—Company B
December 31, 20x2

Note Payable	$12,100	
Less: Discount on Note Payable	0	
Total Long-Term Liabilities		$12,100

Financial statements include many other applications of the concepts similar to those described in the examples above. Although a detailed discussion of these concepts is beyond the scope of this book, similar concepts are applied to capital lease obligations and bonds payable, which are discussed below.

CAPITAL LEASE OBLIGATIONS

A company may enter into rental or lease agreements for equipment, buildings, or other assets as an alternative to financing an actual purchase of those assets on its own. A rental or lease arrangement may be for a short duration, such as renting specialized equipment for a few days, but for buildings and other assets the lease term may span many years. There are many considerations involved in a lease versus buy decision, along with many complex financial reporting issues that are beyond the scope of this book, but we will discuss a couple of examples briefly below.

Let's first examine an example of what might be called an *operating lease*. A company decides to rent office space and signs a one-year lease agreement in December 20x1, pays the first two months in advance, and makes monthly rent payments for the remainder of the lease term. As was discussed in Chapter 3, when financial statements are prepared on December 31, 20x1, one month of rent expense will be reported in the income statement, and the other month paid in advance will be reported as a current asset, prepaid rent, and not an expense until the following year in accordance with the matching principle.

Now let's consider a company that needs its own office building and can either finance the purchase of the building with a 25-year mortgage note payable and make monthly loan payments or enter into a 25-year agreement to lease another office building and make monthly lease payments. If it decides to borrow money and purchase a building, the building will be included in plant assets, and the mortgage note payable will be included in liabilities on the balance sheet.

But what if the company instead decides to lease the other building and is legally obligated to make 25 years of lease payments, along with other terms and conditions? That's a pretty big commitment. If this arrangement is considered to be an *operating lease*, the monthly lease payments would be reported as rent expense in the income statement, but you would not find the obligation for the future lease payments included among the liabilities; in other words, this would be an *off–balance sheet* arrangement (now almost a household term thanks to Enron and its clever arrangements to conceal its activities).

In contrast to an operating lease, a *capital lease* is the term used to describe lease arrangements that more closely resemble financing the purchase of an asset with long-term debt. Regardless of the form of the written agreement, the economic substance should be considered carefully because it may indicate that the arrangement is like a purchase in disguise in an effort to keep debt off a company's balance sheet.

If the 25-year lease arrangement above was determined to be a capital lease, it would be treated much like the actual purchase of the office building with a mortgage note payable. The capital lease obligation would represent the present value of the future lease payments (using concepts similar to the discounted note payable discussed earlier) and would be treated very much like a mortgage note payable, with a portion of each lease payment applied to pay down the capital lease obligation (much like principal payments on a loan) and the remainder of each payment is much like the interest portion of a mortgage loan payment. The building would be capitalized as though it had been purchased, included in plant assets, and depreciated.

BONDS PAYABLE

Bonds are a common form of financing that are used not only by large corporations but also by federal and state governments and agencies, school districts, and many other parties which need to borrow substantial amounts of money for a long period of time. When you purchase a U.S. savings bond, you are lending your money to the government. If you purchase a school district bond, you are making a loan to help pay for the construction of new schools or other improvements. If you purchase a corporate bond, you are lending money the corporation will use to finance expansion and growth either internally or to acquire other companies to achieve external growth.

This book is focused on the financial statements of business entities, and so we will emphasize concepts pertaining to corporate bonds, although many of the concepts are similar for bonds issued by other parties.

Debentures are a form of unsecured bonds (no specific collateral), while other types of bonds may pledge assets or specific revenue sources as collateral. Some bond agreements require the company to make periodic payments into a *sinking fund* which will be used to repay the bonds on the maturity date.

One advantage of this form of long-term borrowing is the company's ability to raise substantial amounts of money that it may not have to repay for years or even decades without relying upon a single lender, such as a bank, to do so. The denomination of a typical corporate bond is $1,000; in theory, if the corporation needs to borrow $10,000,000, it could borrow $1,000 each from 10,000 different parties. Another advantage is that a bondholder (the investor) can sell the bond investment to other parties and not have to wait to be repaid when the bonds mature, which might be many years in the future. Just like stock investments, bonds are purchased and sold daily in the financial markets.

Although the principal (or maturity value) of the bond may not be repaid for many years in the future, a stated amount of interest is owed and generally is paid semiannually. For example, if the corporation issues $10,000,000 of bonds with a stated annual interest rate of 4 percent and pays the interest semiannually, every six months the cash interest payment would be calculated as shown below:

Principal	$\times$	**Interest Rate**	$\times$	**Time**	=	**Interest**
$10,000,000	$\times$	4%	$\times$	6/12 months	=	$200,000

Amounts received by the corporation at the time it issues bonds may differ from the amount it is required to repay when the bonds mature to adjust for differences in the interest rate specified for the bonds and market rates of interest at the time of borrowing. Thus, bonds payable are shown in the balance sheet at their present value, based on implied or imputed interest, similar to the example of the discounted note payable that was discussed earlier in the chapter.

For example, if 4 percent bonds were issued when market rates of interest were higher than 4 percent, the bondholders might pay only $9,200,000 to purchase the bonds but if the bondholders hold their investment to maturity they still will be paid the full $10,000,000 when the bonds mature which compensates them for the additional interest they expected to earn. We would say the bonds are issued at a *discount*, based on concepts similar to the discounted note payable example that was discussed earlier. (The amount paid for the bonds, $9,200,000 in this case, is not a random number. It is based on a mathematical calculation using the timing and amounts of cash payments and an applicable interest rate, a topic beyond the scope of this book.) The bonds would be presented on the balance sheet as shown in Figure 5.45.

Figure 5.45   Balance Sheet Reporting: Bonds Payable Issued at a Discount

Long-Term Liabilities		
Bonds Payable (4% interest rate, maturing in 20 years)	$10,000,000	
Less: Discount on Bonds Payable	(800,000)	
Total Long-Term Liabilities		$9,200,000

By contrast, if the market rate of interest at the time the bonds are issued is less than 4 percent, the corporation will issue the bonds at a higher price; for example, the bonds might sell for $10,800,000. (Again, this is not a random number; it is computed using calculations that provide the bondholders with a lower interest rate that the market is willing to accept at the time.) This lower effective interest rate of return is achieved because the company will repay only $10,000,000 at maturity, reducing its overall effective interest cost. We would say the bonds are issued at a *premium*, and the bonds would be presented in the balance sheet as shown in Figure 5.46.

Figure 5.46   Balance Sheet Reporting: Bonds Payable Issued at a Premium

Long-Term Liabilities		
Bonds Payable (4% interest rate, maturing in 20 years)	$10,000,000	
Add: Premium on Bonds Payable	800,000	
Total Long-Term Liabilities		$10,800,000

COVENANTS, COLLATERAL, AND SINKING FUNDS

The terms and conditions for long-term borrowing arrangements can be very detailed and complex, and the agreement may specify conditions that must be met throughout the term of the loan or may impose restrictions. These conditions and restrictions, which are referred to as loan *covenants*, may limit the amount of cash dividend payments to the stockholders, require the company to meet certain financial benchmarks (including certain ratios that will be discussed in Chapter 8), or require it to pledge specific assets as collateral for the loan in the event of default. Some agreements require that money be set aside and invested in a fund that will be used to repay the loan at maturity, such as the *sinking fund* that was discussed in the section on long-term investments. The financial statement footnotes for long-term debt will provide considerable additional information, including key covenants, pledged assets, stated and effective interest rates, maturity dates, and scheduled payments or sinking fund requirements for each of the next five years.

DEFERRED INCOME TAXES

Corporations are considered legal entities separate from their owners and a corporate entity must file tax returns and pay federal and state income taxes on its profits. A corporation makes quarterly estimates of its taxable income for the current year and makes quarterly estimated tax payments; any unpaid taxes owed for the current year are reported under current liabilities as *income taxes payable*.

By contrast, amounts reported as *deferred income tax liabilities* represent income taxes which may become payable in later years and are related to differences in accounting and taxable income. According to the matching principle, the amount reported as *income tax expense* in the current year's income statement represents the tax due on the basis of the revenues and expenses including in accounting income for that year.

However, according to tax law, not all revenues are taxable income in the same year they are considered to have been earned under financial accounting concepts. Likewise, not all expenses are tax-deductible in the same year they were incurred and reported in the income statement.

Accounting for income tax liabilities is a very complex issue that is beyond the scope of this book, but a brief example may help explain the concept. Deferred income taxes commonly arise when the depreciation methods used in the financial statements (discussed earlier in this chapter) differ from the depreciation methods and tax deductions specified in the tax law, although there are many other examples.

Assume a corporation recently purchased equipment and capitalized a cost of $100,000. It expects to use this equipment for 10 years, after which the trade-in value is presumed to be zero, and even if it could be sold for its scrap value, that would be a negligible amount. It will depreciate $10,000 per year for a total of $100,000, using the straight-line method of depreciation explained earlier in this chapter.

According to the matching principle, income tax expense in the income statement is based on the accounting income earned in that period that will be subject to income taxation but not necessarily reported on the tax return for that particular year. Assume income before depreciation is $500,000 and the income tax rate is 40 percent. As shown in Figure 5.47, the company will report income tax expense of $196,000 in its 20x1 income statement, based on accounting depreciation of $10,000.

Figure 5.47   Income Statement: Calculation of Income Tax Expense

Income before Depreciation Expense	$500,000
Depreciation Expense	*(10,000)*
Income before Taxes	490,000
Income Tax Expense ($490,000 × 40%)	*(196,000)*
Net Income	$294,000

However, for income tax purposes, assume that this asset qualifies for a shorter five-year life and that depreciation is based on the MACRS method discussed earlier in this chapter (Figure 5.32). A total of $100,000 of depreciation will be taken, with a depreciation deduction in the income tax return of $20,000 in the first year of use. Taxable income and income taxes currently payable would be determined as shown in Figure 5.48.

Figure 5.48   Tax Return: Calculation of Income Tax Currently Payable

Taxable Income before Depreciation Deduction	$500,000
Depreciation Deduction	*(20,000)*
Taxable Income	480,000
Income Tax Rate	×40%
Income Taxes Currently Payable	*$192,000*

Assuming the company has not paid its 20x1 income taxes yet, its year-end balance sheet would include the information shown in Figure 5.49.

Figure 5.49   Balance Sheet: Income Tax Liabilities

Current Liabilities	
Income Taxes Payable	$192,000
Long-Term Liabilities	
Deferred Income Tax Liability	$ 4,000

The amount reported as *income taxes payable* of $192,000 represents the income tax the corporation is obligated to pay for the 20x1 income tax year. Most corporations pay estimated income taxes owed on a quarterly basis and so the amount reported as a current liability may be only the unpaid fourth quarter installment (or $48,000 in this example).

The *deferred income tax liability* of $4,000 at December 31, 20x1, represents the additional income taxes the corporation expects to pay in a future year (or years) when taxable income is greater than accounting income. In the early years of the asset's useful life, the tax deduction for depreciation is greater than depreciation expense in the income statement, and the deferred income tax liability will increase as the corporation postpones paying income taxes it eventually will owe. However, in later years, when the income tax deduction is lower (or zero), the income taxes that were postponed or deferred become payable.

The total amount of depreciation for both income tax and accounting purposes is $100,000 in this example. If all other factors are held constant, the total amount of income tax paid would equal the total amount of income tax expense that was reported in the income statement for the ten years the asset is used and depreciated. However, in individual years the timing and the amounts differ, which is aptly referred to as a *timing difference*. You can think of the deferred income tax liability arising in 20x1 as the timing difference between tax depreciation ($20,000) and income statement depreciation ($10,000) times the 40 percent income tax rate, which is $4,000; in other words, the income taxes that were deferred or postponed for the time being but must be paid in the future.

You also may find *deferred income tax assets* on the balance sheet. In this case, certain revenues may be taxable income before the revenue is earned according to the revenue recognition principle and reported in the income statement, and certain expenses reported in the income statement may not be tax-deductible until a later year. In this case, it is almost as though the corporation had prepaid its income tax, but this prepayment is referred to as a deferred income tax asset on the balance sheet because it is quite different from other prepaid expenses such as rent or insurance. The financial accounting treatment of deferred income taxes is a very complex area.

Owners' Equity and Changes in Owners' Equity

Owners' equity represents the residual claims of the owners to the assets of the business and sometimes is referred to as *net assets* or *net worth*. The balance sheet shows the total amount of owners' equity at a point in time and includes the amounts invested by the owners and the profits retained or reinvested in the business. The statement of owners' equity shows any additional investments made during the year, the profit or loss, and the amounts withdrawn by or distributed to the owners.

We will begin by discussing the basic characteristics and concepts of owners' equity for three types of business entities: sole proprietorships, partnerships, and corporations. In the final portion of this chapter, we will discuss corporations in more detail.

SOLE PROPRIETORSHIPS

A *sole proprietorship* is a business with a single owner, often the person who manages the business. Legally, the business is not considered separate from the owner; the owner is personally responsible for business actions and can be personally liable for business debts. However, according to the business entity assumption as discussed in Chapter 2, business activities are reported separately from the personal activities of the owner. Personal expenses of the owner paid by the business and the owner's salary are treated as withdrawals and not as business expenses. The results of business activities are included on the owner's personal income tax return, and the owner personally pays income taxes on business profits; the business entity is not taxed.

In the case of a sole proprietorship, the owner's equity is referred to as *capital*, which includes the owner's investments and profits retained by the business presented as a single amount on the balance sheet, as shown in Figure 5.50.

Figure 5.50 Sole Proprietorship: Balance Sheet (Partial)
December 31, 20x1

Owner's Equity	
Swithin, Capital	$400,000

An additional financial statement, the statement of owner's equity, shows the cause of any changes in owner's equity that occurred during the year. Figure 5.51 shows the statement of owner's equity for 20x2, the second year of business operations.

Figure 5.51 Sole Proprietorship Statement of Owner's Equity
For the Year Ended December 31, 20x2

Capital, January 1, 20x2	$400,000
Add: Owner Investments	20,000
Net Income for 20x2	80,000
Total	500,000
Less: Withdrawals	(40,000)
Capital, December 31, 20x2	$460,000

This statement shows that the owner invested $20,000 of additional capital in the business during the year, the increase in owner's equity when the business earned a profit of $80,000, and that the owner withdrew $40,000 of the profits for personal use, but the remainder of the earnings were reinvested or retained by the business. The year-end capital balance of $460,000 includes the amounts invested by the owner as well as the profits which were retained or reinvested in the business.

PARTNERSHIPS

A general partnership is a voluntary association of two or more owners which can be based on a simple verbal agreement but ideally should be based on a written contract. Partners may consist of individuals, other business entities, estates or trusts, or other parties. In fact, many business joint venture activities are structured as partnerships.

Similar to a sole proprietorship, a general partnership is not considered to be a legal entity separate from its owners, although the business is considered a separate accounting entity. The partners are personally responsible for business actions and can be held personally liable for business debts. Personal expenses paid by the partnership and the partners' salaries are treated as withdrawals and not as business expenses.

The partnership files an informational income tax return and reports each partner's share of the income to the taxing authorities. However, the partnership entity is not taxed on its income; each partner's share of the income is reported and taxed on each partner's separate income tax return.

If the business in the earlier example had been structured as a partnership with two owners, the 20x2 financial statements would include the information presented in Figure 5.52. From Chapter 4, recall that the partnership had two owners: Swithin invested and owned a one-fourth interest and Patrick invested and owned the other three-fourths of the partnership. Partnership income can be divided among the partners in any manner to which they agree, but in the absence of an agreement, each is considered an equal partner and is entitled to an equal share of the profits. However, in this example, we assumed that the partners agreed to divide the profits on the basis of the relative capital invested, with one-fourth ($^1/_4$) going to Swithin and three-fourths ($^3/_4$) to Patrick. The withdrawals might be the share of the partnership profit each partner is allowed to withdraw in lieu of a salary.

Figure 5.52   Statement of Partnership Equity
For the Year Ended December 31, 20x2

	Swithin	Patrick	Total
Capital, January 1, 20x2	$100,000	$300,000	$400,000
Add: Capital Investments	5,000	15,000	20,000
Net Income for 20x2	20,000	60,000	80,000
Total	125,000	375,000	500,000
Less: Withdrawals	(10,000)	(30,000)	(40,000)
Capital, December 31, 20x2	$115,000	$345,000	$460,000

Balance Sheet (Partial) December 31, 20x2

Partnership Equity		
Swithin Johnson, Capital	$115,000	
Patrick Johnson, Capital	345,000	
Total Partnership Equity		$460,000

Partnerships and Related Business Forms

The discussion above was based on what might be called a *general partnership*, but there are many partnership-like variations for entities with multiple owners. Some are more like partnerships and others are more like corporations, with a range of variations in between. Each form has its unique advantages and disadvantages,

often pertaining to which owners have the authority to manage the business and make decisions, the risk of personal liability of the owners, or differences in the way business income and distributions are taxed. The characteristics, advantages, and disadvantages of each of these business forms should be investigated and understood before one selects a particular form of business entity, based on expert accounting and legal advice.

Although a detailed discussion of various forms of entities is beyond the scope of this book, we provide short explanations for the more common ones below:

- **General Partnership**: In a general partnership, each partner has the right to conduct business on behalf of the partnership, is entitled to a share of the profits, and has a residual interest in the net assets, but can be held personally liable for actions against the partnership and for partnership debts.
- **Limited Partnership**: There must be at least one general partner with decision-making authority and personal risk in a limited partnership entity. The limited partners are more like passive investors; they provide capital to the business and usually are guaranteed a return on their investments. They do not participate in the management of the business and are not personally liable for partnership debts.
- **Limited Liability Partnership (LLP)**: A limited liability partnership is similar to a general partnership in terms of the rights to participate in management, a share of the profits, and a residual interest in net assets. However, the individual partners generally are protected from personal liability unless it is caused by a partner's own personal negligence or malpractice.
- **Limited Liability Company (LLC)**: A limited liability company is a bit more like a corporation as the owners are not liable for business debts but similar to a general partnership in the distribution and taxation of profits. The owners of an LLC are referred to as members.

CORPORATIONS

A *corporation* is both a separate legal entity and a separate accounting entity and is formed subject to the laws of the state in which it is incorporated. Ownership in a corporation is evidenced by shares of stock; the equity of an individual stockholder is based on the proportion of the total stock that is owned. If the corporation is *publicly held*, its shares of stock may be purchased and sold readily by investors, and the individual owners of the corporation may change frequently. A *nonpublic* or *closely held* corporation may establish limitations pertaining to the type of parties permitted to own stock or the conditions for selling stock to other parties. A corporation may have a single stockholder, a few owners or hundreds, and the owners may be individuals, partnerships, estates or trusts, corporations, or other parties.

Because a corporation is a legal entity that is separate from its owners, the stockholders do not participate in its management or operations unless they also happen to be officers or employees. Stockholders are not personally liable for business activities or business debts. A corporation files a tax return and also pays income taxes on the income earned by the corporation. In addition, the stockholders also may be individually subject to income taxation on earnings distributed as cash dividends, other distributions, and gains and losses from the sale of their stock investments.

In the case of a corporation, owners' equity is referred to as *stockholders' equity*. Owners receive shares of stock as evidence of their ownership and investment in the corporation, typically *common stock*, although there are other types. A public corporation may have hundreds of stockholders, and ownership can change daily as shares of stock are traded in the financial markets. As a result, a corporation reports the amounts originally invested (contributed) by the stockholders and the profits retained by the corporation rather than the equity of individual owners. Figure 5.53 shows how stockholders' equity is presented if the business is structured as a corporation.

Figure 5.53 Corporation Balance Sheet (Partial)
December 31, 20x1

Stockholders' Equity		
Common Stock, 40,000 shares	$ 80,000	
Retained Earnings	320,000	
Total Stockholders' Equity		$400,000

Although the equity of an individual stockholder is not presented in the financial statements, this can be determined by calculating the *book value* of a share of stock. In this case by dividing total stockholders' equity of $400,000 by 40,000 shares of stock, the book value is $10 for one share of stock. The equity of an individual stockholder who owns 10,000 shares, or one-fourth of the stock, is $100,000 (10,000 shares × $10 book value per share), which is equivalent to the amount of Swithin's capital balance in the previous partnership example.

Figure 5.54 shows the statement of stockholders' equity that would be presented in the corporation's 20x2 financial statements. Stockholders invested an additional $20,000 by purchasing additional common stock. The corporation earned a profit of $80,000, of which $40,000 was distributed to its stockholders in the form of cash dividends and the remaining profit earned in 20x2 was retained or reinvested. At December 31, 20x2 the corporation has $100,000 of common stock which represents the amounts stockholders invested, and retained earnings of $360,000 which represents the cumulative amount of profits earned to date that were retained by the corporation.

Figure 5.54 Statement of Stockholders' Equity
For the Year Ended December 31, 20x2

	Common Stock	Retained Earnings	Total
Balances, January 1, 20x2	$ 80,000	$320,000	$400,000
Add: Common Stock Issued	20,000		20,000
Net Income for 20x2		80,000	80,000
Less: Dividends Declared		(40,000)	(40,000)
Balances, December 31, 20x2	$100,000	$360,000	$460,000

Balance Sheet (Partial) December 31, 20x2

Stockholders' Equity		
Common Stock	$100,000	
Retained Earnings	360,000	
Total Stockholders' Equity		$460,000

Building on the basic stockholders' equity concepts above, the final portion of this chapter will focus on additional concepts and terminology likely to be found in the financial statements of a corporation.

COMMON STOCK

The corporate charter indicates the types and amount of stock a corporation is authorized to issue. Most corporations have *common stock* or *capital stock*. Common stockholders are the true owners of the business and are entitled to one vote for each share of stock owned. Stockholders do not participate directly in the management of the business unless they also happen to be directors, officers, or employees.

Stockholder participation is based on exercising voting rights to elect the board of directors and certain other matters. One may control a corporation by owning more than 50 percent of the stock, although control may be achieved with lesser ownership if other stockholders do not unite and vote as a unit or by other means. Common stockholders have the right to receive a proportionate share of cash dividends if and when they are declared by the board of directors, but common stock does *not* carry a stated or guaranteed cash dividend. Common stockholders also have the first right to purchase a proportionate share of any additional stock issued, and to receive a proportionate share of corporate assets upon liquidation, but only after creditor claims and other claims have first been paid.

PREFERRED STOCK

Corporations may also be authorized to issue other types of stock, such as *preferred stock*, which may appeal to a different set of investors than those who invest in common stock. Despite its name, preferred stock is not necessarily a better or a preferred type of investment; rather, the term preferred is used for a category of stock which conveys specific or preferential rights that common stockholders do not receive. Preferred stockholders do not have voting rights; however, there is a stated cash dividend that will be paid to preferred stockholders and must be paid before distributions to the common stockholders can be made. In most cases, preferred stock dividend rights are *cumulative*; if a corporation is unable to pay the required preferred stock dividend in a particular year, the amounts accumulate and must also be paid before any distributions to the common stockholders. If a corporation has past-due or *dividends in arrears*, it will disclose this information in the financial statement footnotes.

Preferred stockholders have other special rights; they will be paid a stated amount for their stock if the corporation retires or redeems it, and if the corporation liquidates and creditors have been paid, the preferred stockholders will be paid for their equity before any distributions can be made to the common stockholders.

PAR OR STATED VALUE

The corporate charter may specify a *par value* or *stated value* associated with a share of stock. Par value is a legal concept that generally specifies the minimum amount stockholders must invest in the corporation at the time the stock is first issued and a minimum amount of capital the corporation must maintain. In theory this provides some protection to corporate creditors whose claims can be paid only from corporate assets (and not from the personal assets of the owners as might happen in the case of a sole proprietorship or partnership). For common stock, the par or stated value is usually a nominal amount and should not be viewed as an indication of the current market price or value of one share; in fact, the par value of some companies common stock is one penny. The amount stockholders invest typically is greater than the par value of the common stock, and the excess is reported separately as *contributed capital in excess of par value*.

For preferred stock the par value is the amount on which the stated dividend will be based. For example, a share of preferred stock with par value of $100 and a 10 percent dividend rate will be paid a $10 cash dividend each year.

RETAINED EARNINGS, DEFICITS, AND RESTRICTIONS

Let's use a simple example to illustrate what we mean by retained earnings or reinvested earnings and explain why even a profitable corporation may not distribute its profits to its stockholders. Assume a corporation's net income for its first year of operations was $100,000, and it has $100,000 in cash in the bank at year-end. Rather than paying cash dividends to its stockholders now, the company can grow bigger and faster if it reinvests those earnings in a building it needs, and so it purchases a building with the $100,000 in cash. At year end it has $100,000 of retained earnings but no cash because its earnings were reinvested in the building it purchased.

Next year its net income is $200,000, but it still has no cash; it paid for all of its operating expenses but has not collected the $200,000 its customers still owe from this year's sales even though it expects it will collect this amount early next year. At this point, the corporation has earned a total of $300,000 of net income and has $300,000 of retained earnings, but still it has not paid the stockholders any cash dividends. However, if the corporation reinvests its earnings and continues to per-form well, the market price of its stock may increase over time and the stockholders will be better off in the long run than they would be if they received cash dividends now and purchased some other type of investment.

A company may have profits but no cash. It may have retained earnings but no cash. It may have profits and cash but can create greater value in the long run by reinvesting its earnings and cash instead of paying cash dividends.

Instead of retained earnings, a corporation may have a *deficit*. Most people asso-ciate this term with news broadcasts about the economy and the federal govern-ment. Deficit spending means that the government is spending more than it brings in from income tax revenues and other sources. A trade deficit means that the value of goods the United States imports exceeds the value of the goods it exports to other countries. In the case of a corporation, a deficit means that since the time of incor-poration its cumulative losses have exceeded its cumulative profits and this is defi-nitely not a good signal.

Retained earnings that are earmarked for particular purposes or are legally unavailable for distribution to the owners are disclosed in the financial state-ments or the footnotes. Some borrowing agreements may restrict the amount of earnings available for dividends until the loans are repaid, but a corporation may restrict its earnings voluntarily as a signal of its plans for future expansion or for other reasons.

DIVIDENDS

Dividends are a distribution of past or present earnings to the stockholders, but they are not expenses of the corporation and do not appear on the income statement. Dividends are similar to owner withdrawals in a sole proprietorship or a partner-ship; however, it is the board of directors, not the owners, which determines the amount and timing of dividend payments. Preferred stockholders are entitled to a specified dividend stated on the stock certificate: a fixed dollar amount or a percent-age of the par value.

Common stock ordinarily does not have a specified dividend rate. The amount of dividends declared is at the discretion of the board of directors even if the corporation has paid regular cash dividends in the past.

Rather than distributing cash, the corporation may declare a *stock dividend*, and each stockholder receives a proportionate amount of the stock distributed. When a company's stock price continues to rise, it may declare a *stock split* to keep the price of a share in a more reasonable zone. For example, if the market price of one share of stock has risen to $200, the corporation may declare a two-for-one stock split. Each owner will have twice as many shares as before the split, but each share will be worth half as much because the market price would be expected to decline to $100 after the stock split.

TREASURY STOCK

Just like any other investor, a corporation can purchase shares of stock in other companies or even its own stock. *Treasury stock* represents a corporation's own shares of stock which were issued to its stockholders but have been reacquired by the corporation. As was discussed in other sections of this chapter, investments in the stock of other companies may be found under several different balance sheet classifications, depending on the purpose and intended holding period. However, when a corporation purchases (reacquires) its own stock from existing stockholders, it is not considered an asset; instead, it is shown as a deduction from total stockholders' equity as less stock owned by outside investors.

A corporation may purchase its own stock for many reasons. If the market price is falling, it can purchase the shares at a low price and perhaps sell (reissue) them later when the price goes up. It may purchase shares to avoid a hostile takeover of the company or to distribute to key executives later as additional compensation or to sell to employees as part of an employee stock ownership plan. Shares held in the treasury have no voting or dividend rights; treasury stock represents shares that were issued but are no longer *outstanding* for voting and dividend purposes.

Treasury stock is shown as a deduction from total stockholders' equity in the balance sheet, along with disclosure of the number of treasury shares held and any restrictions placed on retained earnings. If the shares later are reissued at a price higher or lower than their price when purchased, those gains or losses are reflected as increases or decreases in stockholders' equity, not in the income statement. A corporation cannot report profits or losses from dealing in its own stock.

ACCUMULATED OTHER COMPREHENSIVE INCOME

From our earlier discussions of short-term and long-term investments in marketable securities, you learned that *trading* and *available for sale securities* are adjusted to market value on the year-end balance sheet. The *unrealized holding gain or loss* on trading securities is reported in the income statement; however, if the investments are classified as available for sale, the unrealized gain or loss is reported in stockholders' equity, not included in net income or in the year-end retained earnings.

Accounting guidelines firmly support the notion that all revenues and/or gains and expenses and/or losses be reported in the income statement, with proper classifications and disclosures. However, there are a handful of exceptions, including the unrealized holding gain or loss on available for sale securities and some others which are beyond the scope of this book. Since these gains and losses bypass the income statement, thus are not reflected in retained earnings at year-end, stockholders' equity includes these unique types of gains and losses in a separate caption, referred to as *accumulated other comprehensive income.*

On the basis of the additional concepts discussed above, Figure 5.55 provides a more detailed illustration of the stockholders' equity portion of the balance sheet. Note that the amounts invested by the preferred and common stockholders are shown first under the heading of *contributed capital* and the income reinvested in the corporation is shown separately as *retained earnings.*

Figure 5.55   Balance Sheet: Stockholders' Equity
December 31, 20x2

Contributed Capital		
10% Preferred Stock, $100 par value, 1,000 shares authorized, 100 shares issued and outstanding	$10,000	
Common Stock, $5 par value, 50,000 shares authorized, 5,000 shares issued, of which 100 are held as treasury stock	25,000	
Contributed capital in excess of par value on common stock	65,000	
Total Contributed Capital		$100,000
Retained Earnings		360,000
Accumulated Other Comprehensive Income		30,000
Less: Treasury Stock, 100 shares (at cost)		(3,000)
Total Stockholders' Equity		$487,000

As you review Figure 5.55, note that each type of stock is shown separately, along with some additional information. For example, the corporate charter authorized the corporation to issue 1,000 shares of preferred stock, but to date it has issued only 100 of the 1,000 shares authorized. It can issue additional preferred stock at a future date without having to amend its charter. The preferred stock has a par value of $100 and a 10 percent stated dividend rate; the annual dividend requirement is $10 per share, and preferred stock dividends must be paid before the common stockholders receive any distributions.

The corporate charter authorized the issue of 50,000 shares of common stock, but only 5,000 of those shares have been issued to date; additional stock can be issued at a later date if the corporation needs to raise more capital to finance growth and expansion. The par value of the common stock, typically a nominal amount, is only $5 per share; the amount reported as common stock represents the par value of the 5,000 shares issued or $25,000. However, when the common stock was issued, the market price must have been much higher than $5 per share. The common stockholders contributed (invested) $65,000 more than the par value, for a total investment of $90,000; thus, the 5,000 shares of common stock were issued at an average market price of $18 a share.

Sometime after the common stock originally was issued, the corporation reacquired 100 shares of its own stock, which appears as a deduction from stockholders' equity, not as an investment in the asset section of the balance sheet. The $3,000 amount reported as *treasury stock* is based on the cost at the time the stock was reacquired. Thus, the market price when the 100 shares were reacquired must have been at an average price of $30 per share.

Finally, note that the corporation reports $30,000 as *accumulated other comprehensive income*. Perhaps this is the unrealized holding gain on available for sale securities that was discussed in an earlier section of this chapter; this signifies that the company has investments in available for sale securities for which the current market value is $30,000 greater than their cost.

Summary

This chapter has covered a lot of ground. Building on the foundation introduced in Chapter 4, we focused on the specific and unique characteristics of many balance sheet items and the relationship of those items to income statement reporting. You also learned that financial statements include assumptions and estimates, the statements do not always include precise information, and alternative acceptable accounting methods for items such as depreciation and inventory cost produce different financial statement results.

We are now ready to move on to the last of the four financial statements: the statement of cash flows. Once we have completed the study of the financial statements, the remainder of the book will acquaint you with how to read and use financial statements and discuss ways in which a company may misstate its results fraudulently.

Quiz for Chapter 5

1. According to the matching principle, bad debts expense should appear in the income statement in the time period in which the:
   a. Sales revenue was earned
   b. Specific customer account balance was written off as uncollectible

2. Customers owe a company $100,000. If the company reports accounts receivable (net) of $94,000 on its balance sheet:
   a. The estimated amount the company expects to collect from its receivables is $94,000.
   b. The company has established an allowance for doubtful accounts of $6,000
   c. The company included an estimate of uncollectible accounts in the operating expenses reported in its income statement.
   d. All of the above are true.
   e. None of the above are true.

3. On November 1, year 1, a company accepts a $2,000, 12 percent, six-month note receivable from a customer. When preparing its financial statements at December 31, year 1, which of the following is true?
   a. $40 of interest income will be reported in the income statement.
   b. $40 will be included in the accrued receivables in the balance sheet.
   c. When the note matures, the company is entitled to collect $2,000 and $120 interest.
   d. All of the above.
   e. None of the above.

Use the following information to answer questions #4 & #5:

During the year, a company purchased three units of inventory for $2,000, $2,400, and $2,500, respectively. It sold two units and has one left in ending inventory. Determine the amounts that would be reported as cost of goods sold and ending inventory by using the cost-flow assumptions in the next two questions.

4. Using FIFO, the amounts would be:
   a. Cost of goods sold $4,400 and ending inventory $2,500
   b. Cost of goods sold $4,900 and ending inventory $2,000
   c. Cost of goods sold $4,600 and ending inventory $2,300

5. Using LIFO, the amounts would be:
   a. Cost of goods sold $4,400 and ending inventory $2,500
   b. Cost of goods sold $4,900 and ending inventory $2,000
   c. Cost of goods sold $4,600 and ending inventory $2,300

6. A cost that is capitalized rather than being expensed immediately is:
   a. Included in the cost of a plant asset and will be reflected in depreciation expense later
   b. The cost of an addition made to an existing asset, such as a new wing to an office building
   c. Significant improvements or substantial repairs/replacements made to an existing asset which are expected to extend its useful life
   d. All of the above
   e. None of the above

7. Equipment was purchased at an original cost of $200,000. Its useful life is estimated to be 5 years or 600,000 units, and its salvage value is estimated to be $50,000. Using the straight-line method, year 2 depreciation expense will be:
   a. $30,000
   b. $40,000
   c. $60,000
   d. $80,000

8. A company incurred $2 million of research and development costs which ultimately led to a patent on a new cancer treatment medication, and the patent was registered at a cost of $100,000. The balance sheet value of the patent will be:
   a. $2,100,000
   b. $2,000,000
   c. $100,000

9. All but which of the following are true pertaining to corporate bonds?
   a. The issuing corporation must rely on a single lender to raise the money it needs.
   b. The principal or maturity value of the bonds will be repaid on a specified future date.
   c. The issuing corporation promises to pay a stated amount of interest on the bonds, usually twice a year.
   d. The amount the corporation receives at the time of borrowing can be greater or less than the amount it must repay at maturity to adjust for differences in the stated interest rate and the market rates of interest.
   e. All of the above are true.

10. Which of the following is true regarding a partnership?
    a. The partnership entity pays income tax on its profits.
    b. Partners can be held personally liable for business debts.
    c. Ownership is limited to individual persons only; a partnership cannot be owned by other companies or parties.
    d. All of the above are true.
    e. None of the above are true.

CHAPTER 6

Statement of Cash Flows

In this chapter we conclude our detailed discussions of each separate financial statement by taking a closer look at the statement of cash flows. We will review the basic concepts and format of the statement of cash flows and then discuss each of the cash-flow classifications in greater detail. The chapter concludes with a comprehensive example that illustrates all four of the financial statements Case Company prepares at year end to comply with generally accepted accounting principles (GAAP). Despite the relative simplicity of this example, it will reinforce several of the basic financial reporting concepts introduced and discussed in various ways throughout the first five chapters. The Case Company example also will illuminate how information provided within each individual financial statement is related to that provided in one or more of the other financial statements.

Basic Format

The statement of cash flows presents a summary of the cash flows of the business during a period of time and the change in the cash balance. This financial statement helps explain the change in the cash balance as well as changes in other assets and liabilities on the balance sheet and shows why net income differs from the cash generated or used in routine business activities. Cash flows are classified as arising from operating, investing or financing activities, and certain noncash activities also are disclosed.

Figure 6.1 presents a condensed version showing the basic form and content of the statement of cash flows for Case Company. Cash flows from each significant activity are disclosed separately under the classifications of operating, investing, and financing activities. The net increase or decrease in cash during the year is also shown, along with the resulting year-end cash balance which is also the amount reported as cash in the year-end balance sheet.

Figure 6.1   Case Company Statement of Cash Flows
For the Year Ended December 31, 20x1

Net Cash Flows from		
Operating Activities	$45,000	
Investing Activities	(1,000)	
Financing Activities	(45,000)	
Net Decrease in Cash during 20x1		$(1,000)
Cash Balance, December 31, 20x0		4,000
Cash Balance, December 31, 20x1		$ 3,000

OPERATING ACTIVITIES

Operating activities are those arising from primary business activities. Revenues and expenses reported in the income statement usually generate or use cash, though the period in which revenue is earned or an expense is incurred may differ from the timing of the actual receipt or payment of cash, and some revenues and expenses do not involve cash. Receipts from cash sales, collections on receivables, and dividends and interest received on loans and investments as well as cash payments to suppliers and employees and for operating expenses, interest, and income taxes are included in net operating cash flows.

INVESTING ACTIVITIES

Investing activities pertain to assets acquired and used by the company, such as plant assets, natural resources, and intangibles, as well as investments. Cash flows

from investing activities include cash receipts and payments arising from the purchase or sale of these types of assets.

FINANCING ACTIVITIES

A company finances its formation and growth with owners' investments and borrowed funds. Cash flows from *financing activities* include cash receipts and cash payments arising from borrowing and repaying loans, cash invested in the business by the owners, and cash withdrawals or dividends paid to the owners.

NONCASH INVESTING AND FINANCING ACTIVITIES

Not all investing or financing activities involve a cash receipt or payment; for example, the purchase of equipment financed with a note payable is both an investing activity (equipment purchase) and a financing activity (borrowing). These activities are disclosed but do not appear in the actual statement of cash flows.

Case Company: A Comprehensive Example

Case Company will be used as a comprehensive example in this chapter. Although this business is a sole proprietorship, the simplest form of business organization, the applicable accounting concepts are identical to those involving partnerships and corporations even though the specific terminology or underlying transactions may differ slightly in those cases.

Cash Flows From Operating Activities

Although the income statement is viewed as the primary statement for reporting the results of operating activities, cash flows arising from these activities are also of great importance as they affect the liquidity and financial flexibility of the business. The statement of cash flows presents cash receipts and cash payments arising from the related revenues and expenses reported in the income statement, although the actual cash receipt or payment may occur in a different period.

Cash receipts from operating activities include cash sales and collections from customers on account, dividends received from investments in stock, and interest received on loans and investments. Cash payments for operating activities include cash paid to suppliers for raw materials or goods acquired for resale, payments to employees, and payments for other operating expenses, taxes, and interest on loans.

A company may need to find temporary cash resources to sustain its routine business operations in the short run. In a given year, if it is unable to generate a sufficient amount of cash sales and customer collections to cover its routine operating expenses, pay its suppliers on time and have enough left to accumulate the funds needed to pay the interest and maturity value of long-term obligations or return profits to its owners, it will face difficulties in borrowing money and/or attracting new owner investments. Operating cash flows are vital to business sustenance and success; the statement of cash flows provides valuable information about cash generated and used in ongoing operations.

CASH FLOWS FROM OPERATING ACTIVITIES: DIRECT METHOD VERSUS INDIRECT METHOD

A company can present its net cash flow from operating activities by using either a direct method or an indirect method approach in the statement of cash flows. The *direct method* presents the specific amounts of cash received and cash paid for each significant item and the resulting net cash flow arising from operating activities. By contrast, the *indirect method* shows only the net effect of items which caused net income and net operating cash flows to differ. We will explain and provide examples to illustrate these concepts below.

We use the condensed income statement for Case Company in Figure 6.2 to discuss basic concepts and illustrate how operating cash flows are reported using both the direct and indirect approaches.

Figure 6.2   Case Company Income Statement (Condensed)
For the Year Ended December 31, 20x1

Sales Revenue	$800,000
Cost of Goods Sold and Operating Expenses	(696,000)
Operating Income	104,000
Interest Income	1,000
Interest Expense	(5,000)
Net Income	$100,000

Direct Method

If Case Company uses the *direct method*, net operating cash flows will be based on the specific amounts of cash received and paid for all significant (material) income statement items, as shown in Figure 6.3.

The detailed cash-flow information presented in the direct method approach is useful in assessing differences between revenues and related cash receipts and between expenses and related cash payments. The information provided can be understood readily by persons with little background in accounting and is useful to

Figure 6.3   Direct Method: Cash Flows from Operating Activities
For the Year Ended December 31, 20x1

Cash Receipts from Operating Activities		
Cash collections from customers	$782,000	
Interest earned on investments	1,000	
Total		$783,000
Cash Payments for Operating Activities		
Merchandise purchases and operating expenses	733,000	
Interest on notes payable	5,000	
Total		(738,000)
Net Cash Flows from Operating Activities		$ 45,000

managers in evaluating budgeted and actual cash flows. For example, you can see that
Case Company earned $800,000 sales revenue, but only $782,000 was received in
cash this year. It had cost of goods sold and operating expenses of $696,000 but its
cash payments for these items was $733,000 during the year. We will discuss the
reasons for these differences in later examples.

Indirect Method

If Case Company uses the *indirect method*, net operating cash flows will be determined by using the differences between net income and cash flows for particular
items. For example, the difference between revenues and actual cash collections is
related to the increase or decrease in customer receivables. Similarly, the difference
between expenses and cash payments is related to prepayments and expenses payable. The format in Figure 6.4 is not exactly what one would see in an actual financial statement, but it illustrates the concept of the indirect method, which will be
discussed and illustrated in more detail later in this chapter.

Figure 6.4   Indirect Method: Cash Flows from Operating Activities
For the Year Ended December 31, 20x1

Net Income	$100,000
Differences between net income and net cash flows from operating activities:	
Revenues earned this period which were not received in cash	(18,000)
Cash payments for expenses of previous or future time periods	(37,000)
Net Cash Flows from Operating Activities	$ 45,000

As you can see, both methods arrived at net cash flows from operating activities of $45,000. The direct method shows the specific amounts of actual cash receipts and payments, while the indirect method shows the differences between revenues earned and cash received and the differences between expenses incurred and actual cash payments for those expenses. Although most revenues earned and expenses incurred will also be received or paid in the same financial statement period, some cash flows may occur before the revenues are earned or the expenses incurred and some cash flows may occur in a later period.

CASH FLOWS FROM OPERATING ACTIVITIES: COMPREHENSIVE EXAMPLES

We expand our discussion of operating cash flows in the next few examples, using more specific information and the more detailed version of Case Company's income statement presented in Figure 6.5.

Figure 6.5   Case Company Income Statement
For the Year Ended December 31, 20x1

Sales Revenue		$800,000
Cost of Goods Sold		
Inventory, January 1	$ 40,000	
Purchases	525,000	
Cost of goods available for sale	565,000	
Inventory, December 31	(65,000)	
Cost of goods sold		500,000
Gross Profit		300,000
Operating Expenses		
Salaries and wages	130,000	
Depreciation	10,000	
Advertising	20,000	
Telephone and utilities	15,000	
Supplies and postage	7,000	
Insurance	9,000	
Property taxes	5,000	
Total operating expenses		196,000
Operating Income		104,000
Other Income and Expense		
Interest income	1,000	
Interest expense	(5,000)	
Total other income and expense		(4,000)
Net Income		$100,000

Example 1: Sales Revenue versus Cash Receipts from Customers

Case Company started the year with $13,000 of accounts receivable from the prior year's sales, all of which were collected in cash this year. It earned $800,000 of sales revenue this year, all from credit sales. Of that amount, $769,000 was collected in cash and the remaining $31,000 is in year-end accounts receivable. A visual representation of the information is presented in Figure 6.6.

Figure 6.6   Sales Revenue versus Cash Receipts

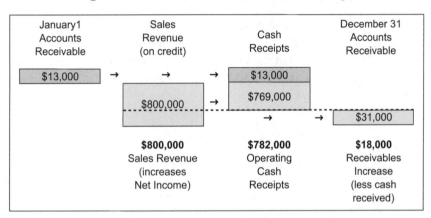

Figure 6.7 shows how this information might appear in the financial statements. The income statement reports the $800,000 of sales revenue earned during the year in accordance with the revenue recognition principle. In the statement of cash flows, the direct method shows the amount actually collected in cash of $782,000, which includes the beginning accounts receivable of $13,000 and $769,000 of the current year's credit sales.

Figure 6.7   Financial Statements (Partial): Sales Revenue versus Cash Receipts

INCOME STATEMENT	
Sales Revenue Earned	$800,000
STATEMENT OF CASH FLOWS	
Cash Flows from Operating Activities, Direct Method	
Cash receipts from customers	$782,000
OR	
Cash Flows from Operating Activities: Indirect Method	
Net Income	$100,000
Less: Increase in Accounts Receivable	(18,000)

By contrast, the indirect method shows only the $18,000 difference between sales revenue ($800,000) and actual cash receipts ($782,000) as a deduction from net income due to the increase in accounts receivable. An increase in accounts receivable means that not all of this year's revenue earned from credit sales were collected in cash; thus, operating cash flows were $18,000 less than net income. If receivables had decreased, rather than increased, this amount would be added to net income signifying that cash collections were greater than the amount of sales revenue earned.

Example 2: Cost of Goods Purchased versus Cash Paid to Merchandise Suppliers

Case Company started the year with $36,000 of accounts payable from the prior year's purchases of merchandise, all of which were paid in cash this year. It purchased $525,000 this year, all on credit. Of this amount, $509,000 was paid in cash and the remainder of $16,000 is in year-end accounts payable. A visual representation of the information is presented in Figure 6.8.

Figure 6.8 Purchases versus Cash Payments

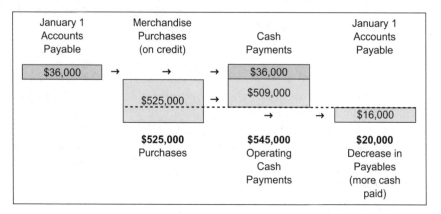

Figure 6.9 shows how this information might appear in the financial statements. Recall that the cost of inventory purchased is not an expense in the income statement until the inventory has been sold. As will be discussed in the example to follow, the amount reported as cost of goods sold is based on not only the $525,000 of inventory purchased, but also the amounts of inventory on hand at the beginning and end of the year.

The direct method shows the cash payments to suppliers of $545,000 as an operating cash outflow; this amount includes the payment of the $36,000 accounts payable owed at the beginning of the year and $509,000 cash payments for some, but

Figure 6.9 Financial Statements (Partial): Purchases versus Cash Payments

INCOME STATEMENT		
Cost of Goods Sold:		
Inventory, January 1	$xxx,xxx	
Add: Purchases	525,000	
Cost of Goods Available for Sale	xxx,xxx	
Less: Inventory, December 31	(xx,xxx)	
Cost of Goods Sold		($xxx,xxx)
STATEMENT OF CASH FLOWS		
Operating Activities: Direct Method		
Cash paid to suppliers		($545,000)
OR		
Operating Activities: Indirect Method		
Net Income		$100,000
Less: Decrease in accounts payable		(20,000)

not all, of the inventory purchased on credit during the year. The indirect method shows only the $20,000 difference between the amount of inventory purchased on credit ($525,000) and the cash payments to suppliers ($545,000) as a deduction from net income. A decrease in accounts payable means that the company paid more cash to suppliers than the amount of inventory it purchased during the year. If accounts payable instead had increased, it would signify that cash payments to suppliers were less than the amount of credit purchases, and this difference would be added to net income.

Example 3: Cost of Goods Purchased versus Cost of Goods Sold

The previous example focused on the difference between cash payments to suppliers and inventory purchased on credit during the year, but any difference between the amount of inventory purchased versus the amount sold also must be considered. In previous chapters you learned that inventory costs are expenses when the inventory is sold and matched with the sales revenue reported in the income statement for that period, and not as expenses in the period when purchased. Continuing on with the previous example, the difference between the amount of inventory purchased versus the amount sold is also considered and illustrated below.

Case Company started the year with $40,000 of merchandise inventory which it purchased during the previous year and had $525,000 of additional credit purchases of inventory this year; thus, during the year a total of $565,000 of inventory was on hand and available for sale. Of this amount, goods which cost $500,000 were sold and the remaining $65,000 were still on hand and included in year-end inventory. A visual representation of the information is presented in Figure 6.10.

Figure 6.10   Purchases versus Cost of Goods Sold

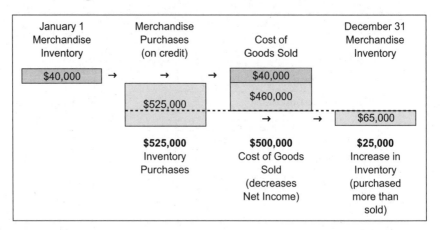

Figure 6.11 shows the financial statement effects for cost of goods sold and cash payments to suppliers, taking into consideration the differences between credit purchases versus cash payments to suppliers, as well as the additional effects of the difference between the amounts purchased versus the amount of inventory sold that was discussed above in Example 3 (the continued example).

The $45,000 difference between cost of goods sold of $500,000 (treated as an expense in the income statement) and the $545,000 cash paid to suppliers (treated as an operating cash outflow in the statement of cash flows) arose for two reasons. First, Case Company's cash payments to suppliers on account were $20,000 more the cost of the inventory it purchased on credit, which resulted in a $20,000 decrease in accounts payable by year-end (see Figure 6.8). Second, Case Company purchased $25,000 more inventory than it sold during the year, which resulted in a $25,000 increase in merchandise inventory by year-end (see Figure 6.10).

When reported operating cash flows are based on the direct method, the specific amount of cash paid to suppliers of $545,000 is shown. By contrast, if Case Company reports operating cash flows based on the indirect method, the adjustments to net income reveal that: 1) cash payments to suppliers exceeded the amount purchased on credit – accounts payable decreased and 2) inventory purchased on credit exceeded the amount sold – inventory increased. Figure 6.11 shows the income statement and the statement of cash flows effects for both the direct and the indirect methods.

Figure 6.11 Financial Statements (Partial):
Cost of Goods Sold versus Cash Payments

INCOME STATEMENT		
Cost of Goods Sold:		
Inventory, January 1	$ 40,000	
Add: Purchases	525,000	
Cost of Goods Available for Sale	565,000	
Less: Inventory, December 31	(65,000)	
Cost of Goods Sold		$(500,000)
STATEMENT OF CASH FLOWS		
Operating Activities: Direct Method		
Cash paid to suppliers		$(545,000)
OR		
Operating Activities: Indirect Method		
Net Income		$ 100,000
Less: Decrease in Accounts Payable		(20,000)
Less: Increase in Merchandise Inventory		(25,000)

Example 4: Depreciation Expense

Depreciation expense is a bit different from most other types of operating expenses reported in the income statement and is also handled in a different manner in the statement of cash flows. Recall that depreciation, depletion, and amortization allocate a portion of the cost of an asset as an expense during each period of use according to the matching principle and that these do not represent operating expenses that will require the payment of cash. Any cash paid at the time of purchase is considered an investing and not an operating cash flow, and if the purchase was financed with borrowed funds, the principal amounts repaid are considered financing, not operating activities. Depreciation expense is used in determining net income, but as a noncash expense it is either omitted from operating activities in the direct method approach or added to net income as a noncash item in the indirect method approach, as shown in Figure 6.12.

Concepts similar to those discussed in the examples above also apply to most other types of revenues and expenses. Visual representations and financial statement results for Case Company's other revenues and expenses are presented and briefly discussed in the examples which follow.

Figure 6.12 Financial Statements (Partial): Depreciation Expense

INCOME STATEMENT	
Depreciation Expense	$(10,000)
STATEMENT OF CASH FLOWS	
Cash Flows from Operating Activities: Direct Method (not applicable, no cash paid)	
OR	
Cash Flows from Operating Activities: Indirect Method	
Net Income	$100,000
Add: Depreciation Expense	10,000

Example 5: Salaries and Wages Expense versus Cash Payments to Employees

Case Company incurred salary and wage expenses of $130,000, of which $125,000 was paid in cash and the remaining $5,000 is owed to employees and included in year-end salaries and wages payable. It also paid the $4,000 of salaries it owed to employees at the end of the prior year. The $1,000 increase in salaries and wages payable represents the difference between the current year's salary and wages expense ($130,000) and the cash payments made to employees ($129,000). A visual representation of this information appears in Figure 6.13, and the financial statement results are presented in Figure 6.14.

Figure 6.13 Salaries Expense versus Cash Payments

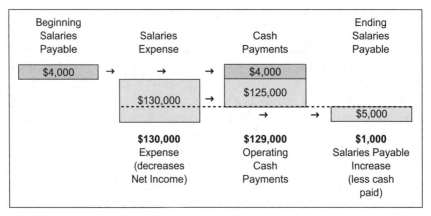

Figure 6.14 Financial Statements (Partial):
Salaries Expense versus Cash Payments

INCOME STATEMENT	
Salaries and Wages Expense	$(130,000)
STATEMENT OF CASH FLOWS	
Cash Flows from Operating Activities: Direct Method	
Cash paid to employees	$(129,000)
OR	
Cash Flows from Operating Activities: Indirect Method	
Net Income	$100,000
Add: Increase in Salaries and Wages Payable	1,000

Example 6: Supplies and Postage Expense versus Cash Payments for Supplies Purchased

Case Company used $7,000 of supplies during the year but purchased and paid for only $6,000 of supplies; thus, its supplies inventory decreased by $1,000. It used the $2,000 of supplies on hand at the beginning of the year and $5,000 of the $6,000 of the supplies purchased and has $1,000 of supplies on hand at year-end. A visual representation of this information appears in Figure 6.15, and the financial statement results are presented in Figure 6.16.

Figure 6.15 Supplies Expense versus Cash Payments

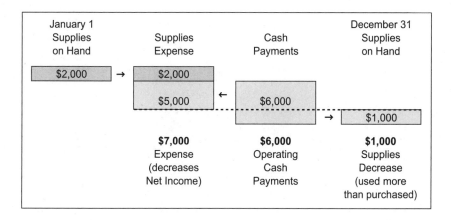

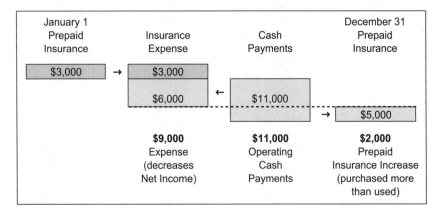
Figure 6.16 Financial Statements (Partial): Supplies Expense versus Cash Payments

INCOME STATEMENT	
Supplies and Postage Expense	$ (7,000)
STATEMENT OF CASH FLOWS	
Cash Flows from Operating Activities: Direct Method	
Cash paid to purchase supplies and postage	$ (6,000)
OR	
Cash Flows from Operating Activities: Indirect Method	
Net Income	$100,000
Add: Decrease in Supplies and Postage on Hand	1,000

Example 7: Insurance Expense versus Cash Payments for Insurance

Case Company purchased $11,000 of insurance during the year, but only $9,000 was an expense of this year; thus, its year-end prepaid insurance increased by $2,000. The prepaid insurance at the beginning of the year was used, but only $6,000 of the additional insurance purchased during the year was used, and so year-end prepaid insurance is $5,000. A visual representation of this information appears in Figure 6.17, and the financial statement results are presented in Figure 6.18.

Figure 6.17 Insurance Expense versus Cash Payments

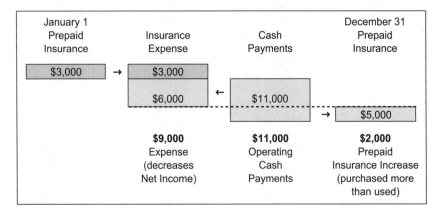

Figure 6.18 Financial Statements (Partial):
Insurance Expense versus Cash Payments

INCOME STATEMENT	
Insurance Expense	$ (9,000)
STATEMENT OF CASH FLOWS	
Cash Flows from Operating Activities: Direct Method	
Cash paid to purchase insurance	$(11,000)
OR	
Cash Flows from Operating Activities: Indirect Method	
Net Income	$100,000
Less:Increase in Prepaid Insurance	(2,000)

Example 8: Property Tax Expense versus Cash Payments for Property Taxes

Case Company incurred property tax expense of $5,000, paid $4,000 of this amount in cash and the remaining $1,000 is in year-end property taxes payable. Property tax payments totaled $7,000, which included the payment of $4,000 of the current year's property tax expense and the $3,000 it owed from the prior year. The $2,000 decrease in property tax payable signifies that the cash payments ($7,000) were greater than the current year's property tax expense ($5,000). A visual representation of this information appears in Figure 6.19, and the financial statement results are presented in Figure 6.20.

Figure 6.19 Property Tax Expense versus Cash Payments

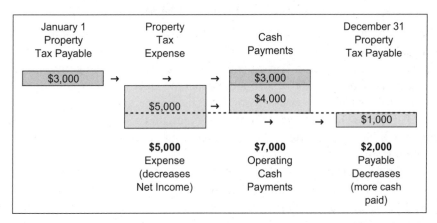

Figure 6.20 Financial Statements (Partial): Property Tax Expense versus Cash Payments

INCOME STATEMENT	
Property Tax Expense	$ (5,000)
STATEMENT OF CASH FLOWS	
Cash Flows from Operating Activities: Direct Method	
Cash paid for property taxes	$ (7,000)
OR	
Cash Flows from Operating Activities: Indirect Method	
Net Income	$100,000
Less: Decrease in Property Taxes Payable	(2,000)

Example 9: Revenues Earned and Received and Expenses Incurred and Paid in the Same Period

Other revenues and expenses in Case Company's income statement were received or paid in cash during the same year, such as the $1,000 of interest income, the $5,000 of interest expense, and the $20,000 for advertising and $15,000 for telephone and utility expenses. The specific amounts of cash received or paid for these revenues and expenses are presented as operating cash flows when using the direct method approach. If operating cash flows are reported using the indirect method approach, there is no need to show adjustments to net income because the amounts reported as revenues and expenses under the accrual basis of accounting are identical to the amounts of the cash received or paid during the same time period.

Example 10: Nonoperating Gains and Losses

In addition to the net income and net operating cash flow differences discussed and illustrated earlier, there is one more concept you may encounter when reviewing a company's statement of cash flows: the treatment of *nonoperating gains and losses*. Although Case Company did report interest income and interest expense separately from the revenues and expenses arising from its routine and ongoing operations, it did not have any *gains* or *losses* to report this year, and so a different and unrelated example will be used to explain how nonoperating gains and losses are treated in the statement of cash flows.

As was discussed in earlier chapters, when a company sells a plant asset or an investment it owns, the difference between the selling price and the book value of the asset or investment is reported as a gain or as a loss in its income statement. As you learned earlier in this chapter on the statement of cash flows, purchases and sales of assets used by the business or investments it owns are considered to be investing activities, and not operating activities; thus, the cash received from the sale of such an asset or investment is classified as an investing activity cash flow and does not appear in the operating cash flows when the direct method approach is used. However, when the indirect method approach is used to report operating cash flows, any nonoperating gains that are included in the amount of net income reported in the income statement should be deducted, and any nonoperating losses should be added to net income. The cash received from the sale of an asset or investment, whether sold at a gain or at a loss, is classified as an investing cash inflow.

For example, assume both accounting income and operating cash flows were $100,000, excluding any effects from the sale of equipment. If equipment with a book value of $20,000 was sold for $25,000, a $5,000 gain from the sale would be included in the amount of net income reported in the income statement. In the statement of cash flows, the sale of equipment is considered an investing activity, and the $25,000 cash proceeds from the sale should be reported as an investing cash inflow. If the indirect method is used to report operating cash flows, the $5,000 nonoperating gain must be deducted from net income as it did not produce an operating cash flow. The financial statements would include the information shown in Figure 6.21. Notice that the net *operating* cash flow of $100,000 was not affected by the equipment sale; the $25,000 cash received from the equipment sale was an *investing* activity cash flow, not an operating cash flow.

Figure 6.21 Financial Statements (Partial): Sale of Equipment and Gain

INCOME STATEMENT		
Operating Income	$100,000	
Other Income and Expense:		
Gain on sale of equipment	5,000	
Net Income		$105,000
STATEMENT OF CASH FLOWS		
Operating Activities: Direct Method (cash received from equipment sale is an investing, not an operating cash flow)		$100,000
OR		
Operating Activities: Indirect Method		
Net Income	$105,000	
Less: Gain on sale of equipment	(5,000)	
Net cash flows from operating activities		$100,000
Investing Activities		
Cash received from sale of equipment		$ 25,000

If instead the equipment had been sold for $18,000, a $2,000 loss from the sale would have been deducted in arriving at the amount of net income reported in the income statement. Similar to the previous example, the $18,000 cash proceeds from the sale should be reported in the statement of cash flows as an investing activity. If the indirect method is used to report operating cash flows, the $2,000 nonoperating loss which reduced net income but did not result in a cash outflow must be added back to net income to arrive at the proper amount of operating cash flows. The financial statements would include the information shown in Figure 6.22. As in the previous example, the net *operating* cash flows of $100,000 has not changed; the equipment sale generated an $18,000 *investing* activity cash flow and did not affect operating cash flows.

Figure 6.22   Financial Statements (Partial): Sale of Equipment and Loss

INCOME STATEMENT		
Operating Income	$100,000	
Other Income and Expense		
Loss on sale of equipment	(2,000)	
Net Income		$ 98,000
STATEMENT OF CASH FLOWS		
Operating Activities: Direct Method (cash received from equipment sale is an investing, not an operating cash flow)		$100,000
OR		
Operating Activities: Indirect Method		
Net Income	$ 98,000	
Add: Loss on sale of equipment	2,000	
Net cash flows from operating activities		$100,000
Investing Activities		
Cash received from sale of equipment		$ 18,000

Case Company Operating Cash Flows

The examples above illustrated and explained why the amount of a specific revenue or expense that was reported in the income statement may differ from the amount of the related cash receipt or cash payment during the same time period. Let's take a look at the operating activity section of Case Company's statement of cash flows which incorporates the specific revenue and expense examples that were discussed separately above. Figure 6.23 shows net cash flows from operating activities using the

direct method approach. Figure 6.24 also presents net operating cash flows, but as they would be reported using the *indirect method* approach.

Figure 6.23 Direct Method: Operating Cash Flows

Case Company
Statement of Cash Flows (partial)–Direct Method
For the Year Ended December 31, 20x1

Cash Flows from Operating Activities		
Cash Receipts		
Cash collections from customers	$782,000	
Interest on investments and loans	1,000	
Total Cash Receipts		$783,000
Cash Payments		
Merchandise purchases	545,000	
Salaries and wages	129,000	
Advertising	20,000	
Telephone and utilities	15,000	
Supplies and postage	6,000	
Insurance	11,000	
Property taxes	7,000	
Interest	5,000	
Total Cash Payments		(738,000)
Net Cash Flows from Operating Activities		$ 45,000

Figure 6.24 Indirect Method - Operating Cash Flows

Case Company
Statement of Cash Flows (partial)–Indirect Method
For the Year Ended December 31, 20x1

Net Income		$100,000
Adjustments to reconcile net income to		
net cash flow from operating activities		
Increase in accounts receivable	$(18,000)	
Increase in merchandise inventory	(25,000)	
Decrease in accounts payable	(20,000)	
Increase in salaries and wages payable	1,000	
Depreciation expense	10,000	
Decrease in supplies on hand	1,000	
Increase in prepaid insurance	(2,000)	
Decrease in property taxes payable	(2,000)	
Total Adjustments		(55,000)
Net Cash Provided by Operating Activities		$ 45,000

Which Method to Use: Direct or Indirect?

The accounting profession encourages the use of the direct method, with additional disclosure using the indirect method in a supplemental schedule that is referred to as the *schedule reconciling net income to net cash flows from operating activities*. However, it is permissible to use only the indirect method in the statement of cash flows. In fact, and perhaps unfortunately, the indirect method is used more widely in published financial statements. Although the indirect method does make sense and provides valuable information, it is not as straightforward or easily understood as the direct method.

Accrual Basis Versus Cash Basis

In summary, when you compare the income statement results with the operating activities section of the statement of cash flows, there are some similarities and some differences. The income statement and the operating activities section of the statement of cash flows are similar in that both present information about the primary business activities: the income earned and cash flows from providing services or selling goods.

However, the income statement and the cash flow statement differ in that the income statement shows revenues earned, expenses incurred, and the resulting net income or loss without regard to cash flows, using the accrual basis concept. Preparing the operating activities section of the statement of cash flows is much like preparing the income statement, but using the cash basis of accounting. Although cash basis information is important and valuable, an income statement prepared on the cash basis generally is not considered the best measure of a company's operating performance.

In the next section, we will discuss investing and financing activities and the way they are reported in the statement of cash flows, as well as the concept of cash equivalents.

Investing Activities

Investing activities may be viewed as transactions involving the assets of the business; they generally consist of the purchase and sale of investments and assets used by the business. Investing activities also may include cash loans and collections of the principal amounts of those loans, although the dividends and interest collected on loans and investments are classified as operating activities. The investing activities section of a company's statement of cash flows may include the items shown in Figure 6.25.

Figure 6.25   Statement of Cash Flows Reporting: Investing Activities

Cash Flows from Investing Activities		
Cash Inflows		
Sale of equipment	$ 10,000	
Sale of investments	200,000	
Collection of note receivable	20,000	
Total		$ 230,000
Cash Outflows		
Purchase of land and building	(600,000)	
Purchase of investments	(30,000)	
Cash loaned in exchange for a note receivable	(20,000)	
Total		(650,000)
Net Cash Flows from Investing Activities		$(420,000)

Note that net cash flows from investing activities is a negative amount; in the example above, the company used more cash for investing activities than it took in. It might have financed the purchase of additional investments and other assets internally, using excess cash generated from its routine operating activities. However, it might have been necessary to find and use other resources to finance the acquisition of new plant assets and other investments.

Financing Activities

Financing activities may be viewed as transactions involving the parties which provide resources to the business: the creditors, and the owners. Transactions with creditors include borrowing and repaying the principal amount of loans, although the interest on loans is treated as an operating activity. Transactions with owners include investments by the owners, distributions to the owners such as withdrawals and cash dividends, the purchase of treasury stock, and the retirement of outstanding stock. The financing activities section of a company's statement of cash flows may include the items shown in Figure 6.26.

It was mentioned in the earlier discussion of investing activities that a company can finance its growth internally or through external means. In the short run, a company may finance expansion and growth or even overcome liquidity problems using capital provided by owners (sole proprietor, partners, or stockholders) or using borrowed funds (bank loans, mortgage loans, bonds payable). However, if a company is to be viable in the long run it ultimately must be able to repay the amounts

Figure 6.26   Statement of Cash Flows Reporting: Financing Activities

Cash Flows from Financing Activities		
Cash Inflows		
Bonds payable issued	$400,000	
Common stock issued	300,000	
Total		$700,000
Cash Outflows		
Repayment of long-term note payable	(160,000)	
Cash dividends paid	(30,000)	
Purchases of treasury stock	(10,000)	
Total		(200,000)
Net Cash Flows from Financing Activities		$500,000

borrowed, distribute dividends, and/or increase the market price of its stock to reward its investors. If the company cannot sustain itself through profits and cash flows it should be able to generate from its ongoing and routine business activities, it will be difficult or perhaps impossible, to attract new capital investments or to find additional lending sources.

On the basis of the examples of investing and financing activities illustrated in Figures 6.25 and 6.26, in the short run, it appears that this company has financed a significant portion of its plant asset expansion by issuing bonds payable and by issuing (selling) additional common stock. Will it be able to repay the interest and principal amounts it has borrowed? Will it be able to distribute some of its profits to stockholders via cash dividends and/or generate a higher market price for its stock and reward its investors in this way? A review of a company's statement of cash flows can provide some important hints or clues, as would a review of any of the other financial statements. However, key questions are more likely to be answered by analyzing the financial statements and footnote disclosures in their entirety, by taking a look at how things are developing for a company over time, and how a given company compares to a competitor. The additional topics covered in Chapters 7 to 10 will provide you with some additional tools and further insight that might help you in finding answers to some of your important questions about a company's health.

Gross Versus Net Cash Flows

Cash flows from investing and financing activities generally are based on the amounts of cash received or paid for significant items; this is more relevant and useful information than a simple report of the net amount of cash received or paid for each item. For example, if $10,000 was paid to purchase equipment and other equipment was sold for $2,000, under investing activity cash flows, both the cash payment of $10,000 and the cash receipt of $2,000 would be presented, rather than just the net cash paid of $8,000. Similarly, if $60,000 was borrowed and $5,000 was repaid, both the borrowing and the repayment would be shown rather than the net cash receipt of $55,000.

There is an exception which permits net reporting for certain types of borrowing activities if the turnover is quick, the amounts are large, and the maturities are three months or less. For example, assume your banker permits you to borrow to meet seasonal cash requirements with a series of one-month loans. During the course of the year, you take several such loans for a total of $100,000 and repay a total of $95,000. In this case, it is permissible to report only the net amount of cash borrowings of $5,000 because the turnover of the loans was quick and the amounts of the loans were relatively large.

Noncash Investing and Financing Activities

The statement of cash flows reports only those activities which result in receipts or payments of cash. However, a business may engage in investing or financing activities which do not directly result in cash receipts or cash payments; information about such activities is relevant and useful because it can help the financial statement user to predict future cash flows pertaining to these items. Consequently, the accounting profession requires disclosure of significant noncash investing and financing activities. Noncash investing and financing activities include the purchase of assets financed with a note or mortgage payable, acquiring the long-term rights to the use of an asset via a capital lease agreement, repayment of debt with noncash assets, and settling a debt by issuing stock instead of a cash repayment. For example, a company's financial statements or footnotes disclosures for noncash investing and financing activities may include the items shown in Figure 6.27.

Let's take a look at the investing and financing activities Case Company presents in its statement of cash flows and its supplemental disclosures, as shown in Figure 6.28.

As you can see, Case Company's only investing activity was the purchase of equipment, for which it used $1,000 in cash; the remainder was financed through

Figure 6.27 Schedule of Noncash Investing and Financing Activities

Cost of land and buildings purchased	$500,000	
Less: Cash paid	(100,000)	
Land and buildings financed with mortgage note payable		$ 400,000
Bonds payable retired by issuing common stock		$5,000,000

Figure 6.28 Investing and Financing Activities

Case Company
Statement of Cash Flows (partial)
For the Year Ended December 31, 20x1

Cash Flows from Investing Activities		
Cash payments for equipment purchases		$ (1,000)
Cash Flows from Financing Activities		
Additional investment by owner	$ 10,000	
Owner withdrawals	(50,000)	
Principal payment on mortgage note payable	(5,000)	
Net Cash Flows from Financing Activities		$(45,000)
Schedule of Noncash Investing and Financing Activities		
Cost of equipment purchased		$ 5,000
Less: Cash down payment		(1,000)
Portion of equipment cost financed with note payable		$ 4,000

borrowing, specifically, a $4,000 note payable. The financing activities included $10,000 of additional cash invested by the owner, $50,000 of cash withdrawn by the owner, and $5,000 of cash paid on the principal balance of the long-term mortgage note payable (the interest paid was an operating activity). The cash flow information combined with the noncash disclosures can assist you in determining the cause of changes in asset, liability, and equity accounts which may be explained only partially by the other financial statements.

Cash and Cash Equivalents

The final section of the statement of cash flows shows the change in cash and cash equivalents during the year, and the amount of cash and cash equivalents at year-end. Cash consists of cash on hand or on deposit with banks or other financial institutions. A business may invest its idle cash in a variety of ways to generate earnings until the cash is needed for business activities. Cash equivalents, as discussed in Chapter 5, are a special category of temporary investments of cash in highly liquid, readily marketable securities that may be converted into known amounts of cash. Cash equivalents generally consist of investments in U.S. Treasury bills, money market funds, and commercial paper, if such investments are purchased within three months of their original maturity date.

In the balance sheet, cash and cash equivalents are combined and shown as a single amount, the change in the total amount of cash and cash equivalents is shown, and the policies used to determine cash equivalents should be disclosed. The change in cash and cash equivalents and accounting policy disclosure for Case Company appear in Figure 6.29.

Figure 6.29 Change in Cash and Cash Equivalents

Case Company
Statement of Cash Flows
For the Year Ended December 31, 20x1

Net Cash Flows arising from:		
Operating Activities	$45,000	
Investing Activities	(1,000)	
Financing Activities	(45,000)	
Decrease in Cash and Cash Equivalents		$(1,000)
Cash and Cash Equivalents*, December 31, 20x0		4,000
Cash and Cash Equivalents, December 31, 20x1		$ 3,000

*Accounting Policies:
   Cash and Cash Equivalents include cash on hand, cash in banks and other financial institutions, and investments in US Treasury Bills and money market funds.

Even though cash equivalents are comprised of specific types of investments, purchases and sales of cash equivalents are not reported because they are considered to be much like actual cash on hand. For example, assume a business has $4,000 in cash. If it invests $1,000 in a money market fund and has $3,000 in cash, total cash and cash equivalents has not changed; it is still $4,000. If it sells $200 of the investment in the money market fund, it still has $4,000 in cash and cash equivalents; $3,200 cash and $800 of cash equivalents. However, the interest and dividends received from investments in cash equivalents are reported in the statement of cash flows under operating activities. The $1,000 of interest income Case Company reported was from its investments in cash equivalents; it had no other investments during the year.

Pulling It All Together

As we near the conclusion of this chapter, we provide two additional figures which will help you understand how the information presented in each individual financial statement relates to one or more of the other statements. Figure 6.30 focuses on the differences between the revenues and expenses as reported in the income statement and the cash receipts and cash payments reported as operating activities in the statement of cash flows. Figure 6.31 focuses on the comparative balance sheet and shows the amount of the change for each asset, liability and total owner's equity

Figure 6.30

Case Company
Operating Activities - Explanations of Differences Between
Revenues and Expenses and Cash Receipts and Payments

	Revenue (Expense)	Cash Receipts (Payments)	Difference	Explanation
Sales	$ 800,000	$ 782,000	$(18,000)	Increase in receivables; less collected
Interest Income	1,000	1,000	-	All earned and collected
Cost of Goods Sold	(500,000)	(545,000)	(25,000)	Increase in inventory; more purchased
			(20,000)	Decrease in accounts payable; more paid
Salaries and Wages	(130,000)	(129,000)	1,000	Increase in salaries payable; less paid
Depreciation	(10,000)	-	10,000	Noncash expense
Advertising	(20,000)	(20,000)	-	All incurred and paid
Telephone and Utilities	(15,000)	(15,000)	-	All incurred and paid
Supplies and Postage	(7,000)	(6,000)	1,000	Decrease in supplies; used more
Insurance	(9,000)	(11,000)	(2,000)	Increase in prepaid insurance; more purchased
Property Taxes	(5,000)	(7,000)	(2,000)	Decrease in taxes payable; more paid
Interest Expense	(5,000)	(5,000)	-	All incurred and paid
Total	$ 100,000	$ 45,000	$(55,000)	
	Net Income	Operating Cash Flows	Adjustments to Net Income	

184

Figure 6.31

Case Company
Explanations of Changes in Asset and Liability Amounts During the Year

	End of Year	Beginning of Year	Increase (Decrease)	Explanation
ASSETS				
Current Assets				
Cash and cash equivalents	$ 3,000	$ 4,000	$(1,000)	See Statement of Cash Flows
Accounts receivable	31,000	13,000	18,000	Sales earned but not collected
Inventory	65,000	40,000	25,000	Purchased more than sold
Prepaid insurance	5,000	3,000	2,000	Purchased more than used
Supplies on hand	1,000	2,000	(1,000)	Used more than purchased
Total Current Assets	105,000	62,000		
Plant and Equipment				
Land	10,000	10,000		No change
Building (net)	60,000	64,000	(4,000)	None purchased, $4,000 depreciation
Equipment (net)	23,000	24,000	(1,000)	$5,000 purchased; $6,000 depreciation
Total Plant and Equipment	93,000	98,000		
Total Assets	$198,000	$160,000		
LIABILITIES AND EQUITY				
Current liabilities				
Accounts payable	$ 16,000	$ 36,000	(20,000)	Paid more than purchased
Salaries payable	5,000	4,000	1,000	Paid less than incurred
Property tax payable	1,000	3,000	(2,000)	Paid more than incurred
Note payable	4,000	-	4,000	Borrowed to finance purchase of equipment
Current mortgage	5,000	5,000		No change, $5,000 to be paid in coming year
Total Current Liabilities	31,000	48,000		
Long-term Liabilities				
Mortgage note payable	40,000	45,000	(5,000)	Repaid a portion of the loan
Total Liabilities	71,000	93,000		
Owner's Equity				
Case, Capital	127,000	67,000	60,000	See Statement of Owner Equity
Total Liabilities and Equity	$198,000	$160,000		

In Figure 6.30, the revenue (expense) column shows the amounts reported in the income statement, resulting in accrual basis net income of $100,000. The cash receipts (payments) column shows the amounts reported as operating cash flows using the direct method, resulting in a net operating cash inflow of $45,000, which can be viewed as cash basis net income. Notice that net operating cash flows were $55,000 less than accrual basis net income. The differences between individual revenue/expense and cash receipt/payment amount s represent the adjustments to net income that are shown when reporting net operating cash flows using the indirect method approach.

Figure 6.31 focuses on the comparative balance sheet and shows the amount of the change; it also provides a brief explanation for each item. As you will notice, the changes in each item were reported in or explained by one or more of the other financial statements. The balance sheet shows the financial position at a point in time. The transactions and events that took place during the year were reported in the income statement, the statement of owner's equity, and/or the statement of cash flows and produced the amounts reported in the year-end balance sheet.

We conclude this chapter by presenting the complete set of financial statements Case Company might include in its application for a bank loan or in a year-end annual report to stockholders if Case Company was a corporation instead of a sole proprietorship. In this example, we assume that Case Company has elected to use the direct method to report its operating cash flows and to present the indirect method and its noncash investing and financing activities in separate schedules or footnote disclosures. Of course, there would be many additional disclosures for other financial statement items included in the accompanying financial statement footnotes, along with the information provided in this example. This complete set of financial statements for Case Company is shown in Figure 6.32.

Summary

We introduced you to basic financial accounting and reporting concepts in Chapters 1 and 2 and then discussed and illustrated each financial statement in much more detail and made frequent reference to how the basic financial accounting and reporting concepts applied in each case. The income statement was discussed in Chapter 3, the balance sheet and the statement of owners' equity were discussed in Chapters 4 and 5, and we concluded with a discussion of the statement of cash flows in this chapter.

Building on this foundation, in the chapters which follow we will discuss some additional financial reporting issues and the information found in a company's annual report, including the report of the independent auditor, and will introduce you to financial statement analysis tools and techniques. We will conclude the book with a discussion of fraudulently misstated financial statements.

Figure 6.32   Case Company - Financial Statements

Case Company
Income Statement
For the Year Ended December 31, 20x1

Sales Revenue		$ 800,000
Cost of Goods Sold		
Inventory, January 1	$ 40,000	
Purchases	525,000	
Cost of Goods Available for Sale	565,000	
Inventory, December 31	(65,000)	
Cost of Goods Sold		500,000
Gross Profit		300,000
Operating Expenses		
Salaries and wages	130,000	
Depreciation	10,000	
Advertising	20,000	
Telephone and utilities	15,000	
Supplies and postage	7,000	
Insurance	9,000	
Property taxes	5,000	
Total operating expenses		196,000
Operating Income		104,000
Other Income and Expense		
Interest income	1,000	
Interest expense	(5,000)	
Total other income and expense		(4,000)
Net Income		$100 ,000

Case Company
Statement of Owner's Equity
For the Year Ended December 31, 20x1

Case, Capital, December 31, 20x0		$ 67,000
Add: Additional investment by the owner		10,000
Net Income		100,000
Total		177,000
Less: Owner withdrawals		(50,000)
Case, Capital, December 31, 20x1		$ 127,000

Comparative Balance Sheets
As of December 31

	20x1	20x0
ASSETS		
Current Assets		
Cash and cash equivalents	$ 3,000	$ 4,000
Accounts receivable	31,000	13,000
Merchandise inventory	65,000	40,000
Prepaid insurance	5,000	3,000
Supplies on hand	1,000	2,000
Total Current Assets	105,000	62,000
Plant and Equipment		
Land	10,000	10,000
Building (net of accumulated depreciation)	60,000	64,000
Equipment (net of accumulated depreciation)	23,000	24,000
Total Plant and Equipment	93,000	98,000
Total Assets	$198,000	$160,000
LIABILITIES AND OWNER'S EQUITY		
Current liabilities		
Accounts payable	$ 16,000	$ 36,000
Salaries and wages payable	5,000	4,000
Property taxes payable	1,000	3,000
Note payable	4,000	-
Current portion of mortgage note payable	5,000	5,000
Total Current Liabilities	31,000	48,000
Long-term Liabilities		
Mortgage note payable	40,000	45,000
Total Liabilities	71,000	93,000
Owner's Equity		
Case, Capital	127,000	67,000
Total Liabilities and Owner's Equity	$198,000	$160,000

Case Company
Statement of Cash Flows
For the Year Ended December 31, 20x1

Cash Flows from Operating Activities		
Cash Receipts		
Cash collections from customers	$782,000	
Interest	1,000	
Total Cash Receipts		$783,000
Cash Payments		
Merchandise purchases	545,000	
Salaries and wages	129,000	
Advertising	20,000	
Telephone and utilities	15,000	
Supplies and postage	6,000	
Insurance	11,000	
Property taxes	7,000	
Interest	5,000	
Total Cash Payments		(738,000)
Net Cash Flows from Operating Activities		45,000
Cash Flows from Investing Activities		
Cash payments for equipment purchases		(1,000)
Cash Flows from Financing Activities		
Additional investment by owner	10,000	
Owner withdrawals	(50,000)	
Principal payment on mortgage note payable	(5,000)	
Net Cash Flows from Financing Activities		(45,000)
Decrease in Cash and Cash Equivalents		(1,000)
Cash and Cash Equivalents, December 31, 20x0		4,000
Cash and Cash Equivalents, December 31, 20x1		$ 3,000

Schedule of Noncash Investing and Financing Activities

Cost of equipment purchased at year-end	$ 5,000
Less: Cash down payment	(1,000)
Portion of equipment cost financed with note payable	$ 4,000

Schedule Reconciling Net Income to
Net Cash Provided by Operating Activities

Net Income		$100,000
Adjustments to reconcile net income to		
net cash flow from operating activities:		
Increase in accounts receivable	$(18,000)	
Increase in merchandise inventory	(25,000)	
Decrease in accounts payable	(20,000)	
Increase in salaries and wages payable	1,000	
Depreciation expense	10,000	
Decrease in supplies on hand	1,000	
Increase in prepaid insurance	(2,000)	
Decrease in property taxes payable	(2,000)	
Total Adjustments		(55,000)
Net Cash Provided by Operating Activities		$ 45,000

Quiz for Chapter 6

1. Cash flows from investing activities include all of the following except:
   a. Purchases of plant assets
   b. Dividends and interest earned on investments
   c. Sales of investments
   d. Collection of the principal amount of a note receivable
   e. All of the above are investing activities.

2. Cash flows from financing activities include all of the following except:
   a. Issuing common stock
   b. Cash dividends paid to stockholders
   c. Repayment of bonds payable at maturity
   d. Payment of interest on bonds and notes payable
   e. All of the above are financing activities.

3. Which of the following is true regarding operating cash flows?
   a. Cash sales and customer collections on accounts receivable are included in the amount reported as operating cash flows.
   b. Specific amounts of cash receipts and cash payments will be reported as operating activities using the direct method.
   c. If cash received from customers differs from the amount of sales revenue reported in the income statement, the difference will be reported as an adjustment to net income using the indirect method.
   d. All of the above.
   e. None of the above.

4. Sales revenue for the year was $500,000. Beginning accounts receivable was $10,000, and ending accounts receivable was $15,000. Cash receipts from customers were:
   a. $500,000
   b. $495,000
   c. $505,000

5. Salaries expense for the year was $100,000. Beginning salaries payable was $10,000, and ending salaries payable was $15,000. Cash payments for salaries were:
   a. $100,000
   b. $ 95,000
   c. $105,000

6. Rent expense for the year was $40,000. Beginning prepaid rent was $10,000, and ending prepaid rent was $15,000. Cash payments for rent were:
   a. $40,000
   b. $35,000
   c. $45,000

7. Which of the following is true regarding the reporting of depreciation, depletion, and amortization costs?
   a. These amounts would be ignored in preparing the operating cash flow section using the direct method, as they are noncash expenses.
   b. These amounts would be added to net income in preparing the operating cash flow section using the indirect method, as these expenses reduced net income but did not have an associated cash outflow.
   c. Both of the above are true.
   d. Neither of the above is true.

8. Which of the following is an example of a noncash investing and/or financing activity?
   a. Issuing bonds payable to finance the purchase of land and buildings
   b. Retiring long-term debt by issuing common stock
   c. Trading in an old delivery vehicle for a new model
   d. All of the above
   e. None of the above

9. Which of the following is true pertaining to cash equivalents?
   a. Cash equivalents are a particular category of highly liquid, readily marketable investments.
   b. Cash and cash equivalents often are combined and presented as a single amount on the balance sheet.
   c. The statement of cash flows should include the change in the total amount of cash and cash equivalents from the beginning to the end of the year.
   d. All of the above are true.
   e. None of the above are true.

10. The term *accrual basis of accounting* means that the income statement covering a particular period will include the revenues earned and expenses incurred during that period regardless of the period in which the company received cash from its customers or paid cash for operating expenses.
    a. True
    b. False

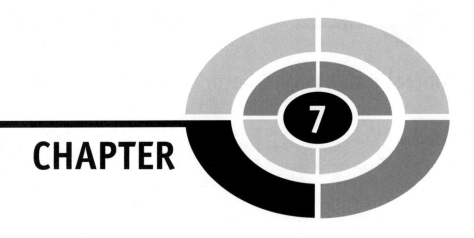

CHAPTER

7

Reading the Financial Statements:

The Auditors' Reports and Financial Statement Footnotes

In the previous chapters, we discussed the four basic financial statements in detail, explaining common terminology and concepts and exploring their interrelationships. In this chapter, we discuss ways to read the set of financial statements with a focus on understanding the auditors' opinions and the financial statement footnotes.

Annual Reports and Form 10-Ks

All publicly traded companies in the United States are required under federal securities laws to publish financial reports every year and submit them to the Securities and Exchange Commission (SEC). Privately held companies are not subject to this requirement, since the public cannot purchase shares of their stock. Consequently, the general public has no need to know the financial details of these companies.

The annual report required by the SEC is referred to as a Form 10-K (a Form 10-Q is submitted for quarterly financial information), and it contains a large amount of detailed information about a corporation. It is not unusual for a corporation's Form 10-K to exceed 100 pages. Anyone can access these filings on the SEC's Web site (www.sec.gov) or the individual corporation's Web site (usually under a tab titled "Investors," "Investor Relations," or something similar).

The 10-K includes the financial statements of the public company, along with additional required information. However, companies do not have the flexibility to choose what type of information they will submit to the SEC or where in the Form 10-K they will provide information. The SEC wants to enhance the comparability of financial information from company to company and dictates what must be included in Form 10-K. Thus, the type of information provided by a company will be similar in content and location from one Form 10-K to another, even among a variety of industries.

For example, let's look at the Form 10-Ks of the following four companies, which are engaged in different types of business operations:

- Target Corporation, which operates large-format general merchandise and food discount stores, for the fiscal year ended February 3, 2007
- Cabela's Incorporated, a large direct marketer and leading specialty retailer of fishing, hunting, camping, and related outdoor merchandise, for the fiscal year ended December 30, 2006
- Coca-Cola Enterprises, Inc., the world's largest Coca-Cola bottler, which markets, sells, manufactures, and distributes a variety of nonalcoholic beverages, for the fiscal year ended December 31, 2006
- Kimberly-Clark Corporation, which principally manufactures and markets a wide range of health and hygiene products, for the fiscal year ended December 31, 2006

You'll find that their Form 10-K tables of contents are identical, as shown in Figure 7.1.

Although a Form 10-K is the annual report a public company is required to file with the SEC, it is not the same as the annual report sent to the shareholders. Shareholders' annual reports often give the appearance of a magazine, with glossy paper, brightly colored photographs and illustrations, and a lot of marketing-type information about the company. Financial statements are included in these annual reports but often appear toward the back

Figure 7.1 Form 10-K Table of Contents for Target Corporation, Cabela's Incorporated, Coca-Cola Enterprises, Inc., and Kimberly-Clark Corporation

Part I.

Item 1.	Business
Item 1A.	Risk Factors
Item 1B.	Unresolved Staff Comments
Item 2.	Properties
Item 3.	Legal Proceedings
Item 4.	Submission of Matters to a Vote of Security Holders

Part II.

Item 5.	Market for Registrant's Common Equity, Related Stockholder Matters, and Issuer Purchases of Equity Securities
Item 6.	Selected Financial Data
Item 7.	Management's Discussion and Analysis of Financial Condition and Results of Operations
Item 7A.	Quantitative and Qualitative Disclosures about Market Risk
Item 8.	Financial Statements and Supplementary Data
Item 9.	Changes in and Disagreements with Accountants on Accounting and Financial Disclosure
Item 9A.	Controls and Procedures
Item 9B.	Other Information

Part III.

Item 10.	Directors and Executive Officers and Corporate Governance
Item 11.	Executive Compensation
Item 12.	Security Ownership of Certain Beneficial Owners and Management and Related Stockholder Matters
Item 13.	Certain Relationships and Related Transactions and Director Independence
Item 14.	Principal Accountant Fees and Services

Part IV.

Item 15.	Exhibits and Financial Statement Schedules

Signatures

of the reports on nonglossy paper, and there typically isn't as much financial data as there is in a Form 10-K. However, some companies reproduce the Form 10-K in its entirety as part of the shareholders' annual report.

Audited versus Nonaudited Financial Statements

The annual financial statements submitted by public companies to the SEC are required to be audited. Private companies are not required by legislation to have their financial statements audited; however, if a private company is applying for a loan, it is likely that the bank will require audited financial statements before approving a loan. Otherwise, the bank will have to take the risk of accepting the financial statements as management has prepared them.

A company will include the report of its independent auditors on the financial statements in both the Form 10-K and the shareholders' annual report. The audit report often is referred to as the *auditors' opinion*, because the auditors are providing an opinion about whether the financial statements are presented fairly in all material respects, based on the evidence gathered during the audit process.

Why is the audit report important? Essentially, management is responsible for designing an accounting information system that will capture all of its business transactions and compile the financial statements. However, anyone outside the company, such as a current or potential investor or creditor, may be concerned about whether management has put the financial statements together without bias. Could management have intentionally or even unknowingly presented some events more optimistically than is warranted? Absolutely. Worse, could management have intentionally included some fictitious revenues, omitted some actual expenses, or performed some other accounting trick so that the company's financial results would appear better than in fact they are? Yes, if management is so inclined. The independent auditors' report is designed to alleviate that concern and give the public assurance that the financial statements can be relied on. *Assurance* is a key word: In fact, it is common in the accounting profession to refer to auditing as an assurance service or attest service because the auditors are providing assurance or attesting (vouching for) to the fairness of the presentation of the information on the financial statements.

It is important to understand exactly how much assurance the auditors are providing in regard to the financial statements and to understand what their opinion means. For quite some time there has been a disconnect between what the accounting profession requires of auditors and what many in the general public believe auditors do. This misunderstanding has been referred to as the expectations gap. We'll attempt to narrow this gap in the next few paragraphs by discussing a few key auditing concepts.

Independent Auditors

The purpose of the audit report is to give the public confidence that it can rely on the financial statements prepared by management. However, what assurance does the public have that it can rely on what the auditors have to say? To enhance the public's confidence in the audit report, auditors are required to be *independent* with respect to the client (the company whose financial statements are being audited). Independence is a critical aspect of auditing. It is so important that if for some reason a public accounting firm discovers during an audit that the firm is not independent with respect to its client, it is required to stop auditing and issue a very short (one sentence) report stating that the public accounting firm is not independent and therefore it cannot and is not issuing any kind of opinion on the financial statements.

To enhance the public's confidence in its work, the audit report is signed with the name of the public accounting firm that performed it, not with the names of the individual auditors on the engagement team. In other words, the entire firm is standing behind their opinion.

To underscore its independence, the public accounting firm is required to include the word *independent* in the title of its audit report. The rules for determining whether a firm is or is not independent are fairly complex but are in place essentially to help ensure that auditors are able to conduct their audits in an objective, unbiased, and impartial manner. In fact, the auditing profession defines independence as the ability to conduct an audit in an unbiased and objective manner. This definition does not imply that auditors automatically assume that management is dishonest, but they also should not assume that management is honest; professional skepticism is to be exercised during the conduct of an audit.

To help ensure independence, there are rules forbidding an auditor's direct financial interest of any amount in a client (even owning one share of stock in a client is prohibited), as well as rules pertaining to the type of employment that an auditor's dependents and other relatives may have with a client. The accounting profession traditionally has been concerned with auditors being not only independent in fact— truly independent with respect to their clients—but also independent in appearance because perception is as important as reality. Thus, some of the independence rules may appear harsh, but the auditing profession believes the public's confidence in their work is worth it.

One factor that complicates the issue of independence is the fact that the audit fee is paid by the client to the auditors. Certainly, if the client becomes unhappy with the auditors for any reason, it can terminate the relationship and hire another public accounting firm to conduct the audit. Critics wonder how independent auditors truly can be when the client writes the check. This issue became even more controversial in the late 1990s, when many public accounting firms provided consulting services to their audit clients for large additional fees. For example, the public accounting firm that audited Enron earned millions more a year in consulting revenue than in audit fees. Many people were concerned that this type of relationship could cause auditors to agree with any questionable financial reporting on the part of their audit clients for fear of losing not only the audit fee but also the substantial consulting revenue. Primarily as a result of the numerous widely publicized corporate scandals of the late 1990s and early 2000s, Congress enacted the Sarbanes-Oxley Act of 2002, which greatly limited the types of nonaudit services public accounting firms can offer to their audit clients.

Reasonable Assurance versus Absolute Assurance

An audit report provides *reasonable assurance* that the financial statements are free of material misstatements, not absolute assurance. In fact the term *reasonable assurance* must be used in the audit report. However, reasonable assurance is never defined precisely in the professional auditing standards. Auditors understand that the term refers to the fact that audits cannot provide 100 percent guarantees that there are no material misstatements in the financial statements, although this is a concept that the public frequently misunderstands. When auditors have obtained reasonable assurance is a matter left to the auditors' judgment.

Why do auditors provide reasonable assurance as opposed to absolute assurance? It is impossible for auditors to audit everything to provide such a guarantee. Even if they audited every single transaction throughout the year, which would be impossible in terms of time and cost, auditors could not know definitely whether there were unrecorded transactions that remained undetected. Thus, it is economically not feasible and impractical to expect auditors to look at everything: they cannot provide absolute assurance about financial statements.

Material Misstatements in Financial Statements

For all practical purposes, auditors cannot be held responsible for finding every misstatement of any amount in the financial statements. Would it really matter to most financial statement readers if the company's inventory was overstated by $1? $10? $100? At some point, it will matter because the misstatement could cause reasonable financial statement users to make decisions different from what they would have decided if the misstatement had not existed. It is at that point that misstatements are considered to be material.

Materiality varies from company to company. For example, overstating inventory by $10,000 may be material for a small business owner. However, when Wal-Mart presents its financial statements in millions of dollars, the $33,685 inventory amount appearing on its January 31, 2007, balance sheet is actually $33,685,000,000 (or nearly $34 billion), a $10,000 overstatement of inventory surely is immaterial.

Because materiality will vary from company to company and even from year to year for a specific company, it is not defined in terms of dollars or percentages throughout the professional auditing standards. Once again, like reasonable assurance, materiality is a decision left to the auditors' judgment. Also, like reasonable assurance, the word *material* is required by professional auditing standards to be in the auditors' report.

The Standard Audit Report

With these basic auditing concepts in mind, let's look at a standard audit report. For our example, we'll use Wal-Mart again (see Figure 7.2).

Figure 7.2   Ernst & Young LLP's Audit Report for Wal-Mart Stores, Inc., Financial Statements as of January 31, 2007

Report of Independent Registered Public Accounting Firm

The Board of Directors and Shareholders,
Wal-Mart Stores, Inc.

We have audited the accompanying consolidated balance sheets of Wal-Mart Stores, Inc., as of January 31, 2007, and 2006, and the related consolidated statements of income, shareholders' equity, and cash flows for each of the three years in the period ended January 31, 2007. These **financial statements are the responsibility of the Company's management. Our responsibility is to express an opinion** on these financial statements based on our audits.

We conducted our audits in accordance with the standards of the Public Company Accounting Oversight Board (United States). Those standards require that we plan and perform the audit to obtain **reasonable assurance** about whether the financial statements are **free of material misstatement**. An audit includes examining, on a test basis, evidence supporting the amounts and disclosures in the financial statements. An audit also includes assessing the accounting principles used and significant estimates made by management, as well as evaluating the overall financial statement presentation. We believe that our audits provide a reasonable basis for our opinion.

In our opinion, the financial statements referred to above **present fairly, in all material respects,** the consolidated financial position of Wal-Mart Stores, Inc., at January 31, 2007 and 2006, and the consolidated results of its operations and its cash flows for each of the three years in the period ended January 31, 2007, **in conformity with U.S. generally accepted accounting principles**.

As discussed in Note 13 to the consolidated financial statements, effective January 31, 2007, the Company adopted Statement of Financial Accounting Standards No. 158, *Employers' Accounting for Defined Benefit Pension and Other Postretirement Plans.*

We also have audited, in accordance with the standards of the Public Company Accounting Oversight Board (United States), the effectiveness of Wal-Mart Stores, Inc.'s internal control over financial reporting as of January 31, 2007, based on criteria established in *Internal Control—Integrated Framework* issued by the Committee of Sponsoring Organizations of the Treadway Commission, and our report dated March 26, 2007, expressed an unqualified opinion thereon.

Ernst & Young LLP (signed)
Rogers, Arkansas
March 26, 2007

The audit report contains quite a bit of information. The professional auditing standards require fairly uniform wording, however, so that financial statement readers can assess the type of opinion being given without getting bogged down in variations in terminology and phrasing. Note in Figure 7.2 that the terms we discussed above—*independent, reasonable assurance*, and *material*—are all present. Note also that the audit opinion is signed with the public accounting firm's name, not the names of the individual auditors who worked on the engagement, because the entire firm is standing behind the opinion.

The opinion shown in Figure 7.2 is called an *unqualified audit opinion*, and it is the best opinion the auditors can give. Often, this is referred to as a *clean opinion*. What the auditors are saying is that the financial statements, in their opinion, follow generally accepted accounting principles (GAAP) in all material respects. The auditors are giving this opinion without any qualifications. That is why the opinion is given the name *unqualified*. A qualification is a discovery by the auditors of some kind of problem; we'll explain that shortly.

To determine whether a company received this best opinion, look for the paragraph that begins with "In our opinion…" and determine whether the auditors are stating that without any exceptions the financial statements "present fairly, in all material respects" (see Figure 7.3).

Figure 7.3   Different Types of Audit Opinions

Type of Audit Opinion	Key Phrase(s)	Translation
Unqualified	In our opinion, present fairly, in all material respects	Best opinion
Qualified	In our opinion, *except for*, present fairly, in all material respects	There's a problem (which the auditors will explain) with some aspect of the financial statements, but other than that, the financial statements as a whole are presented fairly. It is up to the reader to decide if the problem identified by the auditors affects the usefulness of the financial statements.
Adverse	In our opinion, do *not* present fairly in all material respects	Worst opinion: The auditors are telling the readers they can not rely on these financial statements.
Disclaimer	We cannot and do not express an opinion	The auditors cannot give any opinion because of some very serious limitation on their work, either client-imposed or due to circumstances beyond anyone's control (such as the fact that the accounting system is in terrible disarray) or because the auditors lack independence (rare).

The vast majority of audits of public companies result in this best opinion. If the auditors have found a significant misstatement in the financial statements, they will discuss it with management and the company will have an opportunity to adjust the books to the auditors' satisfaction. In almost all cases, management will opt to do this so that it can acquire the best opinion. Why does management strongly prefer to receive an unqualified opinion? Because anything less can affect the reputation of the company adversely and consequently decrease the company's stock price.

The Wal-Mart audit opinion contains the opinion paragraph as the third paragraph. Sometimes public accounting firms begin the report with the opinion because of its importance. However, the key phrases you are looking for do not vary regardless of the placement of the opinion paragraph.

Modifications to the Standard Audit Report

In a few circumstances, auditors may give an unqualified opinion but add an extra paragraph to the report. For example, auditors are required to add an extra paragraph after the opinion paragraph if the company did not apply the same generally accepted accounting principles consistently from last year to this year. Also, auditors must add an extra paragraph after the opinion paragraph if they have serious doubt about the company's ability to continue as a going concern for a period of up to one year past the balance sheet date. Auditors also are allowed to add an extra paragraph to emphasize any matter they wish, but that choice is always at the discretion of the auditor.

Consistency

Auditing standards require the addition of a *consistency* paragraph to indicate to the readers that if the financial statements are different this year (for example, either a higher or lower net income than last year), it could be because the use of accounting principles differed between the two years. In other words, the financial statements may not be directly comparable. However, this does not imply that the company is engaged in anything improper. Companies are allowed to switch from one generally accepted accounting principle (GAAP) to another as long as the change, its effects, and management's justification for the change are disclosed. Further, when the accounting profession issues a new standard that changes the way certain types of transactions previously were accounted for and requires that all companies follow the new standard, consistency comes into play and the auditors must include the additional paragraph again.

For example, take another look at the consistency paragraph in Wal-Mart's audit opinion:

> As discussed in Note 13 to the consolidated financial statements, effective January 31, 2007, the Company adopted Statement of Financial Accounting Standards No. 158, *Employers' Accounting for Defined Benefit Pension and Other Postretirement Plans.*

The auditors added this paragraph to the standard unqualified audit opinion because they are required to do so under auditing standards. Wal-Mart's management properly adopted this new GAAP and properly disclosed it (in Note 13 to the financial statements). If it had not done that and the effects were material, the auditors would have had to give a qualified or possibly an adverse opinion on the financial statements.

Because the accounting profession frequently issues new accounting pronouncements, auditors often include consistency paragraphs in their reports.

Going Concern

Recall that in Chapter 2 we discussed the going concern assumption and explained that accounting methods are based on the assumption that the business will remain in existence indefinitely unless there is evidence to the contrary. Auditors cannot predict the future any better than the average person can, but they are required under auditing standards to add a *going concern paragraph* to an audit opinion if they uncovered evidence during the audit that gives them "substantial doubt" about the company's ability to continue as a going concern for a period of up to one year beyond the balance sheet date. The content of the paragraph is up to the auditors' judgment, but the two terms *substantial doubt* and *going concern* must be included.

The opinion on the historical financial statements still can be unqualified (the best opinion) because the financial statements relate to the past and the opinion states whether they are presented in conformity with GAAP. The auditor will refer the financial statement readers to the financial statement footnote (prepared by management) that discusses the circumstances that have given rise to the going concern issue as well as its plans to mitigate those circumstances. However, the absence of a going concern paragraph is never a guarantee from the auditors that the company will be in existence for a year beyond the balance sheet date.

Emphasis of a Matter

Auditors have the option to add an extra paragraph after the opinion to stress any matter they believe should be emphasized. The professional auditing standards provide only a handful of examples of cases in which auditors may choose to exercise this option, for

example, when the company has experienced an unusually important event subsequent to the date of the financial statements. (This subsequent event would have to have been accounted for adequately and/or disclosed by management; otherwise, GAAP has not been followed and the auditors' opinion probably will be affected.)

Thus, it is important to read the entire auditors' opinion, not just the key phrases in the opinion sentence.

Qualified Opinion

When the auditors give a *qualified opinion*, the words *except for* will be included in the opinion sentence. The auditor is stating that except for the effects of either not following GAAP or not being able to perform a key auditing procedure, the financial statements are presented fairly in all material respects. The auditors will include an extra paragraph—termed an *explanatory paragraph*—before the opinion paragraph to explain to the readers why they believe the financial statements have not been presented completely fairly.

A qualified opinion results from either a material (significant) departure from GAAP or a material limitation in the auditors' ability to conduct the audit in accordance with professional auditing standards. For example, auditors generally are required to observe the client's physical inventory count. If a company conducts its inventory count at the end of its fiscal year, for example, on December 31, and for some reason doesn't hire the auditors until later, say, mid-January, it is not possible for the auditors to observe the count and comply with the auditing standards. If the auditors cannot satisfy themselves about the ending inventory balance (assuming it is material) through any alternative auditing procedures, there is a limitation on the scope of their audit and they must qualify their opinion.

Is a qualified opinion useful? Yes, but it's not as good as an unqualified opinion, and so management generally prefers not to receive a qualified opinion. The auditors are stating that except for the item they have explained, the financial statements have been presented fairly in all material respects. It's up to the readers to decide whether the qualification is important to them and whether they can use the financial statements for their decision-making purposes.

Adverse Opinion

An *adverse opinion*, as the name implies, is the worst audit opinion that can be given. The auditors are stating that the financial statements are not presented fairly in all material respects, not even a portion of them. This is a strong statement coming from auditors, and it essentially means that the auditors are telling the readers that they cannot rely on the financial statements for their decision-making purposes.

Adverse opinions rarely are given because management does not want them for obvious reasons and will work closely with the auditors to make any adjustments the auditors consider necessary to avoid an adverse opinion.

As with a qualified opinion, if the auditors are giving an adverse opinion, there will be at least one explanatory paragraph before the opinion paragraph explaining to the readers why the auditors have come to this conclusion.

Disclaimer of Opinion

A *disclaimer of opinion* is no opinion. Disclaimers are given, as explained earlier in this chapter, when the auditors discover that they are not independent with respect to the client. This discovery should happen rarely because before the acceptance of the audit engagement, the auditors should have investigated and determined the status of their independence diligently.

A disclaimer also is given when there is a highly material (very significant) limitation on the scope of the audit, in other words, when the auditors are unable for some reason to perform some essential audit procedure or procedures and are unable to satisfy themselves about the account balance or balances through any alternative auditing procedures. A disclaimer does not result from the auditors' knowledge that the financial statements are materially misstated; instead, the auditors are unable to form an opinion because of a lack of knowledge that results from their inability to perform one or more essential audit procedures.

Management's Responsibilities versus Auditors' Responsibilities

The audit report makes it clear that the financial statements, including the footnotes, are management's responsibility. The auditors are not responsible for preparing the financial statements or for any aspect of capturing the accounting data throughout the year that eventually generate the account balances reported on the financial statements. Instead, the auditors' responsibility is to express an opinion that is based on the audit work.

Auditors' Report on Internal Control Over Financial Reporting

Before the effective date of the Sarbanes-Oxley Act of 2002 (SOX), audit reports were somewhat shorter than they are today. In response to the numerous corporate scandals that occurred shortly before the act was passed (e.g., Enron), Section 404 of SOX requires that auditors also provide an opinion on the effectiveness of public companies' internal control over financial reporting. The logic behind this requirement is essentially that if a public company has effective internal controls over financial reporting, there is a reduced risk of fraudulently misstated financial statements being published and relied on by the investing public.

The internal control report can be separate or can be combined with the audit opinion on the financial statements. The Wal-Mart example provided in Figure 7.2 is a separate report; note that the auditors refer to their separate report on internal controls over financial reporting. The actual internal control report is on the page that follows the audit opinion in Wal-Mart's annual report.

Internal controls are processes and procedures that management puts in place to help ensure the accuracy of financial reporting as well as to safeguard assets and records and to help ensure compliance with all applicable laws and regulations. Controls are designed to help prevent, detect, and correct any errors (or fraud) that might occur. An example of an internal control is that somebody who has no cash handling or recording responsibilities should reconcile the monthly bank statement with the records to help ensure that there are no mistakes in recording cash. If this responsibility was assigned to someone who also handled cash and recorded cash transactions, it could be a simple matter to steal some cash and then cover up the theft by juggling the books and fudging the bank reconciliation.

Auditors of public companies now are required to perform enough additional audit work to allow them to express an opinion on the effectiveness of the company's internal controls over financial reporting as of the fiscal year end. Management is required to assess the effectiveness of those controls and report their assessment. For the first several years after passage of the SOX Act, auditors also were required to express an opinion on management's assessment.

Thus, if the auditors issued a combined report, there were three opinions stated throughout the report:

- An opinion on whether the financial statements are presented fairly in all material respects, in accordance with GAAP
- An opinion on whether management's assessment of the effectiveness of the company's internal controls over financial reporting as of the fiscal year end is fairly stated in all material respects, based on criteria related to internal controls that were developed by the accounting profession
- An opinion on whether the company maintained in all material respects effective internal control over financial reporting as of the fiscal year end, based on the same criteria used for management's assessment

As of late 2007, however, the Public Company Accounting Oversight Board eliminated the requirement for auditors to give the second opinion listed above (the opinion on whether management's internal control assessment was fairly stated). Management still must give its assessment, and the auditors still give their own opinion on the effectiveness of the internal controls (as well as on the financial statements themselves), but the additional opinion by the auditors on management's internal control assessment no longer is considered necessary.

However, the phrases we have discussed: *present fairly, except for,* or *do not present fairly* (see Figure 7.3) still will be present in regard to the opinion on the financial statements.

Footnotes to the Financial Statements

The footnotes (or notes) to the financial statements can be very extensive, running several pages in an annual report. Generally accepted accounting principles require that certain types of disclosures be made in the footnotes, and so this information should be considered an integral part of the financial statements. When the auditors express an opinion on the financial statements, it includes the footnote disclosures as well. An unqualified opinion by the auditors means that not only are the company's financial statements presented fairly in all material respects in conformity with GAAP, so are the footnotes.

Footnotes are required because of the full disclosure concept discussed in Chapter 2. The accounting profession believes that financial statements are more useful when significant information is disclosed adequately to the readers. If this additional important information were included on the face of the financial statements, it would be difficult to read the statements because of the volume of information. Consequently, this information is included in the notes to the financial statements.

The first footnote required by GAAP is a summary of significant accounting policies in which management explains which GAAP it chose to use when alternatives exist. For example, this first note will answer questions such as the following:

- What method or methods of depreciation are used for property, plant, and equipment?
- Over how long a period are the fixed assets depreciated?
- Which inventory valuation method is used?
- How are advertising costs recognized for financial reporting purposes?
- When are research and development costs recognized?
- What policies does the company follow in recognizing revenue?
- What principally makes up the company's accounts receivable?

The remaining footnotes can appear in any order. For example, the headings of the footnotes for two public companies, Wal-Mart and Kellogg's Company, as presented in their recent annual reports are shown in Figures 7.4 and 7.5.

Figures 7.4 and 7.5 present only the footnote headings and subheadings; the actual footnotes are 17 and 24 pages long, respectively, in the annual reports.

Figure 7.4   Wal-Mart, Inc., 2007 Annual Report Footnote Headings

1. Summary of Significant Accounting Policies
   - Consolidation
   - Cash and Cash Equivalents
   - Receivables
   - Inventories
   - Financial Instruments
   - Capitalized Interest
   - Long-Lived Assets
   - Goodwill and Other Acquired Intangible Assets
   - Leases
   - Foreign Currency Translation
   - Revenue Recognition
   - Sam's Club Membership Fee Revenue Recognition
   - Cost of Sales
   - Payments from Suppliers
   - Operating, Selling, General, and Administrative Expenses
   - Advertising Costs
   - Preopening Costs
   - Share-Based Compensation
   - Insurance/Self-Insurance
   - Depreciation and Amortization
   - Income Taxes
   - Accrued Liabilities
   - Net Income per Common Share
   - Estimates and Assumptions
   - Reclassifications
2. Commercial Paper and Long-Term Debt
3. Financial Instruments
   - Fair Value Instruments
   - Net Investment Instruments
   - Cash-Flow Instruments
   - Fair Value of Financial Instruments
4. Accumulated Other Comprehensive Income
5. Income Taxes
6. Acquisitions and Disposals
   - Acquisitions
   - Disposals
7. Share-Based Compensation Plans
8. Litigation
9. Commitments
10. Retirement-Related Benefits
11. Segments
12. Quarterly Financial Data (Unaudited)
13. Recent Accounting Pronouncements
14. Subsequent Events

Figure 7.5 Kellogg's Company 2006 Annual Report Footnote Headings

1. Accounting Policies
   - Basis of presentation
   - Cash and cash equivalents
   - Accounts receivable
   - Inventories
   - Property
   - Goodwill and other intangible assets
   - Revenue recognition and measurement
   - Advertising
   - Research and development
   - Stock compensation
   - Employee postretirement and postemployment benefits
   - Recently issued pronouncements
     - Uncertain tax positions
     - Fair value
   - Use of estimates
2. Acquisitions, other investments, and intangibles
   - Acquisitions
   - Joint venture arrangement
   - Goodwill and other intangible assets
3. Cost-reduction initiatives
   - Cost summary
   - Specific initiatives
4. Other income (expense), net
5. Equity
   - Earnings per share
   - Stock transactions
   - Comprehensive income
6. Leases and other commitments
7. Debt
   - Subsequent events
8. Stock compensation
   - Stock options
   - Other stock-based awards
9. Pension benefits
   - Obligations and funded status
   - Expense
   - Assumptions
   - Plan assets
   - Benefit payments
10. Nonpension postretirement and postemployment benefits
    - Postretirement
    - Obligations and funded status
    - Expense
    - Assumptions
    - Plan assets
    - Postemployment
    - Benefit payments

11. Income taxes
12. Financial instruments and credit risk concentration
      Cash-flow hedges
      Fair value hedges
      Net investment hedges
      Other contracts
      Foreign exchange risk
      Interest rate risk
      Price risk
      Credit risk concentration
13. Quarterly financial data (unaudited)
14. Operating segments
15. Supplemental financial statement data

Quiz for Chapter 7

1. Which of the following are required to file annual reports on a Form 10-K to the Securities and Exchange Commission?
   a. Not-for-profit and governmental entities
   b. Private companies
   c. Public companies
   d. All of the above

2. Annual reports to shareholders and annual reports filed with the SEC are one and the same.
   a. True
   b. False

3. Form 10-Ks are confidential financial information and are not available to the public.
   a. True
   b. False

4. Which of the following is the best opinion auditors can give a company on its financial statements?
   a. An unqualified opinion
   b. A qualified opinion
   c. An adverse opinion
   d. A disclaimer of opinion

5. Auditors are allowed to give an opinion on the client's financial statements even if the auditors are not independent with respect to the client as long as that fact is fully disclosed.
   a. True
   b. False

6. Auditor independence means the auditors:
   a. Are not paid by the client but instead are paid by the federal government
   b. Must maintain an objective, impartial, and unbiased attitude toward the client both in fact and in appearance
   c. Automatically assume management is dishonest
   d. Can own only immaterial (small) amounts of stock in an audit client

7. A qualified audit opinion:
   a. Is the worst opinion and means that the financial statements are not presented fairly in all material respects, not even a portion of them
   b. Is no opinion because the auditors were unable to complete the audit
   c. Means that except for the effects of not following GAAP or not being able to perform a key auditing procedure, the financial statements are presented fairly in all material respects
   d. Means that under no circumstances should anyone rely on these financial statements.

8. The Sarbanes-Oxley Act of 2002 applies only to public companies, not to private companies.
   a. True
   b. False

9. Which of the following statements is true regarding materiality?
   a. Auditors provide absolute assurance that all material errors and fraud are detected.
   b. Materiality is defined as being at least 10 percent of assets.
   c. The determination of what is material is up to the auditors.
   d. Auditors provide reasonable assurance that all immaterial errors and fraud are detected.

10. Footnotes to the financial statements:
    a. Are required under GAAP
    b. Are usually brief and insignificant
    c. Are not audited by the auditors
    d. Are required because of the materiality concept

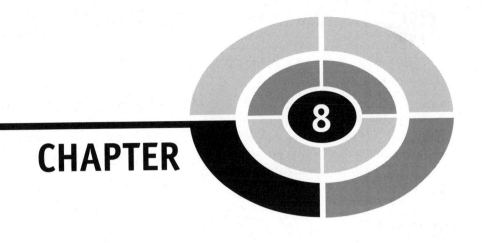

CHAPTER 8

Analysis of Financial Statements

In this chapter, we discuss various techniques readers can use to analyze a set of financial statements.

Horizontal Analysis versus Vertical Analysis

Sometimes it can be difficult to interpret in a meaningful way all the dollar amounts presented in a set of financial statements. For example, if one company has liabilities of $10,000 and another company has liabilities of $10,000,000, is the first company less risky? Maybe, maybe not. It depends in part on the size of the company (how much in assets does each company have?) and the company's industry (what is normal?).

A useful way to analyze financial statements is to perform either a horizontal analysis or a vertical analysis of the statements. These types of analysis help a

financial statement reader compare companies of different sizes, which can be difficult to do when the dollar amounts vary significantly, and evaluate the performance of a company over time.

The horizontal and vertical analysis approaches are similar in that the dollar amounts reported are converted to percentages. The approaches differ in the base used to compute the percentages.

Horizontal Analysis

Horizontal analysis focuses on trends and changes in financial statement items over time. Along with the dollar amounts presented in the financial statements, horizontal analysis can help a financial statement user to see relative changes over time and identify positive or perhaps troubling trends. We will use the income statement information for H. A. Example Company in Figure 8.1 to explain how one might prepare a three year horizontal analysis.

Figure 8.1   Income Statements for Horizontal Analysis

H. A. Example Company
Comparative Income Statements
As of Ended December 31

	20x1	20x2	20x3
Revenue	$100,000	$108,000	$120,000
Cost of Goods Sold	78,000	82,000	90,000
Gross Profit	22,000	26,000	30,000
Operating Expenses	17,500	19,400	21,600
Net Income	$ 4,500	$ 6,600	$ 8,400

In one horizontal analysis approach, a base year is selected and the dollar amount of each financial statement item in subsequent years is converted to a percentage of the base year dollar amount. Assuming 20x1 is the base year, 20x2 and 20x3 revenues were 108% and 120% of the base year amount, as shown in the following calculations:

$$\frac{\text{20x2 Revenue } \$108,000}{\text{20x1 Revenue } \$100,000} = 108\% \qquad \frac{\text{20x3 Revenue } \$120,000}{\text{20x1 Revenue } \$100,000} = 120\%$$

Similar computations would be made for H. A. Example Company's remaining income statement items as shown in Figure 8.2.

Figure 8.2 Horizontal Analysis Example

Horizontal Analysis of Income Statements for
H. A. Example Company
As of December 31
Base Year: 20x1

	20x1		20x2		20x3	
Revenue	$100,000	100%	$108,000	108%	$120,000	120%
Cost of Goods Sold	78,000	100%	82,000	105%	90,000	115%
Gross Profit	22,000	100%	26,000	118%	30,000	136%
Operating Expenses	17,500	100%	19,400	111%	21,600	123%
Net Income	$ 4,500	100%	$ 6,600	147%	$8,400	187%

Some interesting trends can be noted from this analysis. The dollar amounts and percentages for each financial statement item increased each year, but the trends for each item differed. For example, in 20x3 when revenues were 120% of the base year amounts, cost of goods sold was less—only 115% of the base year amount. Perhaps H. A. Example Company raised its selling prices and/or its inventory cost declined? Notice that 20x3 net income was 187% of the base year amount; even though operating expenses had increased to 123% of the base year amount, this was more than offset by the favorable trends in revenues and cost of goods sold.

In addition to base year comparisons, dollar and percentage changes from one year to the next could also be analyzed. For example, 20x2 revenues increased by $8,000 or 8% over the previous year, and 20x3 revenues increased by $12,000 or 11.1% over the previous year, as shown in the following calculations:

$$20x2: \frac{\text{Revenue Increase } \$108,000 - \$100,000}{20x1 \text{ (previous year) } \$100,000} = \frac{\$\ 8,000}{\$100,000} = 8.0\%$$

$$20x3: \frac{\text{Revenue Increase } \$120,000 - \$108,000}{20x2 \text{ (previous year) } \$108,000} = \frac{\$\ 20,000}{\$108,000} = 11.1\%$$

How is the base year selected? That's up to the individual performing the analysis. Fraud examiners who are investigating a case of fraudulent financial reporting, for example, probably will select the last year in which they believe no fraud occurred as the base year in order to estimate the extent of the fraud. In other situations, the choice will depend to some degree on the purpose for which the reader is using the financial statements. Are you trying to decide whether to buy (or sell) stock now that a company has experienced a significant change such as new management or the introduction of a new product line? Then perhaps the base year will be the last year before the change. Essentially, the choice of the base year is up to the individual financial statement user.

Are these proportional increases that we calculated for H. A. Example Company good? Perhaps the competitors in the same industry are increasing even more. To interpret the proportional changes, the reader will need additional information, such as the industry averages and/or the changes for a particular company that the financial statement reader also is considering for investment purposes.

Vertical Analysis

Vertical analysis sometimes is referred to as common-size analysis because all of the amounts for a given year are converted into percentages of a key financial statement component. For example, on the income statement, total revenue is 100% and each item is calculated as a percentage of total revenue. On the balance sheet, total assets are 100% and each asset category is calculated as a percentage of total assets. In the balance sheet equation, total assets are equal to total liabilities plus equity; thus, each liability and/or equity account is also calculated to be a percentage of this total (i.e., total liabilities and equity are 100%). Vertical or common-size analysis allows one to see the composition of each of the financial statements and determine if significant changes have occurred.

We will use the balance sheet information for V. A. Example Company in Figure 8.3 to explain how one might prepare a three year vertical analysis.

Figure 8.3   Balance Sheets for Vertical Analysis

V. A. Vertical Analysis Example Company
Balance Sheets
As of December 31

	20x1	20x2	20x3
Cash	$ 608,000	$ 755,000	$ 783,000
Accounts Receivable	476,000	500,000	556,000
Inventory	500,000	615,000	595,000
Property and Equipment, net	441,000	760,000	591,000
Total Assets	$2,025,000	$2,630,000	$2,525,000
Accounts Payable	$ 115,000	$ 160,000	$ 65,000
Wages Payable	55,000	65,000	60,000
Income Taxes Payable	18,000	35,000	25,000
Notes Payable	87,000	210,000	175,000
Common Stock	400,000	450,000	450,000
Additional Paid-in Capital	600,000	700,000	700,000
Retained Earnings	750,000	1,010,000	1,050,000
Total Liabilities and Stockholders' Equity	$2,025,000	$2,630,000	$2,525,000

After each year's total asset amount is set as 100 percent (or total liabilities plus stockholders' equity, since the amounts must balance), the various accounts' dollar amounts are converted to a percentage of the total assets. When the calculation is complete, the sum of the percentages for the individual asset accounts must equal 100 percent. The sum of the percentages for the various liability and equity accounts also will equal 100 percent (see Figure 8.4).

Figure 8.4   Vertical Analysis Example

**Vertical Analysis of Balance Sheets for
V. A. Example Company
As of December 31**

	20x1		20x2		20x3	
Cash	$ 608,000	30%	$ 755,000	29%	$ 783,000	31%
Accounts Receivable	476,000	23%	500,000	19%	556,000	22%
Inventory	500,000	25%	615,000	23%	595,000	24%
Property and Equipment, net	441,000	22%	760,000	29%	591,000	23%
Total Assets	$2,025,000	100%	$2,630,000	100%	$2,525,000	100%

	20x1		20x2		20x3	
Accounts Payable	$ 115,000	5%	$ 160,000	6%	$ 65,000	3%
Wages Payable	55,000	3%	65,000	3%	60,000	2%
Income Taxes Payable	18,000	1%	35,000	1%	25,000	1%
Notes Payable	87,000	4%	210,000	8%	175,000	7%
Common Stock	400,000	20%	450,000	17%	450,000	18%
Additional Paid-in Capital	600,000	30%	700,000	27%	700,000	27%
Retained Earnings	750,000	37%	1,010,000	38%	1,050,000	42%
Total Liabilities and Stockholders' Equity	$2,025,000	100%	$2,630,000	100%	$2,525,000	100%

Vertical analysis of a balance sheet will answer questions relating to asset, liability, and equity accounts, such as the following:

- What percentage of total assets is classified as current assets? Current liabilities comprise what percentage of total liabilities and stockholders' equity?
- Inventory makes up what percentage of total assets? Is this changing significantly over time? If so, is it increasing or decreasing? (These answers could lead to additional questions such as the following: If it is increasing, could this indicate that the company is having trouble selling its inventory? If so, is this because of increased competition in the industry or perhaps obsolescence of this company's inventory?)

- Accounts receivable makes up what percentage of total assets? Is this changing significantly over time? If so, is it increasing or decreasing? (These answers might lead to additional questions such as the following: If it is increasing, could this indicate that the company is having trouble collecting its receivables? If it is decreasing, could this indicate that the company has tightened its credit policy? If so, is it possible that the company is losing sales that it might have made with a less strict credit policy?)
- What is the composition of the capital structure? In other words, total liabilities make up what percentage of total assets and total stockholders' equity makes up what percentage of total assets?

Vertical analysis of an income statement helps answer questions such as the following:

- What percentage of revenues is cost of goods sold?
- What is the gross profit percentage?
- What is the mix of expenses (in terms of percentages) that the company has incurred in this period?

Since total revenues usually are set at 100 percent, vertical analysis of the income statement essentially shows how many cents of each sales dollar are absorbed by the various expenses. For example, if total revenues were $200,000 and total wage expense was $50,000, total wage expense would equal 25 percent of total revenues. In other words, for every $1 in sales earned, 25 cents goes to employee wages.

In the case of V. A. Example Company, the organization appears to be fairly stable over the three years of data we have. Again, these percentages won't provide you with a lot of insight in and of themselves. The analysis is more meaningful when the percentages are compared with competitors' or industry averages or for a long period of time for one company. However, if some unreasonable fluctuations are noted for one company over time and/or the percentages are significantly different from industry averages, the possibility of fraudulent financial reporting should be considered, a concept we'll cover in Chapter 10.

Financial Statement Ratios

Another method to analyze financial statement information involves the use of ratios. Ratios are useful in showing the relationships among financial statement data and also can be useful in comparing one company with another or analyzing the same company over time.

Ratios often are classified into different categories. Within each category, the ratios measure a common element, such the company's profitability or ability to pay its current debts. Sometimes the terminology of these different categories varies, but even with differing terms, the concepts are the same (see Figure 8.5).

Figure 8.5 Categories of Ratios

Ratio Classifications

Category	Also Called	Measures
Liquidity ratios	Solvency ratios	Company's ability in the near future to pay its debts as they become due
Profitability ratios	Margin ratios	Company's success—or failure—at earning a profit (i.e., generating more revenues than expenses)
Asset management ratios	Turnover ratios Efficiency ratios Activity ratios	Company's effectiveness at using various assets
Leverage ratios	Coverage ratios Capital structure ratios	Company's long-term ability to pay debt as it becomes due

We'll discuss the more common financial ratios next and calculate them using the Ratio Analysis Example Company financial statements in Figures 8.6 and 8.7.

Figure 8.6 Income Statement for Ratio Analysis

Ratio Analysis Example Company
Income Statement
For the Year Ended June 30, 20x1

Net Sales	$ 10,907,000
Cost of Goods Sold	(6,082,000)
Gross Margin	4,825,000
Operating Expenses	(3,059,000)
Operating Income	1,766,000
Other Income or (Expense), net	(320,000)*
Earnings before Income Taxes	1,446,000
Income Tax Expense	(467,000)
Net Income	$ 979,000

*For purposes of some of our later ratio analysis, $307,000 of this total represents interest expense. This information typically can be gathered from a company's financial statements and/or its footnotes.

Figure 8.7   Balance Sheet for Ratio Analysis

Ratio Analysis Example Company
Balance Sheet
June 30, 20x1

Cash	$ 411,000		
Accounts Receivable, net	945,000		
Inventory	824,000		
Prepaid Expenses	248,000		
Total Current Assets		$2,428,000	
Property and Equipment, net		6,916,000	
Intangible Assets		1,371,000	
Total Assets			$10,715,000
Wages Payable	$ 311,000		
Current Portion of Long-Term Debt	723,000		
Notes Payable	1,268,000		
Accounts Payable	911,000		
Accrued Liabilities	655,000		
Income Taxes Payable	152,000		
Total Current Liabilities		$4,020,000	
Long-Term Debt		4,624,000	
Total Liabilities			$ 8,644,000
Common Stock	$ 105,000		
Additional Paid-In Capital	293,000		
Retained Earnings	1,673,000		
Total Stockholders' Equity			2,071,000
Total Liabilities and Stockholders' Equity			$10,715,000

Liquidity Ratios

Debts cannot be paid with assets such as accounts receivable and buildings but must be paid with cash. Thus, ratios that help measure a company's ability to pay its current debts as they become due often are called liquidity ratios since the term *liquidity* means nearness to cash. Cash is the most liquid asset a company can have; you can't get closer to cash than having cash itself. Accounts receivable are less liquid; they will be converted into cash once the customer pays the company. Inventory is even less liquid; it must be sold first, and if it is sold on account, time must pass before the resulting account receivable is converted into cash. If a company can pay its debts when they are due, the company is said to be solvent, and so liquidity ratios sometimes are referred to as solvency ratios.

A company's balance sheet may report that it has $1,000,000 in cash (or $10,000,000 or perhaps only $1,000). Is that enough to pay the bills that will be coming due in the near future, such as a year or less? It's impossible to answer that question with information on only the dollar amount of cash on hand. The answer depends on the amount of current liabilities that are also on the balance sheet. Furthermore, the company may have accounts receivable or other current assets such as short-term investments that can be converted easily into cash and used to pay bills as the need arises. Thus, answering the question requires a comparison of the relationship between various amounts on the balance sheet. Useful ratios for making this comparison include the current ratio and the quick ratio.

CURRENT RATIO

The current ratio is calculated as follows:

$$\textbf{Current Ratio} = \textbf{Current Assets} \div \textbf{Current Liabilities}$$

Recall from Chapter 5 that current assets are assets that will be converted into cash, sold, or used typically within a year and include assets such as cash, short-term investments, accounts receivable, interest receivable, inventory, and prepaid expenses. Note that prepaid expenses never will be converted into cash but will be expensed or used up within a year. Current liabilities are the debts that will be paid or settled within a year by providing goods or services and include items such as accounts payable, the portion of any long-term debt (such as a mortgage) that is due typically within a year, interest payable, wages payable, taxes payable, accrued liabilities, and unearned revenues.

The current ratio for Ratio Analysis Example Company is computed as follows:

$$
\begin{aligned}
\textbf{Current Ratio} &= \textbf{Current Assets} \div \textbf{Current Liabilities} \\
&= \$2,428,000 \quad \div \$4,020,000 \\
&= .60 \text{ to } 1
\end{aligned}
$$

This computation means that for every $1 of debts that will become due within a year, the company currently has 60 cents of assets that will be converted into cash or used up within the year with which to pay those debts. There are no hard and fast rules about the range in which any ratio should fall; one wants to consider a variety of factors rather than any single ratio. However, a current ratio of at least 1.0 implies exactly enough current assets with which to pay the debts that will come due in a year, with no cushion. Even then, the composition of the current assets is important because if a significant portion consists of prepaid expenses, those expenses will not be converted into cash to pay the bills. It is not unusual for banks, when writing loan agreements for a business, to include requirements that must be met or the loan will be due back in full immediately. Often the requirements state that certain minimum ratios must be maintained, such as a current ratio of 2.0 or 3.0, to help ensure continued liquidity but also allow a cushion. Does this imply that the higher a current ratio, the better? To an extent; however, if the current ratio becomes too high, that also can be cause for concern. Perhaps a company is keeping too much of its assets in liquid form when possibly the organization could become more profitable if, for example, the assets instead were placed in long-term investments and/or used to purchase additional fixed assets by which the company could increase operating activities.

In the case of Ratio Analysis Example Company, one probably would want to read management's discussion and analysis of the company's financial condition and results of operations, which is contained in the Form 10-K as well as the annual report to shareholders. Perhaps the current ratio of .60 is not troublesome as the company is expecting a significant inflow of cash early in the following year, as is normal in its industry. In contrast, perhaps there is increased competition in the industry, and the company is having trouble.

QUICK RATIO

The quick ratio (sometimes called the acid test ratio) is a more conservative liquidity measure. It gets its name from the fact that the numerator contains the assets that can be turned into cash most quickly. The formula is

$$\text{Quick Ratio} = \frac{(\textbf{Cash} + \textbf{Short-Term Investments} + \textbf{Receivables})}{\textbf{Current Liabilities}}$$

In other words, inventory and prepaid expenses are removed from the current assets total so that the most liquid current assets remain in the numerator. For this reason, creditors often consider this ratio more meaningful than the current ratio.

Why are inventory and prepaid expenses removed? Inventory is slower to convert to cash: It first must be sold, and if it is sold on credit, the receivable must be collected, all of which will take some time. Further, some of the inventory may be obsolete or otherwise difficult to sell. Also, prepaid expenses will not be converted into cash; these are expenses, such as advertising or rent, which the company has paid for in advance. As time passes and the benefits of the payments are received (e.g., the advertising services), the company will follow the matching principle discussed in Chapter 2 and gradually write off the prepaid expenses from the balance sheet to an expense on the income statement.

For our example company, the quick ratio is computed as follows:

$$\textbf{Quick Ratio} = (\$411,000 + \$945,000) \div \$4,020,000$$
$$= .34 \textbf{ to } 1$$

Quick ratio that is much smaller than a current ratio indicates that the company has quite a bit of resources tied up in inventory and/or prepaid expenses. Conversely, when the two ratios are close to equal, it indicates that the company does not have much inventory and/or prepaid expenses. In Ratio Analysis Example Company's case, the quick ratio indicates that there is only 34 cents available for every $1 of debts that are soon to be due. Before pushing the panic button, one would want to look at recent previous years of the company and also read management's discussion and analysis, which also is contained in the annual report to shareholders. Has something unusual happened recently?

Profitability Ratios

Profitability ratios measure a company's success (or failure) in earning a profit. Recall that profit exists when revenues exceed expenses. Profitability ratios are not the same as liquidity ratios because a company can be profitable but have liquidity problems. How can this be the case? Perhaps a company has made many credit sales rather than cash sales, and so the revenue is recorded and profits have increased. But perhaps many customers have not paid what they owe the company, and so the cash hasn't flowed in yet. Bills cannot be paid with accounts receivable but must be paid with cash. Thus, it is possible for a company to be profitable and insolvent at the same time.

   Liquidity ratios are important for a company's short-term success (how long can a company stay in business if it cannot pay its bills when they are due?). Profitability ratios are important for a company's long-term success (how long can a company stay in business if its expenses exceed its revenues on a continuous basis?).

   Profitability ratios compute the relationship between profit and some other financial statement item, such as assets, sales, equity, or shares of common stock outstanding. The more common profitability ratios include the following:

- Gross margin on sales
- Profit margin on sales (return on sales)
- Return on assets
- Return on equity
- Earnings per share
- Dividend payout ratio
- Price-earnings ratio

GROSS MARGIN ON SALES

Recall from Chapter 3 and our discussion of the income statement that gross margin (also called gross profit) is the excess of sales revenue over the cost of goods sold. Thus, gross margin represents the amount of sales revenue left, after covering the cost of the product sold, to pay all remaining business expenses and have some profit left over.

Gross margin ratios vary widely from industry to industry. In the Ratio Analysis Example Company case, the gross margin on sales is computed as follows:

Gross Margin on Sales = Gross Margin ÷ Net Sales
= $4,825,000 ÷ $10,907,000
= 44%

This computation indicates that for every dollar in net sales that the company generates, the product sold cost 56 cents and there is 44 cents left to cover all remaining expenses and, the company hopes, constitute a profit.

PROFIT MARGIN ON SALES

Profit margin on sales takes the bottom line (net income or net profit) after all expenses are subtracted from revenues and compares it with net sales revenue. Again, this can vary widely from industry to industry. This ratio sometimes is called return on sales and is computed as follows:

Profit Margin on Sales = Net Income ÷ Net Sales

For our company, the return on sales is computed as follows:

Profit Margin on Sales = $979,000 ÷ $10,907,000 = 9%

Thus, for every dollar in sales revenue, 9 cents remains for bottom-line profit and 91 cents is spent on goods sold and all other expenses.

RETURN ON ASSETS

The return on assets (ROA) ratio measures how effectively management is using its assets to generate a profit. It is computed as follows

Return on Assets = Net Income ÷ Average Total Assets

For the Ratio Analysis Example Company (using year-end assets for simplicity), the return on assets is

Return on Assets = $979,000 ÷ $10,715,000 = 9.1%

This ratio is interpreted to mean that for every dollar invested in assets, the company earned 9.1 cents. Is 9.1 percent an adequate return on the investment the company has made in its assets? Comparison to the return on assets over time for this company, to competitors, and to the industry average would be useful. It should at least exceed the return that could be earned by investing in low-risk investments; otherwise it might make more sense for the company to cease doing business and instead invest in these alternatives (and earn a higher return).

RETURN ON EQUITY

The return on equity (ROE) ratio measures how well management is maximizing the return on the stockholders' (owners') investment in the business. For this reason, the ratio sometimes is referred to as return on investment. It is computed as follows:

Return on Equity = Net Income ÷ Average Stockholders' Equity

For the Ratio Analysis Example Company (using year-end stockholders equity for simplicity), the return on equity is

Return on Equity = \$979,000 ÷ \$2,071,000 = 47.3%

This computation indicates that for every dollar the stockholders have invested in the company, 47.3 cents was earned this year; that is a fairly impressive return. However, as with all ratios and other types of analysis, one will want to consider other benchmarks. Furthermore, risk is an important consideration. "Higher risk, higher reward" is not a cliché: If an investment in a particular company presents a greater risk, the higher degree of uncertainty should be rewarded with a greater potential return.

EARNINGS PER SHARE

Earnings per share (EPS) was discussed briefly in Chapter 3 in the analysis of the income statement. It represents a measure of the earnings associated with a single share of stock.

This ratio is unique in that under generally accepted accounting principles require that it be presented by public companies on their income statements; no other ratios are required to be reported. Many investors and creditors track EPS closely; consequently, management also pays it close attention because it is a highly visible profitability number and can affect a company's stock price.

The formula for basic (or simple) EPS is

$$\text{Basic EPS} = \frac{\text{Net Income} - \text{Preferred Dividends}}{\text{Weighted Average Number of Shares Outstanding}}$$

Preferred stock is a different type of ownership interest from that represented by common stock and nearly always involves a preference in regard to dividends (a fixed amount of dividends must be paid to the preferred stockholders each year; further, the preferred stockholders are first in line to receive dividends, and so common stockholders receive nothing until the preferred stockholders are paid). Dividends are not an expense or a cost of doing business but a distribution of the profits of the business to its owners. Since they are not an expense, they are not reported on the income statement. Therefore, subtracting dividends from net income does not double-count the dividends. Instead, with this deduction, the numerator in the formula above represents the year's net income that is available to the common stockholders. Some corporations may have no preferred stock outstanding, in which case the numerator is simply net income.

The denominator represents the number of shares of common stock outstanding during the year, weighted by the period of time in which the shares were outstanding. *Outstanding* means the shares are owned by the common stockholders; the shares have been issued to the stockholders, and they hold the shares. These shares must be weighted by the period in which they were outstanding; otherwise, the resulting EPS number will be distorted. For example, if a company reported net income of $1,000,000 for the year (but had no preferred stock outstanding) and had 1,000,000 shares of common stock outstanding as of year end, it appears the EPS would be $1.00. But what if 750,000 shares were issued on the last day of the fiscal year? In that case, only 250,000 shares were outstanding during the year, and so the EPS would be a more impressive $4.00 ($1,000,000 ÷ 250,000). The capital (money) that was generated by selling the remaining 750,000 shares was not available throughout the year for the company to use to generate profits, and so those shares should be weighted accordingly (in this case, with less than a day left in the year, not weighted at all).

For the Ratio Analysis Example Company, assume that the par value of the common stock is 25 cents per share. With $105,000 reported on the balance sheet as the amount of common stock issued, this translates to $105,000 ÷ $0.25, or 420,000 shares. Assume that these shares were outstanding since the beginning of the year, therefore, no weighting by period of time outstanding is required. Thus, basic EPS is computed as follows:

$$\$979,000 \div 420,000 = \$2.33$$

Since the balance sheet does not report any preferred stock outstanding, there cannot be any preferred dividends to subtract from the net income in the numerator.

If the example company had any potentially dilutive securities present, the company also must report a second type of EPS: diluted EPS. Examples of potentially dilutive securities include bonds or preferred stock shares issued that give the holder the choice of converting the bonds or shares into a preestablished number of shares of common stock. Stock options are also potentially dilutive and often are given to employees as a form of additional compensation. Options give the employee the choice to purchase a set number of shares of stock at a preestablished price and can result in considerable compensation to the employee when the market price is above the preestablished purchase price. Diluted EPS takes into consideration how these additional securities can reduce the reported EPS number, primarily through the increased number of common shares outstanding in the denominator, even though the securities have not been exchanged for shares of common stock. The computation

is more complex than that for basic EPS and typically is covered in more advanced courses in financial accounting. If a company has dilutive securities, that company is required under generally accepted accounting principles (GAAP) to present dilutive EPS along with basic EPS on the income statement. Since the example company does not have any convertible bonds, convertible preferred stock, or stock options issued, no dilutive EPS computation is required.

DIVIDEND PAYOUT RATIO

The dividend payout ratio is often of interest to investors because it indicates how much of a company's wealth is distributed to the common stockholders. Preferred stockholders typically have a fixed, stated amount that will be received as dividends each year, and so this ratio is calculated for the common stockholders as follows:

$$\text{Dividend Payout Ratio} = \frac{\textbf{Cash Dividends Paid to Common Stockholders}}{\textbf{Net Income} - \textbf{Preferred Dividends}}$$

The denominator represents the net income available to common stockholders.

In the Ratio Analysis Example Company, recall that there is no preferred stock outstanding per the balance sheet. The dividends paid during the year to the common stockholders would appear on the statement of stockholders' equity, and if the dividends were all paid in cash during the year (rather than declared but not yet paid), they also will appear as a cash outlay on the statement of cash flows. We did not present either of those two statements for the example company, and so if we assume that $450,000 was paid during the year to the common stockholders, the dividend payout ratio becomes

$$\$450,000 \div \$979,000 = 46\%$$

Once a company begins to distribute dividends, investors often expect to receive them consistently. Further, some investors will expect a relatively high payout ratio to receive what they consider an acceptable return on their investment.

PRICE-EARNINGS RATIO

The price-earnings ratio (PE ratio) is computed as its name implies:

PE Ratio = Market Price per Share of Common Stock ÷ Earnings per Share

This ratio gives readers an idea how much the earnings of the company cost an investor who wishes to purchase shares of the company's stock. The market price tells the investor the cost of a share but by itself does not give the investor an idea of the quality of that purchase. Is the price reasonable considering the profitability of the company?

In the Ratio Analysis Example Company case, assume that the current market price per share of common stock is $42. The PE ratio is computed as follows:

$$\$42 \div \$2.33 = 18 \text{ times}$$

This result means that investors are paying 18 times the current earnings to purchase a share of stock. Is this reasonable? As with all ratios, one will want to compare this to other benchmarks, such as the PE ratio of competitors and the industry average. There is no single benchmark for what a PE ratio "should" be, and the rules of thumb have changed over time.

Asset Management Ratios

Asset management ratios (also called turnover, efficiency, and sometimes activity ratios) indicate the company's effectiveness at using its various assets. The asset management ratios we will discuss here are the following:

- Days sales outstanding
- Accounts receivable turnover
- Inventory turnover
- Days inventory supply
- Asset turnover

DAYS SALES OUTSTANDING

This ratio calculates the number of days it takes the company to collect its accounts receivables on average. The lower this number is, the better, because a company cannot pay its bills with receivables, only with cash.

The formula is as follows:

$$\text{Days Sales Outstanding} = \frac{\text{Accounts Receivable} \times 365}{\text{Net Sales}}$$

For the Ratio Analysis Example Company, the days sales outstanding (sometimes called days of accounts receivable, receivable days, or average collection period) is

$$(\$945,000 \times 365) \div \$10,907,000 = 31.6 \text{ days}$$

This calculation gives you an idea of how liquid the receivables are. Recall that we are including accounts receivable in the current ratio and quick ratio computations, and so if we consider the accounts receivable to be liquid, it is useful to have an idea of exactly how liquid they are.

ACCOUNTS RECEIVABLE TURNOVER

The accounts receivable turnover ratio is closely related to the days sales outstanding. Instead of computing the average number of days that accounts receivable are outstanding, this ratio calculates the number of times accounts receivable are collected during the year. In the example above, we calculated the days sales to be 31.6; since there are 365 days in a year, this translates to the receivables turning over about 11.5 times a year ($365 \div 31.6$). In other words, it measures the number of times on average the company collects its accounts receivable during the year. The formula for accounts receivable turnover is

Accounts Receivable Turnover = Net Sales $\div$ Average Accounts Receivable

When computing receivables turnover, there are some important things that should be considered. First, if a significant amount of the net sales consists of cash sales, those sales should be excluded since they never result in accounts receivable (assuming the reader can gather this information from the financial statements). Often, the reader will not be able to obtain this information. However, if the proportion of cash and credit sales remains fairly constant, the ratio will not be affected by using total net sales.

Second, since the balance sheet shows account balances at a point in time, simply using the end of year (balance sheet) amount for accounts receivable in the denominator could lead to a distorted result if the ending balance is not representative of the typical balance. A more representative result can be obtained by using an average accounts receivable balance, which is calculated as follows:

(Beginning Receivables + Ending Receivables) $\div$ 2 = Average Accounts Receivable.

Thus, as with all ratio analysis, the reader will not want to rely on any single measure or even a handful. The more pieces of the puzzle one looks at, the better the overall resulting picture will be.

INVENTORY TURNOVER

This ratio indicates how quickly on average inventory is sold (i.e., turns over). How long does inventory sit on shelves before it is sold? The formula is

Inventory Turnover = Cost of Goods Sold $\div$ Average Inventory

Note that the denominator consists of average inventory, and not year-end inventory for reasons similar to those we discussed for receivables turnover above.

For the Ratio Analysis Example Company (assuming that beginning inventory as determined from the previous year's balance sheet is $717,000), the inventory turnover is

$$\$6,082,000 \div [(717,000 + 824,000)/2] = 7.9 \text{ times}$$

Thus, inventory was sold and replaced 7.9 times that year. Inventory turnover and its variation—days inventory supply, which is discussed next—are an indication of the liquidity of inventory.

Days Inventory Supply

A variation of inventory turnover is days inventory supply, which is a measure of the average number of days sales for which the company has inventory available. It is calculated as follows:

Days Inventory Supply = (Average Inventory × 365) ÷ Cost of Goods Sold

For the Ratio Analysis Example Company, days inventory supply is calculated as follows:

$$([(\$717,000 + \$824,000)/2] \times 365) \div \$6,082,000 = 46.2 \text{ days}$$

If we've already calculated the inventory turnover, the days inventory supply for the year is more easily calculated this way:

365 ÷ Inventory Turnover = 365 ÷ 7.9 times = 46.2 days

This calculation indicates that if we stop purchasing inventory, we have enough still on hand to maintain sales for about 46 days. Is this sufficient? As was indicated earlier, it depends on the industry. If the company sells jewelry or other expensive luxury items, the days inventory supply of 46 suggests that business is good and the product is moving quickly. However, if the company sells fresh fruit or other perishable items, the days inventory supply of 46 suggests that business is sluggish. Thus, inventory turnover and its variation days supply of inventory are useful in determining whether a company is carrying too much inventory, which can be caused by poor inventory management or sluggish sales.

If a company is carrying too much inventory, it may mean that the inventory is becoming obsolete, and the company will not be able to sell the inventory without reducing prices. Too much inventory also strains a company's resources, as it represents a use of cash and can lead to additional storage and display costs. However, if a company is carrying too little inventory, that can indicate a problem in

production or purchasing. Further, the company may not be able to meet customer demand and as a result could lose sales now and in the future.

ASSET TURNOVER

The asset turnover ratio is computed as follows:

$$\text{Asset Turnover} = \text{Net Sales} \div \text{Average Total Assets}$$

Average total assets is computed as follows:

$$\text{Average Total Assets} = (\text{Beginning Total Assets} + \text{Ending Total Assets}) \div 2$$

The beginning total assets will be the total assets shown on the prior year's balance sheet, since last year's ending balance equals this year's beginning balance.

Since all assets are included in the computation, this is a more general indication of how efficiently a company uses its assets to generate sales. Specifically, it indicates how many dollars of sales are produced for every dollar invested in assets.

For the Ratio Analysis Example Company, the asset turnover (assuming beginning total assets equals $10,575,000) is

$$\$10,907,000 \div [(\$10,575,000 + \$10,715,000)/2] = 1.02 \text{ times}$$

This calculation indicates that the company generated $1.02 in sales in the year for every $1.00 it invested in assets. Whether this is an acceptable amount again depends on the industry as this ratio can vary widely from one industry to another. Generally, a company with a low asset turnover needs more capital (whether from stockholders or from creditors) to generate additional sales. In contrast, a company with a higher asset turnover can generate additional sales with a smaller influx of capital.

Leverage Ratios

Leverage ratios (sometimes called coverage or capital structure ratios) measure a company's long-term ability to pay its debts as they become due. Leveraging means using other people's money to generate profit for a company. The leverage ratios we will introduce are

- Debt-to-equity ratio
- Debt ratio
- Times interest earned

DEBT-TO-EQUITY RATIO

The debt-to-equity ratio, as the name implies, is computed as follows:

Debt-to-Equity Ratio = Total Liabilities ÷ Total Stockholders' Equity

This ratio calculates how much debt a company has in relation to its owners' equity. If the ratio is 1.0, the company has exactly the same amount of debt as it has owners' equity. With a ratio greater than 1, the company has more debt than owners' equity; in other words, the company owes more than it owns. The higher the ratio becomes, the more heavily burdened with debt the company is. Creditors often prefer that this ratio be low because it suggests that the company is less likely to default as it can pay back its loan with the owners' investments if necessary. Usually if the ratio is low, it indicates that there is greater long-term financial safety and more flexibility to borrow in the future, if necessary. (In fact, these leverage ratios sometimes are referred to as safety ratios.)

For the Ratio Analysis Example Company, the debt-to-equity ratio is

$8,644,000 ÷ $2,071,000 = 4.2 times

This computation indicates that the company has about 4.2 times as much debt as equity. Thus, the company owes much more to others than the stockholders own. You probably can anticipate our next statement: This computation is more meaningful when compared with a benchmark such as the industry average, a particular competitor, and/or this company over time. Further, no single ratio will paint a complete picture.

DEBT RATIO

The debt ratio measures the amount of debt in relation to the total assets of the company. Recall from our discussion in Chapter 1 that the assets came from somewhere: either from outsiders (what you owe) or from owners (what you own). The debt ratio is computed as follows:

Debt Ratio = Total Liabilities ÷ Total Assets

For the Ratio Analysis Example Company, the debt ratio is

$8,644,000 ÷ $10,715,000 = 0.80 or 80%

This computation indicates that about 80 percent of the company's assets are financed by creditors. The higher this ratio is, the greater is the risk that the company may have trouble meeting its debt obligations.

TIMES INTEREST EARNED

Interest must be paid on debt and it must be paid on time or the company risks having its creditors call in the loan. To get an indication of a company's ability to pay the annual interest it owes, times interest earned can be calculated. The formula is as follows:

Times Interest Earned = Income before Interest Expense and Taxes ÷ Interest Expense

Note that the bottom-line net income figure is not used in the numerator, since that already has interest expense deducted. Thus, using the net income figure would distort the computation of the company's ability to pay the interest it owes. Since income taxes are based on income after all expenses, using income before taxes as well helps one compute a more meaningful ratio.

For the Ratio Analysis Example Company, times interest earned is computed as follows:

Times Interest Earned = $1,753,000 ÷ $307,000 = 5.7 times

The numerator, income before interest and taxes, was computed as follows:

Earnings before Income Taxes	$1,446,000
Add back Interest Expense	307,000
Income before Interest and Taxes	$1,753,000

Thus, for this period the company earned 5.7 times what it had to pay in interest. Although there is no single benchmark above which this ratio should be, one hopes the ratio will be greater than 1. Otherwise, the company is earning exactly what it must pay for interest, and that probably will cause concern among the lenders.

Summary

As you undoubtedly appreciate by now, numerous financial ratios can be computed from the financial statements (even more than we have presented here). Figure 8.8 summarizes the ratios we've introduced throughout this chapter. The key is to understand the information provided by the ratios and focus on the ones that are most meaningful for your particular decision, along with any other relevant information.

Figure 8.8   Summary of Ratios

Category	Ratio	Formula	Indicates
Liquidity ratios	Current ratio	Current assets ÷ current liabilities	Whether the company is liquid enough to be able to pay its short-term debts
	Quick ratio	(Cash + short-term investments + accounts receivable) ÷ current liabilities	A more conservative measure of liquidity
Profitability ratios	Gross margin on sales	Gross margin ÷ net sales	The excess of a product's selling price over cost, which is what the company has left to cover all remaining expenses and still make a profit
	Profit margin on sales	Net income ÷ net sales	The percentage of net sales that represents profit
	Return on assets	Net income ÷ average total assets	The amount of income being generated by the company's assets
	Return on equity	Net income ÷ average stockholders' equity	The amount of income being generated by the stockholders' investment
	Earnings per share	(Net income − preferred dividends) ÷ weighted average number of shares of common stock outstanding	The earnings associated with one share of common stock; the only ratio required by GAAP to be presented with the financial statements; typically has a great impact on the market price per share and is watched closely by management
	Dividend payout ratio	Cash dividends paid to common stockholders ÷ (net income − preferred dividends)	How much of the company's earnings are distributed to the common stockholders
	Price-earnings ratio	Market price per share of common stock ÷ earnings per share	How much the earnings of the company cost an investor (how expensive are the earnings?)
Asset management ratios	Day sales outstanding	(Accounts receivable × 365) ÷ net sales	On average, how long it takes the company to collect its accounts receivables from customers
	Accounts receivable turnover	Net sales ÷ average accounts receivable	How many times in the period the company collects its accounts receivable
	Inventory turnover	Cost of goods sold ÷ average inventory	On average, how quickly inventory is sold
	Days inventory	(Average inventory × 365) ÷ cost of goods sold	Using an average rate of sales, how long the company will have inventory until it sells out, assuming no further additions to inventory

Category	Ratio	Formula	Indicates
Asset Management Ratios (cont.)	Asset turnover	Net sales ÷ average total assets	How efficiently the company is using its assets to generate sales
Leverage ratios	Debt-to-equity ratio	Total liabilities ÷ total stockholders' equity	How heavily burdened with debt a company is
	Debt ratio	Total liabilities ÷ total assets	What percentage of the company's assets are financed by creditors
	Times interest earned	Income before interest expense and taxes ÷ interest expense	Whether the company's earnings are sufficient to cover its interest expense for the period

Quiz for Chapter 8

1. Horizontal analysis:
   a. Helps one see the relative changes in accounts over time
   b. Begins by setting the dollar amount of total assets to equal 100 percent, and then everything else on the balance sheet is computed as a percentage of total assets
   c. Also is called common-size analysis
   d. Requires that one compare subsequent years with the immediately preceding year

2. When conducting a horizontal or vertical analysis, one will want to compare the results with:
   a. Competitors
   b. Industry averages
   c. The company over a period of time
   d. Any or all of the above

3. Liquidity ratios measure a company's:
   a. Ability in the near future to pay its debts as they become due
   b. Success or failure at earning a profit
   c. Effectiveness at using various assets
   d. Long-term ability to pay debt as it becomes due

4. Leverage ratios are also known as:
   a. Turnover ratios
   b. Activity ratios
   c. Efficiency ratios
   d. Capital structure ratios

5. Current assets divided by current liabilities is called the:
   a. Quick ratio
   b. Acid test ratio
   c. Current ratio
   d. Return on assets

6. Profitability ratios and liquidity ratios are the same.
   a. True
   b. False

Use the following information to answer questions 7 through 10.

Annie Cooper Corporation reported the following information on its most recent financial statements:
   Net Sales: $1,000,000
   Cost of Goods Sold: $750,000
   Operating Income: $120,000
   Net Income: $100,000
   Total Assets: $500,000
   Total Stockholders' Equity: $400,000

7. What is Annie Cooper Corporation's gross margin on sales?
   a. 10%
   b. 12%
   c. 25%
   d. 33%

8. What is Annie Cooper Corporation's return on sales?
   a. 10%
   b. 12%
   c. 25%
   d. 33%

9. What is Annie Cooper Corporation's return on assets?
   a. 10%
   b. 20%
   c. 24%
   d. 25%

10. What is Annie Cooper Corporation's return on equity?
    a. 15%
    b. 25%
    c. 30%
    d. 62.5%

CHAPTER 9

Additional Issues

Now that we have covered the four financial statements in detail, we will introduce a few additional issues that you occasionally may run into on financial statements. These items do not occur on a regular basis, however, and in fact sometimes are referred to as irregular items. These issues may affect any of the financial statements; they include the following:

- Discontinued operations
- Extraordinary gains and losses
- Changes in accounting principles
- Changes in estimates
- Correction of errors

Discontinued Operations

Sometimes you may find an item on the income statement called a gain or loss from *discontinued operations*. This type of item occurs when a company stops operating a particular component of its business, and upon its disposal, the

company has no significant continuing involvement with that component. Examples are shown in Figure 9.1.

Figure 9.1 Examples of Discontinued Operations

Company	Income Statement for Fiscal Period Ending	Amount Reported on Income Statement	Explanation (Found in the Footnotes to the Financial Statements)
Sara Lee Corporation	July 1, 2006	$401 million gain from discontinued operations (after the tax expense of $65 million)	"As part of the corporation's transformation plan, steps were taken to dispose of several businesses." Six businesses were sold: Direct Selling (Tupperware Corp.), U.S. Retail Coffee, European Branded Apparel, European Nuts and Snacks, U.K. Apparel, and U.S. Meat Snacks
Wal-Mart Stores, Inc.	January 31, 2007	$894 million loss from discontinued operations (after the tax benefits)	Sold its retail businesses in South Korea (16 stores) and Germany (85 stores)
Target Corporation	January 29, 2005	1. Earnings from discontinued operations of $75 million (after the tax expense of $46 million) 2. Gain on disposal of discontinued operations of $1,238 million (after the tax expense of $761 million)	Sold Marshall Field's and Mervyn's businesses
Kimberly-Clark Corporation	December 31, 2004	Income from discontinued operations of $29.8 million (after the tax expense of $29.4 million)	Completed a spin-off of Neenah Paper, Inc., a wholly-owned subsidiary that owned the corporation's Canadian pulp business and its U.S. fine paper and technical paper businesses

Generally accepted accounting principles (GAAP) require that this be shown separately on the income statement after income from continuing operations is computed. Why can it not be combined with other revenues and expenses? Because it is logical for the reader of a financial statement to assume that unless there is evidence to the contrary, next year's net income will be reasonably close to this year's net income. However, by definition, discontinued operations will not affect net income in the future in either a positive or a negative direction. Thus, the impact on net income this year should be disclosed separately. When this is done, income from continuing operations also will be identified separately, and this information should be useful to anyone trying to approximate what next year's net income will be.

Taxes must be paid on all income, including income from discontinued operations. The tax effect of discontinued operations also must be separated, and the result is that an after-tax gain or loss from discontinued operations will be shown on the income statement (often described as *net of tax* on the income statement). If taxes have to be paid on income, why would there be any tax effect of a loss? If there is a loss from discontinued operations, there will be a tax benefit—or a reduction in tax expense—in total for the company.

When a company has discontinued operations, two items are shown: the gain or loss from the component's operations during the period before disposal and the gain or loss from the actual disposal of the component. These amounts can be combined on the face of the income statement, with disclosure of the two items in the footnotes. For example, in Figure 9.1, only one of the four companies displayed both items on the face of its income statement. However, the other three companies provided the required information in the footnotes.

Extraordinary Gains and Losses

Extraordinary gains and losses do not occur nearly as frequently as discontinued operations; in fact, by definition they are quite rare. To be classified as an extraordinary item, the event must be material (large in dollar amount) and must be unusual and occur infrequently. In fact, it may be easier to rule out what cannot be treated as an extraordinary gain or loss than it is to specifically identify what is. Examples that do *not* qualify as extraordinary items include the following:

- The writing off of accounts receivable as uncollectible
- Gains or losses from discontinued operations (these are classified as discussed above)
- The effects of a strike (whether against the company or against its competitors or major suppliers)
- Gains or losses from selling or abandoning business property or equipment

None of these items qualify as extraordinary because they are considered to be usual business activities.

However, if the loss from abandoning business property occurred because of a major natural disaster that normally does not occur in the area (e.g., a hurricane, an earthquake, a flood), it might qualify as an extraordinary item. Whether the catastrophe normally occurs in the location is a key criterion to consider (see Figure 9.2).

Figure 9.2 Examples of Possible Extraordinary Items

Event (Date)	Were the Financial Losses That Resulted from This Event Classified as an Extraordinary Item?	Explanation
Eruption of Mount St. Helens in Washington state (May 1980)	Yes	Mount St. Helens had not erupted in over 130 years.
Terrorist attacks in New York City, Pennsylvania, and Washington, D.C. (September 2001)	No	Although the accounting profession acknowledged that the terrorist attacks were extraordinary, it also decided that it was too difficult to separate the financial effects of the attacks from economic conditions that predated the attacks (a sluggish economy); further, the financial impact was pervasive for affected organizations, and placing the financial impact into an extraordinary classification would not provide useful information for financial statement readers, who might try to project the future impact of those events on the companies' financial results.
Hurricane Katrina on the Gulf Coast (August 2005)	No	Hurricanes do not meet the criteria for classification as an extraordinary item in the Gulf Coast since they are not unusual in nature nor infrequent in occurrence. The magnitude of the hurricane and its extensive and unparalleled devastation are not criteria for classification as an extraordinary item on financial statements.

The accounting profession requires that extraordinary items be classified separately toward the bottom of the income statement rather than included in the regular ongoing income statement accounts so that readers will recognize that the financial impact is an anomaly this year that shouldn't be expected to occur in the foreseeable future. Consequently, it should be easier for readers to predict what future net income and cash flows will be, and that may be useful information for their decision-making purposes.

It has become increasingly rare to find an item classified as an extraordinary gain or loss. Several recent analyses of public companies' financial statements have found that perhaps only 2 percent or less report an extraordinary gain or loss.

Changes in Accounting Principles

A change in an *accounting principle* occurs when a company switches from one generally accepted accounting principle to another (i.e., from one GAAP to a different GAAP). When management selects a particular GAAP to follow, such as the last-in, first-out (LIFO) inventory costing method (discussed in Chapter 5), over other acceptable methods, management is not obligated to use that principle for the rest of time. However, it generally is expected that once a company selects a particular accounting principle to follow, it will not change principles year after year arbitrarily and capriciously. Many financial statement readers would frown on this practice because it suggests that management may be trying to play games with the company's bottom-line net income figure since the selection of accounting principles affects how and when revenues and expenses are recorded, thus affecting net income. Further, it makes comparability next to impossible.

When management chooses to change its selection of an accounting principle, however, it is required to provide details in the financial statement footnotes that state the nature of the change and explain why the new method is preferable. The details also will include the financial impact on affected accounts, income from continuing operations, and net income. This information must be provided to aid financial statement readers in making predictions about future earnings levels and cash flows, especially when it may otherwise be difficult to determine if changes in a company's performance are due to actual economic events versus those caused by a change in the method used to account for an event. Without this information, it also is difficult to compare the company's past financial statements with those of the present. To aid in comparability, the accounting profession now requires that when a change occurs, the company adjust all prior year financial statements that are presented as though the newly adopted principle had been used in those years as well.

Recall from Chapter 7 that auditors are required to add a paragraph to their opinion to bring attention to situations in which a company has not applied accounting principles consistently this year compared to the prior year. Paradoxically, this paragraph often is referred to as a *consistency paragraph* even though it is included only when the company has *not* been consistent in its use of accounting principles from the prior year. The auditors' paragraph will refer the reader to the financial statement footnote in which management has provided the details of the change.

When the accounting profession issues a new accounting standard requiring a change in the proper accounting for a particular type of transaction, organizations have to comply with that standard. Otherwise, assuming that the effect of noncompliance is material, the auditors must give the company something less than the most desirable audit opinion (the unqualified opinion). Because the Financial Accounting Standards Board issues new accounting standards often, it is not unusual to see changes in accounting principles (see Figure 9.3).

Figure 9.3 Examples of Changes in Accounting Principle

Company	Annual Report	Change in Accounting Principle, as Explained in the Audit Report (All Required Because of the Issuance of a New Accounting Standard)
eBay Inc.	2006	"As discussed in Note 1 to the consolidated financial statements, the Company changed the manner in which it accounts for share-based compensation in 2006."
Kraft Foods Inc.	2006	"As discussed in Note 15 to the consolidated financial statements, Kraft Foods Inc. changed the manner in which it accounts for pension, postretirement and postemployment plans in fiscal 2006."
Coca-Cola Enterprises Inc.	2006	"As discussed in Notes 2, 9, 11, and 13 in 2006 the Company adopted Statement of Financial Accounting Standards ("SFAS") No. 123 (revised), "Share-Based Payment" and the recognition provisions of SFAS No. 158, "Employers' Accounting for Defined Benefit Pension and Other Postretirement Plans."

Note that in some cases it is clear from the auditors' consistency paragraph that the change is driven by the issuance of a new professional standard, whereas in other cases it is not as clear but can be determined by reading the financial statement footnotes.

What kinds of changes would not be considered by the accounting profession to be changes in accounting principle? Examples include the following:

- Changing from non-GAAP to GAAP (such as from using the cash basis to using the accrual basis of accounting); this is considered a correction of an error.
- Changing the salvage value or service life used in depreciation calculations for property, plant, and equipment; this is a change in estimate.
- Correctly applying an accounting principle this year when it had been applied incorrectly in the past; this is a correction of an error.
- Increasing the write-down of inventory as a result of obsolescence because of new information obtained; this is a change in estimate (discussed next).

Changes in Estimates

Although on the surface it may appear that accounting is quite black and white in nature, in reality many estimates are inherent in the process of preparing financial statements. Examples of how estimates are built into financial statement numbers include the following:

- Salvage value and useful life used for calculating depreciation
- Percentage of net credit sales or accounts receivable that will be uncollectible

- Percentage of products sold that will be returned under warranty and the dollar amount of the warranty repairs and replacements
- Amount to write down inventory because of obsolescence

Because estimates are essentially educated guesses, they are bound to change as time passes and the company gains experience or as new information arrives. How are changes in estimate handled? For example, with the sudden economic recession that developed in late 2008, undoubtedly many companies will increase their estimate of the bad debts that will arise from the year's sales. Imagine the confusion and the resulting lack of confidence in reported financial information if companies were required to revise and reissue past financial statements every time an estimate was changed. For that reason the accounting profession decided that any changes should be incorporated into the financial statements currently and prospectively, in other words, in the period in which the change occurred and any future periods affected. No prior period statements are restated.

The use of estimates is disclosed in the first footnote (summary of significant accounting policies). For example, the 2006 annual report of Johnson & Johnson includes as part of the first financial statement footnote under the heading "Use of Estimates" the following:

> The preparation of consolidated financial statements in conformity with accounting principles generally accepted in the U.S. requires management to make estimates and assumptions that affect the amounts reported. Estimates are used when accounting for sales discounts, rebates, allowances and incentives, product liabilities, income taxes, depreciation, amortization, employee benefits, contingencies and intangible asset and liability valuations. For instance, in determining annual pension and post-employment benefit costs, the Company estimates the rate of return on plan assets, and the cost of future health care benefits. Actual results may or may not differ from those estimates.

For an example of a current and prospective application, assume the following facts:

- A company purchases a piece of equipment for $65,000 and estimates its useful life at six years, with a salvage value at the end of that time of $5,000. ($60,000 total depreciation; $10,000 per year)
- The company depreciates the equipment for four years under the straight-line depreciation method. ($40,000 total depreciation taken to date)
- In the fifth year, the company estimates the useful life to be a total of eight years (instead of six) but still believes the salvage value will be $5,000 at the end of that time. ($65,000 - $40,000 taken - $5,000 salvage = $20,000 remaining depreciation for next four years)

How is this change in estimate reflected in the financial statements (see Figure 9.4)?

Figure 9.4 Example of Prospective Implementation of a Change in Accounting Estimate

Year	Depreciation Calculation	Amount Depreciated	Total Depreciated to Date
1	($65,000−$5,000)÷6	$10,000	$10,000
2	Same as year 1	$10,000	$20,000
3	Same as year 1	$10,000	$30,000
4	Same as year 1	$10,000	$40,000
5	($65,000−$40,000−$5,000)÷4	$5,000	$45,000
6	Same as year 5	$5,000	$50,000
7	Same as year 5	$5,000	$55,000
8	Same as year 5	$5,000	$60,000

In the fifth year, when the estimate changes, the amount shown as depreciation expense on the income statement for this equipment will be $5,000 rather than $10,000 as it had been in each of the previous four years. Assuming no further changes in estimates, by the end of the eighth year, the equipment will be fully depreciated ($60,000). Since it cost $65,000, it will have a book value of $5,000 (the estimated salvage value at the end of the eighth year).

Depending on how the estimate changes, the affected calculation can be increased or decreased, and the amount of change can be material. If the effect is material, companies will disclose the change in estimates in the footnotes. Similarly, if the change affects multiple periods, companies are required to disclose the effect of the change. In light of the numerous estimates built into financial statement data and the fact that management does not have a crystal ball with which to see accurately into the future, it is not surprising that changes in estimates are very common.

Correction of Errors

Just as changes in estimates are very common, so are errors. Regardless of the checks and balances a company may have built into its accounting system, no system (or group of accountants) is perfect. Examples of errors include the following:

- Recording expenses in the wrong period
- Incorrect application of an accounting principle
- Recognizing revenue in the wrong period
- Math errors such as incorrect computation (and recording) of sales discounts
- Misclassifying an item such as recording an accounts receivable as a note receivable
- Changing from non-GAAP to GAAP, such as switching from the cash basis to the accrual basis of accounting

Errors are unintentional honest mistakes. Intentional errors are considered to be financial statement fraud, as is discussed in Chapter 10. As soon as a company discovers it has made an error, it must correct the error. When the error affects prior financial statements, they must be restated if they are presented again. If this occurs, the auditors' report will include a short paragraph bringing this to the reader's attention since the correction represents a lack of consistency. For example, in the 2006 financial report of Sara Lee Corporation, the auditors included the following paragraph in their opinion:

As discussed in Note 1 to the consolidated financial statements, the Corporation has restated its fiscal 2005 and 2004 consolidated financial statements.

Management provides the details about the error or errors and the correction in the financial statement footnotes.

Quiz for Chapter 9

1. Discontinued operations are:
   a. Shown on the balance sheet as a liability
   b. Shown on the balance sheet as an asset
   c. Shown on the income statement as a separate item
   d. Shown on the income statement but combined with other revenues and expenses

2. Income and expenses from discontinued operations have no impact on income taxes.
   a. True
   b. False

3. Extraordinary gains or losses:
   a. Must be unusual and occur infrequently
   b. Occur infrequently but can be a normal business activity as long as they are highly material
   c. Often are listed on financial statements
   d. Are shown as an asset on the balance sheet

4. Which of the following is an example of an extraordinary item?
   a. Gains or losses from discontinued operations
   b. Losses suffered from the effects of a strike against the company
   c. Losses suffered from abandoning business property and equipment because of damage from a major volcanic eruption that previously had not occurred in the area for over a century
   d. Writing off an accounts receivable as uncollectible

5. Changes in accounting principle:
   a. Rarely occur because once management selects an accounting principle to follow, it is not allowed to change it except in extremely unusual circumstances
   b. Are reflected in the current year and future years only; past financial statements are not restated
   c. Require no additions or changes to the standard audit report
   d. Must be disclosed by management in the financial statement footnotes, stating the nature of the change, explaining why the new method is preferable, and including the financial impact on affected accounts, income from continuing operations, and net income

6. Which of the following is an example of a change in accounting principle?
   a. Changing the service life for equipment in depreciation calculations
   b. Switching from the LIFO method to the FIFO method of inventory valuation
   c. Implementing the accrual basis of accounting after using the cash basis of accounting in prior years
   d. Increasing the amount of bad debt expense recorded because of a downturn in the economy

7. A change in estimate requires that prior year financial statements be restated.
   a. True
   b. False

8. A change in estimate rarely occurs, as very few estimates are built into financial statements.
   a. True
   b. False

9. If a company discovers that its prior year financial statements contain an error, they must be restated before they are presented again.
   a. True
   b. False

10. Which of the following is an example of an error?
    a. Increasing the salvage value of equipment for depreciation calculations as a result of better information
    b. Inadvertently recording revenue this year when it should have been recorded in the following year
    c. Intentionally understating expenses in order to be able to report a higher net income
    d. Switching from one generally accepted accounting principle to another because management now believes that the new principle is preferable and will result in an improvement in financial reporting

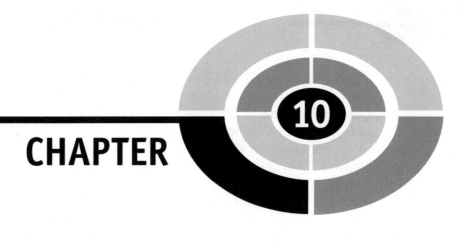

CHAPTER 10

Fraudulently Misstated Financial Statements

Now that you are familiar with the information contained in financial statements, we conclude this book by discussing the topic of fraudulently misstated financial statements.

Not all cases of fraud are discovered and not all discovered frauds are reported, and so there are no solid statistics on the extent to which fraud occurs. Thus, all the statistics are estimates, primarily based on various national and international surveys of different organizations and surveys of people certified in fraud investigation. However, all the surveys are consistent in finding that fraud is pervasive and knows no geographical boundaries. Further, fraud can occur in all types of organizations—private companies, public companies, not-for-profit organizations, universities and other educational institutions, and governmental agencies—and in organizations of all sizes.

The Association of Certified Fraud Examiners (ACFE), headquartered in Austin, Texas, periodically surveys a random sample of Certified Fraud Examiners (CFEs) discussing recent fraud cases they have investigated. These survey responses form the basis for the publication titled *Report to the Nation on Occupational Fraud and Abuse*, first published in 1996 and with subsequent surveys done in 2002, 2004, 2006 and 2008. (These reports can be downloaded free at http://www.acfe.com/fraud/report.asp.)

In its surveys, the ACFE classifies fraud in three broad categories:

1. Asset misappropriation, or the theft of an organization's assets, such as embezzling cash or stealing inventory
2. Fraudulent financial reporting, or the intentional falsification of financial statement information, such as overstating revenues
3. Corruption, or using one's position in an organization wrongfully to obtain a personal benefit, such as accepting kickbacks (cash from a vendor in exchange for having the organization make purchases from that vendor)

The ACFE results suggest that although it is not common, fraudulent financial reporting is occurring more frequently (see Figure 10.1).

Figure 10.1   Rate of Occurrence for Different Categories of Fraud According to the Association of Certified Fraud Examiners Fraud Survey

Category of Fraud	Year of ACFE Report to the Nation* and Frequency of Occurrence				
	1996	2002	2004	2006	2008
Asset misappropriation	85.0%	86.7%	92.7%	91.5%	88.7%
Fraudulent financial reporting	5.0%	5.1%	7.9%	10.6%	10.3%
Corruption	10.0%	12.8%	30.1%	30.8%	27.4%

* Some of the fraud cases studied involved multiple methods of defrauding the organization; thus totals may be greater than 100 percent.

Not only has the occurrence of financial statement fraud increased, as might be expected, the median dollar misstatement caused by fraudulent financial reporting is significantly greater than the median dollar loss in either of the other two fraud categories (see Figure 10.2).

Figure 10.2 Median Fraud Loss/Misstatement for Different Categories of Fraud According to the Association of Certified Fraud Examiners Fraud Survey

Category of Fraud	Year of ACFE Report to the Nation* and Median Fraud Loss or Misstatement			
	2002	2004	2006	2008
Asset misappropriation	$ 80,000	$ 93,000	$ 150,000	$ 150,000
Fraudulent financial reporting	$4,250,000	$1,000,000	$2,000,000	$2,000,000
Corruption	$ 530,000	$ 250,000	$ 538,000	$ 375,000

*These data were not published in the 1996 report.

This disparity in median fraud amounts is caused by the fact that the financial statements are reporting for the entire company, and if management is engaged in fraudulent financial reporting, the amounts will be material; in other words, the fraud is intended to deceive readers into making decisions they would not have made if they had had complete and honest information. Asset misappropriations and corruption typically are perpetrated by an individual who usually does not steal an amount that would be material to the financial statements.

Thus, although fraudulent financial reporting appears not to happen often, when it does occur, it can be devastating.

The ACFE survey results are consistent with those of KPMG, one of the "Big Four" international public accounting firms. KPMG conducted national fraud surveys in 1994, 1998, and 2003. Although comparable data from the 1994 survey were not gathered, KPMG reported that fraudulent financial reporting was the category of fraud that occurred the least but that it increased from 3 percent to 7 percent between 1998 and 2003. Further, the firm reported that the average annual cost of fraudulent financial reporting is by far the highest in all fraud categories, estimated at nearly $258 billion in the 2003 survey.

The Fraud Triangle

In Chapter 9 we discussed how the accounting profession requires that errors in the financial statements be corrected. In this chapter, we are not concerned with errors, which are unintentional and honest mistakes, but with fraud. Fraud involves intent, specifically, the intent to deceive. There is no such thing as unintentional or accidental fraud.

Fraud researchers have discovered that three elements are necessary for fraud to occur: pressure, perceived opportunity, and rationalization. These three elements combined make up what is referred to as the fraud triangle, and all three must be present simultaneously for a fraud to occur (see Figure 10.3). The fraud triangle applies to all three fraud categories: asset misappropriation, fraudulent financial reporting, and corruption.

Figure 10.3 The Fraud Triangle

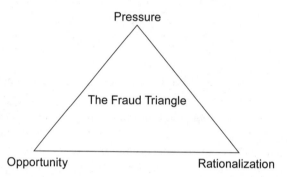

Pressure is the motive to commit fraud, and it may be financial or nonfinancial in nature. Examples of financial pressures include the following:

- Desire to live beyond one's means
- A gambling habit
- Alcohol or drug addiction
- Investment losses
- Excessive personal debts

Examples of nonfinancial pressures include the following:

- A disgruntled employee who wants to get even with the employer
- Perceived peer or family pressure to be successful
- Low self-worth and a belief that one will be well liked if one has more money
- A desire to beat the system

Upper management perpetrates fraudulent financial reporting, not an individual employee, as is often the case with asset misappropriation. Management is in a position to override any internal controls that are in place to help ensure accurate financial reporting, something that would be nearly impossible for an individual employee to do. In fact, fraudulent financial reporting usually is referred to as management fraud, whereas asset misappropriation is termed employee fraud.

Often, management's motive for engaging in this type of fraud is to report better financial results than have occurred to maintain or increase the company's stock price. The stock price may be an important factor in determining the compensation that will be paid to upper management because those individuals may hold a large number of stock options or because their compensation may be tied in other ways to the stock price (or other performance measures that are reported in the financial statements, such as net income and total revenues).

Other reasons to perpetrate this type of fraud include obtaining financing (or obtaining the financing on better terms, such as a lower rate of interest), appearing to meet loan requirements (such as maintaining a minimum current ratio), and encouraging investment in the company through stock purchase (such as by making the company appear to be less risky because of low debt levels). Those in upper management may engage in fraudulent financial reporting to appear more successful than they actually are because of perceived family pressure to do well or the desire to impress stockholders, especially if upper management is relatively new to the company. It is possible, however, that management will report results worse than the real results to pay less in income taxes or to be able to show gradual improvement in results over time.

The second element in the fraud triangle—perceived opportunity—refers to the idea in the perpetrator's mind that he or she will be able to commit fraud and get away with it. Most rational people will not commit fraud if they believe they will be caught. With this element, *perceived* is the key word: There may be internal controls in place that will detect the fraud shortly after it starts, but if the perpetrator is not aware of the controls, he or she will begin to defraud the organization. Of course, the flip side is also true: If a potential perpetrator believes there are controls in place that in reality do not exist that will detect the fraud he or she is considering committing, the person will not commit the fraud.

Management is responsible for establishing the company's internal control system, and so with this thorough knowledge of the system, its members are in a perfect position to override the controls that are in place. Further, because members of management supervise other employees, they often are able to persuade or coerce subordinates (such as accounting personnel) to go along with a fraudulent financial reporting scheme.

The third element of the triangle—rationalization—is unique to fraud perpetrators. Rationalization means that fraudsters must be able to explain in their own minds why their actions are not criminal. In other words, they must be able to make their actions consistent with their personal code of conduct. Common rationalizations include the following:

- I'm only borrowing the money; I'll pay it back.
- Everybody does it.

- I'm not hurting anyone.
- People would understand if they knew how much I need this.
- It's not that serious.
- They owe it to me. I deserve to get paid more.

Members of management may rationalize their fraudulent financial reporting as being only temporary, until the company overcomes a short-term setback. Or they may believe that accounting rules are flexible (we can bend them, but we can't break them). They also may rationalize that no one will be hurt by the inflated stock price because they are too clever to be caught. Regardless of the rationalization, ethical standards are lacking when fraud occurs.

All three elements—pressure, perceived opportunity, and rationalization—must be present simultaneously for fraud to occur. If any of the elements are missing, fraud will not occur. For example, if no pressure or motive to commit fraud exists, why would it occur? Why would a person commit fraud if he believed he would get caught, in other words, if the perceived opportunity was lacking? And how could a person commit fraud if her moral values were strong and she could not rationalize the act? Thus, if any one of the elements is removed, the risk of fraud occurring is minimized greatly.

The fraud triangle concept that all three elements must be present for fraud to occur is similar to that for fire. Heat, fuel, and oxygen all must be present simultaneously for fire to exist. Take away any one of those elements, and the fire is out.

The Auditors' Responsibility for Detecting Fraud

Fooling the auditors is certainly the trick to master when one is engaging in fraudulent financial reporting. On the surface, this may seem difficult, but numerous fraud surveys indicate that auditors seldom detect fraud (see Figures 10.4 and 10.5).

Figure 10.4 Sources of Fraud Detection per KPMG Fraud Surveys

Source	1994	1998	2003
Tips*	134%	161%	173%
Internal control	52%	51%	77%
Internal auditors	47%	43%	65%
Accident	28%	37%	54%
External auditors	5%	4%	12%

*The totals exceed 100 percent because many respondents experienced more than one fraud. Tips came from employees, customers, vendors, regulatory or law enforcement agencies, and anonymously.

Figure 10.5 Sources of Fraud Detection per ACFE Fraud Surveys

Source	2002	2004	2006	2008
Tips*	45%	41%	38%	49%
Accident	19%	21%	25%	20%
Internal auditors	19%	24%	20%	19%
Internal control	15%	18%	19%	23%
External auditors	12%	11%	12%	9%

*Totals exceed 100 percent because for many frauds, there was more than one method of detection.

Again, since not all cases of fraud are discovered and not all discovered frauds are reported, any fraud statistic is an estimate. However, these surveys are consistent in finding that tips are the number one method of discovering a fraud. Further, although these results of detection methods pertain to all categories of fraud, not just fraudulent financial reporting, it is interesting to note how seldom auditors (internal or external) detect fraud.

What exactly is the auditors' responsibility for detecting fraud? External auditors—the auditors from a public accounting firm who are hired by a company to audit its financial statements and render an opinion on them—are required under professional auditing standards to plan and conduct the audit to provide reasonable assurance about detecting material misstatements regardless of whether the material misstatement is due to errors or to fraud. However, recall that the dollar amount of some frauds may not have a material effect in the financial statements for the company as a whole. Note the following points:

- The auditor has no responsibility to detect immaterial fraud (where materiality is defined in relation to the financial statements as a whole); recall that an item is considered material if its misstatement or omission would cause a reasonable person to make a decision different from the decision that would be made if the item had been stated correctly.
- The auditors' responsibility to detect material frauds is no different from their responsibility to detect material errors (unintentional misstatements).
- The auditors do not provide absolute assurance or any kind of guarantee that all material fraud will be detected.

Internal auditors are employees of the company and as such are not considered independent in the required sense for rendering an opinion on financial statements. Therefore, they cannot audit a company's financial statements. However, they provide useful services to management, such as assisting in the design and implementation of internal controls and monitoring the effectiveness of those controls over time.

The professional standards for internal auditors require that those auditors have sufficient knowledge to identify fraud indicators; however, they are not expected to have the same level of fraud expertise as an individual whose primary responsibility is fraud investigation. Internal auditors can assist in fraud deterrence by evaluating the effectiveness of the internal control system, identifying areas of the organization that may be vulnerable to fraud, and implementing controls to help minimize that risk.

In light of the different functions of external and internal auditors, it is not surprising that few fraud cases are detected by external auditors or that more instances are caught by internal auditors, who work year-round at the same company on a closer and more detailed level. The moral of the story is that auditors, both internal and external, cannot be relied on to detect fraud. However, audited financial statements are still preferable to unaudited financial statements (some assurance is better than no assurance).

Further, recall from our discussion in Chapter 7 on reading the auditors' report that the Sarbanes-Oxley Act of 2002 (SOX) was passed in response to the numerous widely publicized corporate accounting scandals that had occurred from the 1990s until that time (e.g., Enron, WorldCom, Xerox, Tyco, Waste Management, Global Crossing). Section 404 of the Act requires auditors to provide an opinion on the effectiveness of public companies' internal control over financial reporting. The logic behind this requirement is essentially that if a public company has effective internal controls over financial reporting, there is a reduced risk of fraudulently misstated financial statements being published and relied on by the investing public.

Methods of Fraudulently Misstating Financial Statements

The majority of cases of fraudulent financial reporting involve making a company's financial health appear better than it really is. There are a number of methods by which this can be accomplished:

- Overstating revenues
- Understating expenses
- Understating liabilities

- Overstating assets
- Improper disclosures

Often, a combination of methods is used. For example, a company may "hold the books open" and record revenue this year when the revenue should be recorded in the following year (overstating revenues). At the same time, the company may delay the recognition of some expenses and record them in the following year when the proper recognition of the expenses should have occurred this year (understating expenses).

OVERSTATING REVENUES

Because net income equals revenue minus expenses, any time revenues are overstated, net income also will be overstated (see Figure 10.6).

Figure 10.6   Effect on Net Income of Fraudulently Overstating Revenues

Example Company
Income Statement
For the Year Ended December 31, 20x1

	If Properly Reported	As Fraudulently Reported
Revenues	$ 900,000	$1,000,000
Expenses	(700,000)	(700,000)
Net Income	$ 200,000	$ 300,000

Overstating revenues has the effect of overstating net income by the same amount

Revenue can be overstated by doing the following:

- Recording fictitious revenue
- Recognizing revenue prematurely
- Understating sales returns

Fictitious revenue can be created by recording sales to customers who do not exist (ghost customers) or by recording inflated sales to actual customers. If the latter method is chosen, management will need to take care not to overbill the actual customers, and so although fake documentation will be required, careful records must be kept. The lengths to which some managers go to perpetrate this kind of fraud can be amazing (see Figure 10.7).

Figure 10.7   Example of Fraudulent Financial Reporting with Fictitious Revenues: ZZZZ Best

In the mid-1980s, ZZZZ Best Co., Inc., perpetrated a massive financial statement fraud that fooled the auditors of one of the then largest international public accounting firms, along with ZZZZ Best's investors, who lost a reported $100 million. The company was a carpet cleaning business started by Barry Minkow out of his parent's garage when he was 13 years old. Most of the fraud involved recording fictitious revenues and accounts receivable and was perpetrated to inflate the stock price when the company went public five years after its inception.

The company claimed to earn most of its revenues through lucrative insurance restoration jobs which involved cleaning and repairing buildings damaged by floods, fires, and other major catastrophes. However, the insurance restoration side of the business was entirely bogus, and only the carpet cleaning side of the company was legitimate (it represented approximately 2 percent of the company's total revenue according to its fraudulent financial statements). When the auditors insisted on physically inspecting one multi-million-dollar insurance restoration site, ZZZZ Best management found a large building under construction and was able to persuade the construction foreman to provide them with keys to the building for a weekend on the pretext that they were with a property management firm and were going to provide a tour to a prospective tenant. Before the auditors' visit, they placed signs throughout the building indicating that ZZZZ Best was the contractor for the building's restoration. This building had not been damaged—instead, it was under construction—but the plan went off without a hitch: The auditors were fooled. On another occasion, when the auditors insisted on visiting another multi-million-dollar restoration site, ZZZZ Best had to lease some floors of a new building quickly. For the floors that weren't completed, ZZZZ Best spent approximately $1 million to make the space look realistic, hiring subcontractors to make the floors look restored. All this for a tour with the auditors that lasted perhaps 20 minutes.

Recognizing revenue early—a timing difference—means recording revenue before GAAP allows it to be recorded. Recall from Chapter 2 that the revenue recognition principle states that revenue generally is considered earned and reported in the income statement in the period in which the business provided the service or sold the goods even though the customer may not pay for the services or goods until a later time. For example, it would not affect a company's financial statements to record revenue on July 13 that was earned on July 25, when the fiscal year end is December 31. Thus, this type of fraud occurs around the end of the fiscal year. Companies may record their revenue prematurely at that time if it appears that they may not reach their desired earnings target. Of course, this is like robbing Peter to pay Paul because the revenue cannot be recorded in the subsequent year when it truly is earned since in that case it would be double-counted.

Understating sales returns is another technique that can be used to overstate revenues. Recall from Chapter 3 on the income statement that sales returns are deducted from gross sales to arrive at net sales revenue. Thus, if the amount of

sales returns is understated, net sales revenue and net income will be overstated (see Figure 10.8).

Figure 10.8   Example of Fraudulent Financial Reporting with Understated Sales Returns: Regina Carpet Cleaning Company

> In the mid–1980s, management changed at Regina Company, Inc., a manufacturer of vacuum cleaners. New products were introduced which were less expensive to manufacture, but those vacuums had plastic parts that apparently often melted when the product was used for a period of time, rendering the vacuum cleaner useless. Consequently, the sales returns were increasing greatly, running as much as 16 percent of gross sales revenues.
>
>   The new CEO had a controlling interest in the company, and it had been his idea to meddle with Regina's 100-year-old sterling reputation as a manufacturer of hardy, dependable vacuum cleaners. He had purchased his interest in the company by taking on a large amount of personal debt, and he needed Regina to be profitable so that he could make his debt payments. With the auditors coming soon and the warehouse filling up with returned merchandise, he decided to cook the books with the assistance of other members of management. He rented a warehouse elsewhere to store the useless returned vacuums and altered all the documentation indicating that the sales had been returned. The sales returns were not reflected on the financial statements, and the auditors were fooled. However, this kind of fraud, with the underlying cause of an ineffective product, cannot continue indefinitely. Before long, word of the defective design began to spread among consumers, and sales began to drop. Eventually, the CEO realized he couldn't continue to juggle the numbers and deceive the auditors. Like a house of cards, the company collapsed, and investors and creditors lost a reported $40 million.

UNDERSTATING EXPENSES

Understating expenses is a fraudulent technique that has the same effect on net income as overstating revenues (see Figure 10.9).

Figure 10.9   Effect on Net Income of Fraudulently Understating Expenses

Example Company
Income Statement
For the Year Ended December 31, 20x1

	If Properly Reported	As Fraudulently Reported
Revenues	$ 900,000	$ 900,000
Expenses	(700,000)	(600,000)
Net Income	$ 200,000	$ 300,000

Understating expenses has the effect of overstating net income by the same amount

Because net income equals revenue minus expenses, any time expenses are understated, net income will be overstated. Expenses can be understated by

- Postponing expense recognition
- Capitalizing expenses (i.e., recording an expense as an asset)

Recognizing expenses in a subsequent accounting period violates the matching principle. Recall from Chapter 2 that the matching principle requires that costs incurred by the business generally be recorded as expenses on the income statement in the period in which the related revenue is produced. In other words, revenues are matched with the costs and efforts associated with producing those revenues, resulting in the net income or loss during the specified period. If the expenses are recorded in an accounting period later than the one in which the related revenues were generated, net income will be overstated.

Capitalizing expenses—improperly recording a cost as an asset that will appear on the balance sheet rather than as an expense of the period that will appear on the income statement—is a variation of recognizing expenses later.

Costs that provide benefits to a company over a number of accounting periods, such as the purchase of a company vehicle or manufacturing equipment, should not be expensed immediately in the period of purchase. That action would violate the matching principle since those assets will help the company generate revenues over future periods. Instead, these costs are capitalized—recorded as an asset—and gradually expensed over time as the assets are used. This expense is called depreciation expense and represents nothing more than the allocation of the asset's cost over the periods benefited by the use of the asset (depreciation in accounting terminology has nothing to do with writing an asset down to market value). Figure 10.10 illustrates this concept.

Figure 10.10 Depreciation Expense Example

20x1	20x2	20x3	20x4	20x5	20x6	20x7

Equipment costing $70,000 is purchased at the beginning of 20x1. It is expected to have a seven-year useful life, with no salvage value at the end of that time.

At the end of 20x7, the equipment is determined to have no more useful life and is disposed of at the local dump.

20x1	20x2	20x3	20x4	20x5	20x6	20x7
$10,000	$10,000	$10,000	$10,000	$10,000	$10,000	$10,000

The cost of the equipment is not all expensed immediately in 20x1; instead, it is written off gradually to expense over the seven-year useful life, since it helps generate revenues over that period (matching principle).

If a company is engaged in fraudulent financial reporting, it may decide to capitalize expenses improperly to overstate income. In the earlier example in this chapter, the company had purchased a piece of equipment and properly capitalized it and depreciated it over its seven-year useful life. But what if the $70,000 outlay had been for employees' wages and the company decided to capitalize that expense? Sound improbable? Capitalizing operating expenses was a technique used by WorldCom to misstate its financial statements by a reported $3.8 billion.

The proper accounting technique would be to expense the $70,000 for wages in that one period since there is no future benefit; the employees worked that year and helped generate revenues that year. However, if the company instead decided to record the $70,000 payment as the purchase of computer equipment, the effect on the financial statements would be to report much less expense (only through gradual depreciation) than would be the case if the entire $70,000 had been expensed and affected net income that year. Thus, the effect of improperly capitalizing expenses is to do the following:

- Overstate assets (which makes the balance sheet look better)
- Understate expenses (which makes net income and the income statement look better)
- Overstate stockholders' equity (net income increases year-end equity and so assets and equity are both overstated, and, the more equity, the better)

UNDERSTATING LIABILITIES

The fewer liabilities—or the less debt—a company has, the healthier and less risky it appears. Because the balance sheet must remain in balance, it will appear that more of the company is owned than owed (see Figure 10.11).

Figure 10.11 How Fraudulently Understating Liabilities Affects the Balance Sheet

Example Company
Balance Sheet
December 31, 20x1

	If Properly Reported		As Fraudulently Reported	
Assets		$1,000,000		$1,000,000
Liabilities	$700,000		$600,000	
Equity	300,000		400,000	
Total Liabilities and Equity		$1,000,000		$1,000,000

Understating liabilities has the effect of overstating equity by the same amount.

This effect occurs because if a liability is understated, there is usually an expense that is not recorded (giving rise to the debt). As was explained in the previous section, if expenses are understated, net income is overstated, which in turn overstates equity. Note that these fraudulent financial reporting schemes are not necessarily mutually exclusive.

Liabilities can be understated by

- Completely omitting some of them from the financial statements or
- Recording them at an amount lower than what is proper

Any liability can be understated if the company decides to do so. For example, a company may decide to omit recording contingent liabilities: liabilities that become debts contingent on a future event occurring. GAAP states that contingent liabilities must be booked if they are "probable" and the amount can be "reasonably estimated." For example, a company must estimate and record a liability for future warranty obligations if it sells products with a warranty. It is probable that some products will fail or be defective in some manner during the warranty period and will be returned. Further, the amount can be estimated reasonably on the basis of past experience.

Another type of liability that a company may omit is unearned revenues. Recall that when a company receives cash from a customer in advance of performing a service or providing goods, the revenue has not been earned. Instead, the cash is recorded as received (an asset has increased) and a liability is also recorded (unearned revenue). The company must either provide the customer goods or services or return the money back to the customer if for some reason it does not provide the service or the goods. Warranty service contracts, sales of gift cards, and frequent flier and other awards programs fall into this category of unearned revenues.

Depending on how bold the company is in its fraudulent financial reporting scheme, it may decide to stash unpaid bills in desk drawers or filing cabinets until it can pay them and fail to include these amounts as liabilities. It is more difficult for auditors to detect an unrecorded item that should be included than to detect an error of an item that has been recorded but using the wrong amount. If an item has been recorded, it can end up being selected to appear in the auditors' sample of items to test. In contrast, if an item has not been recorded, it is not possible for the auditors to select that item for testing from the population of recorded items.

OVERSTATING ASSETS

Overstating assets will achieve the same objectives as understating liabilities. The more assets a company has, the healthier it appears. Because the balance sheet must remain in balance, it will appear that more of the company is owned than owed (see Figure 10.12).

Figure 10.12   Example of How Fraudulently Overstating Assets Affects the Balance Sheet

Example Company
Balance Sheet
December 31, 20x1

	If Properly Reported		As Fraudulently Reported	
Assets		$1,000,000		$1,200,000
Liabilities	$700,000		$700,000	
Equity	300,000		500,000	
Total Liabilities and Equity		$1,000,000		$1,200,000

> Overstating assets has the effect of overstating equity by the same amount.

This effect occurs because if an asset is overstated, the company is not going to record a corresponding nonexistent or overstated debt for the nonexistent or overstated asset. Rather, there is usually a revenue that also was recorded. As was explained earlier in this chapter, if revenues are overstated, net income is overstated, which in turn overstates equity. Again notice how these fraudulent financial reporting schemes are not necessarily mutually exclusive.

Any asset can be overstated, but commonly the following assets are targeted:

- Inventory
- Accounts receivable
- Fixed assets (property, plant, and equipment)

For a manufacturing or retail business, inventory usually constitutes a large proportion of total assets. Auditors are required under professional auditing standards to observe a client's inventory count physically at the end of the fiscal year if inventory is material to the financial statements. This requirement is from one of the first auditing standards issued, which resulted from a major inventory fraud that occurred in 1938 at McKesson & Robbins. Despite this requirement, the auditors still can be fooled if management is intent on doing that (see Figures 10.13 and 10.14).

Figure 10.13 Example of Fraudulent Financial Reporting—Overstated Assets: Phar-Mor, Inc.

In the late 1980s and early 1990s, Phar-Mor, Inc.—a deep discount retail chain store—began to manipulate its reported inventory. The number of stores and the states in which the stores were located grew at a phenomenal rate during that time. The COO (chief operating officer) who was also the president and founder of Phar-Mor claimed that profits and growth were due to the company's ability to successfully engage in "power buying," a term the COO used to describe his approach of buying large quantities of products when the vendors were offering their lowest prices. He also employed a strategy of offering low prices to Phar-Mor customers in order to compete with competitors such as Wal-Mart. However, the prices were so low on so many products that Phar-Mor stopped earning a legitimate profit in 1988.

The losses suffered by the company never were reflected in the financial statements since the COO and several top executives began to engage in fraudulent financial reporting. Inventory was one of their prime targets, and the company began to overstate inventory by inflating the amount of reported inventory for each individual store. But how could this go undetected by the auditors when they were required to observe the client's inventory counts at year end? Auditors cannot observe all stores' inventory counts when there are many stores and they are geographically dispersed, but in this case, the auditors chose to observe the counts annually at only 4 or 5 stores out of over 300. Furthermore, it was reported that the auditors told Phar-Mor executives ahead of time which stores they would be observing. That slip made it a simple matter for the company to ensure that the records and counts would be accurate at those few stores.

Figure 10.14 Example of Fraudulent Financial Reporting—Overstated Assets: Crazy Eddie

Crazy Eddie, Inc., was a consumer electronics retail store in the Northeast during the 1980s. It began as a small family-owned business but went public in 1983 to raise capital to finance further expansions. The company employed an aggressive television advertising campaign: A wildly energetic actor posing as Crazy Eddie would be frantically showing merchandise and shouting, "Crazy Eddie: Our prices are INSANE!" These eye-catching commercials sometimes were parodied on the television show *Saturday Night Live* in its early years, giving the company some national notoriety.

Crazy Eddie, Inc., used a variety of techniques to misstate its financial statements fraudulently, including the overstatement of inventory. The company's methods for misstating inventory were quite bold: It would pressure vendors to ship merchandise around the end of the year but hold off on billing them until the next fiscal year, ship merchandise from one store to another overnight so that it would be double-counted, and even unlock the auditors' briefcases while they were out and alter the inventory numbers on the audit workpapers. The fraud was uncovered in 1987 after a hostile takeover. The new owners had their own inventory count conducted and discovered that inventory had been overstated by approximately $65 million.

The company's CPA was Eddie's cousin, who, with other members of management, helped perpetrate the fraud. After the downfall of the company, he appears to have reformed and now works as a forensic accountant, educating others about fraudulent financial reporting (for much more information about the Crazy Eddie fraud, see his Web site at http://www.whitecollarfraud.com/index.html).

Accounts receivable also may be overstated. Recall that when a receivable is recorded, so is the related revenue. Thus, not only are assets overstated, so are revenues (and net income and therefore equity).

Auditors nearly always will confirm a sample of receivables, however. When auditors confirm information, they are requesting that an independent third party, such as a customer, directly verify to the auditors, usually in writing, that some specific information is correct (e.g., the amount the customer owes the client as of the end of the fiscal year). However, the auditors can be fooled if management is so inclined. In the ZZZZ Best case (Figure 10.7), management persuasively talked the auditors out of confirming its fictitious receivables by pressuring them not to "harass" its customers. Instead, management was able to persuade the auditors to accept internal documentation relating to its receivables, which of course had been manufactured by management.

Fixed assets also may be overstated, but, in a method that is unique to them, management may intentionally understate the depreciation expense each year, such as by using an unrealistic service life. The smaller expense translates into a larger net income, which increases equity. The accumulated depreciation contra asset account that appears on the balance sheet also is understated so that the net plant and equipment added on the asset side of the balance sheet is overstated. Thus, the balance sheet still balances.

IMPROPER DISCLOSURES

Recall that GAAP requires that detailed and extensive footnotes accompany financial statements. Thus, there are probably limitless ways in which management can mislead financial statement readers via the footnotes. Damaging information known to management may not be mentioned, or facts can be misstated. Those actions certainly do not conform to the full disclosure principle discussed in Chapter 2, but any method of misstating financial statements fraudulently does not conform to any concept of financial reporting.

The Enron case is a classic example of improper disclosure. Enron developed *special purpose entities (SPEs)* to finance growth and report profits without reporting the related debt on its balance sheet. According to the accounting rules in place at the time, as long as at least 3 percent of an SPE's financing was provided by outside investors, the SPE's financial statements did not have to be combined (consolidated) with Enron's financial statements. Thus, Enron could use the capital raised by the SPE without having to report the related debt on its balance sheet. This debt avoidance was significant since the SPEs were structured to meet the minimum 3 percent rule, meaning that the remaining 97 percent of the capital typically was contributed by loans from banks. Later, investigators discovered that even the minimal 3 percent rule wasn't always followed by Enron. For example, the outside investors providing the 3 percent capital sometimes were individuals within Enron (e.g., Andrew Fastow, Enron's chief financial officer, who was involved in the creation and operation of

several of these entities and named some of them after his children). Fastow reportedly received $30 million in profits on his investments in the Enron SPE investments that he oversaw.

Enron used the these entities for other purposes as well. It sold some of its assets at grossly overstated amounts to its SPEs, enabling it to report substantial paper gains on its income statement. Further, the SPE loans often were collateralized with Enron common stock. Thus, those SPEs essentially were a convoluted business relationship by which Enron could look financially better off than it was in reality, and Enron's management made sure that the related financial statement footnotes did not portray the true nature of Enron's relationship with the these entities. Wall Street analysts who had years of experience reading financial statements and footnote disclosures found the Enron footnotes pertaining to the SPEs confusing. If those experts could not understand the information provided in the footnotes, how could the average financial statement reader understand it?

Red Flags

How can an investor or a potential investor detect possible fraudulent financial reporting in a company's financial statements? First, keep in mind that fraudulent financial reporting is the exception, not the rule. In the five surveys conducted by the Association of Certified Fraud Examiners, fraudulent financial reporting represented only 5.0 to 10.6 percent of the fraud cases reported by the respondents (see Figure 10.1). This statistic does not mean that fraudulent financial reporting happens up to 10 percent of the time, since these results were not derived from all financial statements produced in any one year, only from fraud cases investigated by the respondents for the most recent year.

Unfortunately, there is no single foolproof method of determining whether financial statements are fraudulently misstated; if there were, all auditors would be aware of that method and use it regularly. However, sometimes a careful look at ratios and their trend over time can be useful, especially when the ratios are compared with industry averages.

Nonsensical Ratios

Keeping in mind the various techniques used to report financial statements fraudulently (overstate revenues, understate expenses, understate liabilities, overstate assets, and/or improperly disclose information), an analysis of the ratios that would be affected by these techniques can help identify potentially misstated financial statements. Any changes in these ratios from one year to the next and over a period of time should make sense. Further, it's reasonable to expect the ratios to be similar to industry averages unless there is a logical explanation for why they are not. Thus, if a company's financial ratios are showing unusual fluctuations that cannot be explained rationally, especially if the ratios are out of line with industry averages, it may be a good idea to reconsider relying on those financial statements.

Industry averages can be obtained fairly easily online, although some Web sites require that an individual pay a subscription fee for their services. On a search engine such as Google, type in "industry averages" and hundreds of thousands of hits will emerge; there are plenty of resources available. One free Web site that provides some industry averages is www.finance.yahoo.com.

For example, in the ZZZZ Best fraud (see Figure 10.7), the financial statements were reporting gross profits of approximately 45 to nearly 60 percent (see Figure 10.15).

Figure 10.15   Examples of Nonsensical Trends and Ratios from ZZZZ Best Co., Inc., Financial Statements

	Fiscal Year 1985 (12 months)	Fiscal Year 1986 (12 months)	First Quarter of Fiscal Year 1987 (3 months)
Gross Profit %	53.5%	57.7%	44.8%
Gross Profit % (Industry Average)	10%	10%	10%
Accounts Receivable	$ 0	$ 693,773	$2,461,098
Net Sales Revenue	$1,240,524	$4,845,347	$5,395,754
General Expenses	$ 306,016	$ 1,125,541	$ 622,811
Cash	$ 30,300	$ 87,014	$ 9,907
Total Assets	$ 178,036	$5,045,671	$8,200,091

However, the industry average was around 10 percent. Recall that nearly all of the sales revenue and related accounts receivable were fictitious in this case. Consequently, the accounts receivable grew from $0 to nearly $700,000 the next year and approximately $2,500,000 only three months after that. Sales increased dramatically in one year from slightly over $1.24 million to just under $4.85 million, a 291 percent increase. In a company doing such booming business, cash increased only from approximately $30,000 to $87,000 during that period. However, almost half of the revenues that year were from only one insurance restoration job (which, of course, was a fake). How could a financial statement reader know this? When an internationally renowned public accounting firm—ZZZZ Best's auditors—couldn't detect the fraud, it's hard to criticize any financial statement reader. But perhaps the idea that this relatively new company was founded and run by a 20-year-old history major with minimal business education and experience should have raised some suspicions. The identity and basic background of a company's CEO should not be a mystery to financial statement readers.

Other red flags were also present. For example, during the year when nearly $4.85 million in net sales was reported, general expenses of approximately $1.13 million also were reported on the income statement. Yet three months later the quarterly financial statements showed nearly $5.4 million in net sales (for three months) while general expenses decreased to approximately $622,000. Total assets on the balance sheet also were skyrocketing. In one year the reported total assets climbed from $178,000 to almost $5.1 million, an increase of over 2,700 percent. Further, the next quarter's financial statements listed total assets of slightly over $8.2 million, which is an increase of over 4,500 percent from the base year only 15 months earlier. This is phenomenal, unheard-of growth.

Ratio and trend analysis also reveal some red flags on the Regina Company, Inc.'s, financial statements (see Figure 10.8). Recall that in this case the vacuum cleaners with the revised product design featuring internal plastic parts were being returned at a fast rate because the plastic parts were melting when the vacuum was operated. Management chose not to book those sales returns properly, which would have reduced the income statement's reported net sales (Figure 10.16).

Figure 10.16   Examples of Nonsensical Trends and Ratios from the Regina Company Financial Statements

	Fiscal Year 1986	Fiscal Year 1987	Fiscal Year 1988
Net Sales	$76,144,000	$128,234,000	$181,123,000
Cost of Goods Sold	$46,213,000	$ 70,756,000	$ 94,934,000
Gross Profit %	39.3%	44.8%	47.6%
Days Inventory Supply	77.1	75.7	112.9
Inventory	$ 9,762,000	$ 19,577,000	$ 39,135,000
Total Assets	$43,202,000	$ 65,241,000	$118,140,000
Accounts Receivable	$14,402,000	$ 27,801,000	$ 51,076,000
Days Sales Outstanding	69.0	79.1	102.9

Consequently, the income statements for three consecutive years showed net sales increasing from approximately $76 million to $128 million to $181 million (increases of 68 percent and 138 percent over the first year). At the same time, cost of goods sold was reported at $46 million, $71 million, and $95 million (increases of 53 percent and 105 percent over the first year). As a result, the gross profit margin changed from approximately 39.3 percent to 44.8 percent to 47.6 percent. Were these increasing gross profit margins due to a more efficient manufacturing process for the revised vacuums, or did they occur because the cost to manufacture vacuum cleaners with plastic parts was lower than the manufacturing costs for the earlier models with steel parts?

Either explanation is rational, but when one also looks at days inventory supply for Regina, a concern arises. Specifically, for the same years, the days inventory supply changed from 77 to 76 to 113. Does this suggest sluggish sales? Inventory increased from $9.7 million to $19.6 million to $39.1 million during those three years, when reported total assets changed from $43.2 million to $65.2 to $118.1 million.

Perhaps many sales were on account, and if that was the case, how quickly were the accounts receivable being collected? In Regina's case, the accounts receivable increased from approximately $14 million to $28 million to $51 million. The resulting days sales outstanding increased from 69 days to 79.1 days to 102.9 days. Was it taking longer to collect the receivables because customers were disputing what they owed for those returned faulty products?

The Exception, Not the Rule

It bears repeating that fraudulent financial reporting is the exception, not the rule. Although numerous corporate accounting reporting scandals have been publicized widely in the last several years, those companies account for only a fraction of 1 percent of all published financial statements.

Quiz for Chapter 10

1. It is impossible to know exactly how much fraud occurs, and as a result, all fraud statistics are estimates.
    a. True
    b. False

2. The Association of Certified Fraud Examiners classifies fraud into three broad categories. Which of the following is not one of those categories?
    a. Embezzlement
    b. Asset misappropriation
    c. Fraudulent financial reporting
    d. Corruption

3. According to the Association of Certified Fraud Examiners, fraudulent financial reporting is the most frequently occurring type of fraud.
    a. True
    b. False

4. Which of the following is not one of the three elements of the fraud triangle?
   a. Pressure
   b. Greed
   c. Perceived opportunity
   d. Rationalization

5. According to recent fraud surveys conducted by both the Association of Certified Fraud Examiners and the Big Four public accounting firm KPMG, tips are the most common manner in which frauds are detected.
   a. True
   b. False

6. Which of the following statements is true? Auditors provide:
   a. Reasonable assurance that they have detected immaterial fraud
   b. Absolute assurance that they have detected material fraud
   c. Reasonable assurance that they have detected material fraud
   d. More assurance that they have detected material fraud than that they have detected material errors

7. Fraudulent financial reporting usually is done to improve a company's financial position. Which of the following approaches is not a common method by which to accomplish this objective?
   a. Overstate revenues
   b. Overstate liabilities
   c. Understate expenses
   d. Improper disclosures

8. One method of overstating net income is to overstate sales returns.
   a. True
   b. False

9. Expenses can be understated by capitalizing expenses.
   a. True
   b. False

10. One useful method to detect fraudulently misstated financial statements is to compare reported results with industry averages.
    a. True
    b. False

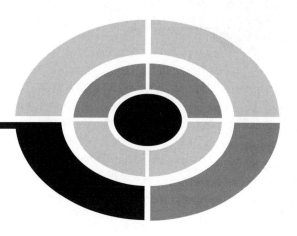

Final Exam

1. Financial statements can be used for a variety of business purposes, including:
   a. Deciding whether to invest in a company
   b. Deciding whether to lend money to a company
   c. Determining the amount of bonuses to be paid to a company's top executives
   d. All of the above

2. Which of the following is not one of the four basic financial statements?
   a. Statement of changes in working capital
   b. Income statement
   c. Balance sheet
   d. Statement of cash flows

3. Which of the following financial statements reports the amount of cash as of the end of the fiscal year?
   a. Income statement and balance sheet
   b. Balance sheet and statement of cash flows
   c. Income statement and statement of cash flows
   d. Statement of cash flows and statement of changes in owners' equity

4. Which of the following financial statements reports an organization's financial position at a specific point in time?
   a. Income statement
   b. Balance sheet
   c. Statement of cash flows
   d. Statement of changes in owners' equity

5. Revenues are the:
   a. Excess of assets over liabilities
   b. Economic resources of the business
   c. Resources flowing into the business primarily from providing services or producing and/or selling goods
   d. Cash flowing into the business

6. If a company reports $500,000 of revenues (of which $350,000 was received in cash) and $100,000 of expenses (of which $25,000 was paid in cash), the amount of net income reported for the period will be:
   a. $250,000
   b. $325,000
   c. $400,000
   d. $425,000

7. The ending balance of owners' equity as computed on the statement of owners' equity also appears on the:
   a. Statement of cash flows
   b. Balance sheet
   c. Income statement
   d. All three of these financial statements

8. The accounting profession requires that accounting information be comparable. This concept means that the information:
   a. Helps financial statement users make predictions of future company performance on the basis of past information
   b. Can be verified
   c. Is presented or reported in a similar manner for different companies
   d. Is presented in the same manner from one period to the next for a particular company

9. Financial statements are based on the assumption that they reflect only the business's transactions and do not include any of the owner's personal transactions.
   a. True
   b. False

10. Financial statements are prepared in accordance with GAAP, which stands for:
    a. Generally antiquated accounting practices
    b. Government approved accounting policies
    c. Generally accepted accounting principles
    d. Generally acceptable auditing procedures

11. Under the revenue recognition principle, revenue is reported on the income statement when:
    a. Cash is received for the goods sold or the services provided
    b. A contract is signed to provide the services or sell the goods
    c. The goods are sold or the services are provided
    d. Cash is paid for the goods or services

12. Companies are required to prepare their financial statements on the cash basis of accounting.
    a. True
    b. False

13. Many guidelines and standards have been developed by the accounting profession that must be followed in preparing financial statements. Primarily, these standards are developed by an organization called the:
    a. Financial Accounting Standards Board
    b. Society of Professional Accountants
    c. Financial Statements Standards Committee
    d. Governmental Accounting Oversight Board

14. Accounts receivable is:
    a. An asset
    b. A liability
    c. A revenue
    d. An expense

15. For one year, a company has received $130,000 in cash from customers and spent $125,000 in cash for expenses. For the same period, it reports revenues of $275,000 and expenses of $150,000. What is the reported net income on the income statement?
    a. $5,000
    b. $125,000
    c. $130,000
    d. $275,000

16. Unearned revenues:
    a. Are reported on the income statement
    b. Represent cash received from a customer in advance of performing a service or selling goods
    c. Equal the cash received during the year
    d. Are an asset reported on the balance sheet

17. Expenses are reported on the:
    a. Income statement
    b. Statement of cash flows
    c. Balance sheet
    d. Statement of changes in owners' equity

18. Which of the following is not an expense?
    a. Employee salaries
    b. Rent for office space
    c. Office supplies used
    d. Prepaid advertising

19. The matching principle requires that:
    a. Expenses paid in cash be matched against cash revenues, with the resulting difference reported on the income statement
    b. Costs of doing business be reported in the same period as the revenues they helped generate
    c. Every item listed on the balance sheet be matched against its counterpart on the income statement
    d. A matching footnote be provided for every item reported on the financial statements

20. *Earnings*, *profit*, *income*, and *net income* are different terms for the same concept.
    a. True
    b. False

21. If a company purchased inventory during the year that cost $250,000, had inventory on hand at the beginning of the year that cost $100,000, had inventory on hand at the end of the year that cost $30,000, and paid $225,000 cash for the inventory purchases, the cost of goods sold for the year would equal:
    a. $295,000
    b. $320,000
    c. $325,000
    d. $380,000

22. Gross margin represents:
    a. The markup on the goods sold
    b. The difference between gross sales revenue and net sales revenue
    c. The excess of profit margin over operating expenses
    d. The difference between cost of goods available for sale and ending inventory

23. For a company that manufactures the goods it sells, overhead represents:
    a. The cost of salaries and wages of employees directly involved in manufacturing the goods
    b. The cost of materials that become part of the finished product during the year
    c. The costs incurred on goods manufactured in prior periods that have not been completed as of the beginning of the year
    d. All the indirect costs of production

24. To determine the amount of dividends paid during the year, one would look at:
    a. The income statement
    b. The statement of cash flows
    c. The balance sheet
    d. The income statement and the statement of cash flows.

25. Earnings per share is a measure of profitability for common stock, not preferred stock.
    a. True
    b. False

26. Current assets are:
    a. Presented on the balance sheet in order of liquidity
    b. Assets that will be converted to cash or sold or used within a year or the operating cycle of the business, whichever is longer
    c. Generally valued at their cost at the time acquired
    d. Reported at a value below the original cost if the value has declined
    e. All of the above

27. Investments classified as long-term would include all of the following except:
    a. A corporate bond which is expected to be held until it is repaid at maturity
    b. Seasonally idle cash which was invested in the common stock of another corporation
    c. Land purchased for speculative purposes
    d. Investments in stocks and bonds set aside to repay bonds payable at maturity
    e. All of the above are long-term investments

28. Investments in marketable securities were purchased for $80,000, and the year-end market value is $90,000.
   a. The investments will be reported on the balance sheet at the market value of $90,000 if they are classified as trading or available for sale securities.
   b. The $10,000 increase in market value is referred to as an unrealized holding gain.
   c. If the investments are classified as available for sale, the unrealized gain will be reported in stockholders' equity, not in the income statement.
   d. All of the above are true.
   e. None of the above is true.

29. For most companies, dividends and interest earned and gains or losses from the sale of investments are included in the routine revenues when reported in the income statement.
   a. True
   b. False

30. Which of the following is true regarding an investment in a corporate bond?
   a. The bondholder will receive a stated amount of interest each year.
   b. The market price of the bond can fluctuate over time.
   c. The bondholder will be repaid a stated amount if the investment is held to maturity.
   d. The bondholder can sell its bond investment to another party.
   e. All of the above are true.

31. A company extends 2/10, n/30 credit terms to its customers. Which of the following is true regarding a customer invoice in the amount of $3,000?
   a. The normal credit terms require the customer to pay the $3,000 balance within 30 days of the invoice date.
   b. If the customer pays the invoice within 10 days, a cash discount of $60 can be taken.
   c. Both of the above are true.
   d. Neither of the above is true.

32. Which of the following would a manufacturing company include in the cost of goods in process inventory on its balance sheet?
   a. The cost of materials used to manufacture the product
   b. Wages paid to the assembly line workers
   c. Depreciation on manufacturing equipment
   d. All of the above
   e. None of the above

33. For which of the following companies would the physical flow of merchandise inventory most closely resemble the FIFO assumption?
    a. Car dealer
    b. Meat shop
    c. Gasoline station
    d. All of the above
    e. None of the above

34. A company using the weighted average cost-flow assumption purchased 200 units at $10 each and 800 units at $11 each. The weighted average unit cost is:
    a. $10.80 per unit
    b. $10.50 per unit

35. During the year, a company purchased three units of inventory and paid $4,000, $4,800, and $5,000, respectively. It sold two units and has one left in ending inventory. Determine the amounts that would be reported using the FIFO cost-flow assumption.
    a. Cost of goods sold $8,800 and ending inventory $5,000
    b. Cost of goods sold $9,800 and ending inventory $4,000

36. In a period of rising inventory prices, which of the following inventory cost-flow assumptions would produce the highest net income?
    a. FIFO
    b. LIFO
    c. Weighted average
    d. Cannot be determined without specific price information

37. In a period of rising inventory prices, which of the following inventory cost-flow assumptions would produce the lowest income tax liability?
    a. FIFO
    b. LIFO
    c. Weighted average
    d. Cannot be determined without specific price information

38. Inventory may be valued at the lower of cost or market when goods on hand are:
    a. Damaged or shopworn
    b. Obsolete
    c. Replacement cost has declined and future selling prices must be reduced regardless of the cost paid at the time of purchase
    d. All of the above
    e. None of the above

39. Investments in marketable securities for which the earnings and ultimate proceeds from the sale of such investments will be used to pay the maturity value of bonds payable should be classified as a long-term investment.
    a. True
    b. False

40. A company owns 30 percent of the common stock of Corporation X and has significant influence. Corporation X had net income of $100,000 and paid cash dividends of $10,000. Using the equity method, the investor would report $3,000 of dividend income in its income statement for the year.
    a. True
    b. False

41. When a company owns 80 percent of another corporation's common stock and has control:
    a. The investor is referred to as a parent company
    b. The company in which the investor owns stock is referred to as a subsidiary company
    c. The investor's financial statements will reflect the combined results of the two companies as though it were a single entity
    d. The consolidated financial statements will show the amount of net income and stockholders' equity attributable to the 20 percent noncontrolling interest
    e. All of the above

42. Which of the following might be included in the property, plant, and equipment classification in the balance sheet?
    a. Land purchased for speculative purposes
    b. Farm equipment held for resale by a farm implement dealer
    c. Building under construction for the company's own use
    d. All of the above
    e. None of the above

43. Which of the following would *not* be included in the amount reported as the cost of equipment on the balance sheet?
    a. The cost to repair damages caused by vandalism
    b. Delivery charges on equipment purchased
    c. Costs to install and adjust equipment before its use in manufacturing operations
    d. The invoice price less the amount of the cash discount taken for early payment
    e. All of the above would be included

44. The cost of a building that a company is constructing for its own use probably would include:
    a. Architectural design fees
    b. Materials and labor costs
    c. Depreciation on equipment used in construction activities
    d. Interest on funds borrowed to finance the construction of the building
    e. All of the above

45. In regard to the accounting concept of depreciation:
    a. The amount reported as depreciation expense each year measures the decline in the current market value of a plant asset
    b. The book value of the asset on the year-end balance sheet is an estimate of its current market value if it was sold on this date
    c. Both of the above
    d. Neither of the above

46. The units of production depreciation method might be used for which of the following assets?
    a. Delivery vehicles
    b. Machinery used to crush mineral ore produced in mining operations
    c. Automated packaging equipment used in manufacturing operations
    d. All of the above
    e. None of the above

Use the following information to answer Questions #47 & #48:

Equipment was purchased at an original cost of $500,000. Its useful life is estimated to be five years or 100,000 units, and its salvage value is estimated to be $20,000.

47. The total amount of depreciation expense that can be taken during the five years of use is:
    a. $500,000
    b. $480,000

48. Using the units of production method, the depreciation rate per unit is:
    a. $5.00 per unit
    b. $4.80 per unit

49. If a company reports an impairment loss in its income statement, this signifies that the value of a long-lived asset declined below its book value and that future earnings from the use or sale of that asset are not sufficient to recover its cost.
    a. True
    b. False

50. Which of the following could be capitalized as the cost of a natural resource?
    a. The cost to purchase rights to harvest timber on state land
    b. Exploration costs incurred by oil and gas companies
    c. Blasting and tunneling costs incurred to construct mine shafts
    d. All of the above
    e. None of the above

51. The depletion cost taken in a particular year:
    a. Is treated in a manner similar to that used for the raw material costs incurred by a manufacturing company
    b. Is a component of the cost of the inventory of the natural resource product on the balance sheet until it is sold
    c. Will be a component of the amount reported as cost of goods sold in the income statement when the natural resource product eventually is sold
    d. All of the above
    e. None of the above

52. Which of the following is true regarding goodwill?
    a. Goodwill is associated with the value of a company as a whole and cannot be identified separately.
    b. Goodwill can be included among the intangible assets on the balance sheet only if it arose from the acquisition of another company.
    c. Goodwill represents the excess paid to acquire a company over the fair value of the identifiable net assets acquired.
    d. All of the above are true.
    e. None of the above is true.

53. The term *depreciation expense* applies to plant assets. What term is used to describe a similar concept pertaining to intangible assets?
    a. Depletion
    b. Amortization

54. Current liabilities:
    a. Are obligations which must be paid or settled within a year or the operating cycle of the business
    b. Will be settled using cash or other current assets or by the creation of other current liabilities
    c. May include obligations for which the amount or specific party owed may not be known at the time the balance sheet is prepared.
    d. All of the above
    e. None of the above

55. Which of the following is true regarding contingent liabilities?
    a. Probable contingent liabilities the amount of which can be estimated must be reported as liabilities in the balance sheet.
    b. Contingent liabilities are disclosed in the footnotes only and should not be reported as liabilities in the balance sheet.
    c. Contingent liabilities are ignored in preparing the financial statements and footnotes because of the uncertainty of whether an actual liability exists at this time.
    d. All of the above are true.
    e. None of the above is true.

56. Which of the following would be reported as accrued liabilities in the balance sheet?
    a. Vacation pay employees have earned but not taken
    b. Rental fees owed for the temporary use of snow removal equipment
    c. Interest owed on a promissory note payable
    d. The unpaid monthly telephone bill
    e. All of the above

57. A one-year, $6,000, 9 percent note payable was signed on November 1, year 1. Which of the following is true?
    a. $540 of interest will be paid when the note matures in year 2.
    b. $90 of interest will be included in accrued liabilities on the December 31, year 1 balance sheet.
    c. $450 of interest expense will be reported in the year 2 income statement.
    d. All of the above are true
    e. None of the above is true.

58. Which of the following is true regarding a capital lease?
    a. The substance of the lease agreement resembles that of financing the purchase of an asset with long-term debt.
    b. The asset under lease will be included in plant assets and depreciated.
    c. The obligation for future lease payments will be included in long-term liabilities.
    d. All of the above are true.
    e. None of the above is true.

59. How should the balance of a long-term mortgage note payable which is repaid in monthly installments be reported in the balance sheet?
    a. As a long-term liability
    b. As a current liability
    c. The principal payments due in the coming year should be reported as a current liability, and the remaining principal balance should be reported as a long-term liability.

60. If at the time a corporation issues bonds payable the current market rate of interest is higher than the specified interest rate the corporation has promised to pay to its bondholders:
    a. The corporation will receive less cash than it has promised to repay on the maturity date
    b. The bonds will be issued at a discount
    c. The bonds will be reported on the balance at the amount the corporation has promised to repay at maturity less the applicable discount
    d. All of the above
    e. None of the above

61. When a corporation issues bonds at a discount, this signifies that the market rate of interest applicable at the time the bonds are issued is:
    a. Higher than the stated interest rate the corporation has promised to pay
    b. Lower than the stated interest rate the corporation has promised to pay

62. When a corporation issues bonds at a premium, this signifies that the market rate applicable at the time the bonds are issued is:
    a. Higher than the stated interest rate the corporation has promised to pay
    b. Lower than the stated interest rate the corporation has promised to pay

63. When a corporation reports deferred income tax liabilities on its balance sheet, this may signify that it paid less income tax this year because of a higher tax depreciation deduction but that additional taxes are expected to become payable in a future year.
    a. True
    b. False

64. Which of the following is not true of a business formed and operated as a sole proprietorship?
    a. The owner's salary is treated as a business expense.
    b. The owner will pay personal income taxes on the business profits.
    c. The capital balance includes the owner's investments and the profits retained by the business.
    d. All of the above are true.
    e. None of the above is true.

65. Which of the following is true regarding a corporation?
    a. The amount of each individual stockholder's equity is shown in the financial statements.
    b. Stockholders have a right to participate in managing and operating the corporation.
    c. The corporation files an income tax return and pays income taxes on its profits.
    d. All of the above are true.
    e. None of the above is true.

66. The terms *par value* and *market value* are synonymous and are used interchangeably.
    a. True
    b. False

67. All of the following are true regarding treasury stock except:
    a. Treasury stock represents shares of the corporation's own common stock that the corporation has reacquired
    b. Treasury stock is reported as an investment on the balance sheet
    c. Shares held in the treasury do not have voting or dividend rights
    d. The balance sheet value for treasury stock is based on the cost at the time it is reacquired
    e. All of the above

68. If a corporation issues common stock and receives an amount greater than the par value, its stockholders' equity will include amounts for both common stock and contributed capital in excess of par value.
    a. True
    b. False

69. A stated amount of cash dividends must be paid on which of the following?
    a. Common stock
    b. Preferred stock
    c. Treasury stock
    d. All of the above
    e. None of the above

70. At the beginning of the year, a corporation had $600,000 of common stock and $1,400,000 of retained earnings. During the year, the corporation issued $400,000 of additional common stock, earned net income of $1,000,000, and paid cash dividends of $200,000. Total stockholders' equity at year end is:
   a. $2,400,000
   b. $3,000,000
   c. $3,400,000
   d. $3,200,000
   e. Some other amount

71. The indirect method of reporting operating cash flows shows the differences between the amounts of revenues and expenses included in the amount of reported net income and the related cash receipts and payments associated with those revenues and expenses.
   a. True
   b. False

72. Cash dividends paid by a corporation to its stockholders will be reported in the statement of cash flows as a(n):
   a. Operating activity
   b. Investing activity
   c. Financing activity

73. Information that would explain the change in the amount reported as equipment (net) from the beginning to the end of the year can be found by reviewing:
   a. The depreciation expense reported in the income statement
   b. Purchases and sales of equipment reported as investing activities in the statement of cash flows
   c. The supplemental schedule of noncash investing and financing activities presented along with the statement of cash flows
   d. All of the above
   e. None of the above

74. An increase in accounts receivable indicates that the amount of cash collected from customers is:
   a. Greater than the sales revenue earned during the year
   b. Less than the sales revenue earned during the year

75. An increase in accounts payable indicates that the amount of cash paid to suppliers is:
   a. Greater than the amount of inventory purchased during the year
   b. Less than the amount of inventory purchased during the year

76. A Form 10-K:
   a. Is a tax form that must be filed by all businesses
   b. Is an annual report required by the Securities and Exchange Commission to be filed by all public companies
   c. Allows companies great flexibility in terms of what information is to be reported
   d. Is limited to containing a company's financial statements

77. Financial statements filed with the Securities and Exchange Commission must be audited.
   a. True
   b. False

78. In an auditors' report, the auditors provide an opinion about whether the financial statements:
   a. Are presented fairly in all material respects in accordance with GAAP
   b. Are presented accurately in accordance with GAAP
   c. Are presented fairly regardless of materiality
   d. Were audited properly in accordance with auditing standards

79. Auditors provide a guarantee that audited financial statements are correct.
   a. True
   b. False

80. Auditors are required, without exception, to be independent with respect to the company whose financial statements are being audited.
   a. True
   b. False

81. Independence when auditing financial statements is important because it helps ensure that the audit is conducted with an unbiased, objective viewpoint, giving the public greater confidence in the auditors' report.
   a. True
   b. False

82. An audit can be conducted in accordance with professional standards and an unqualified opinion can be given, yet the financial statements still can contain large errors or fraud that went undetected by the auditors.
   a. True
   b. False

83. A qualified audit opinion:
   a. Means that the auditors are qualified to render this opinion
   b. Is the best audit opinion that can be given
   c. Is the same as a clean opinion
   d. Means the auditors have discovered some kind of problem with the financial statements

84. A disclaimer of opinion by the auditor means:
    a. The financial statements should not be relied on by anyone because the auditors believe they contain large misstatements
    b. The financial statements can be relied on
    c. The auditors have discovered some problem with the financial statements, but other than that, the statements can be relied on
    d. For some reason, such as the inability to gather enough evidence pertaining to one or more matters, the auditors are not rendering any kind of opinion

85. Since the passage of the Sarbanes-Oxley Act of 2002, auditors of public companies are required to issue an opinion on:
    a. The effectiveness of the company's internal control over financial reporting as of the end of the fiscal year
    b. The business decisions made by management during the year
    c. Management's qualifications to run the company
    d. The efficiency of the company's operations

86. The auditors' opinion on the financial statements includes the footnote disclosures.
    a. True
    b. False

87. Vertical analysis:
    a. Involves computing changes in an account from one year to the next for several subsequent years
    b. Involves converting all the amounts on a financial statement for one year to a percentage of some other amount, such as total revenues
    c. Allows one to see the relative change in any account over time
    d. Requires that several ratios be computed

88. Horizontal analysis can help answer questions such as:
    a. What percentage of total assets is classified as current assets?
    b. What is the gross profit percentage?
    c. Accounts receivable this year are what percentage of the base year's accounts receivable?
    d. Inventory makes up what percentage of total assets?

89. Profitability ratios include:
    a. Return on assets and gross margin on sales
    b. The current ratio and the quick ratio
    c. Times interest earned and the debt-to-equity ratio
    d. Inventory turnover and days' sales outstanding

90. If a company reports net sales of $500,000, cost of goods sold of $300,000, total operating expenses of $50,000, cash of $400,000, and total assets of $1,000,000, the profit margin on sales is:
    a. 30%
    b. 50%
    c. 60%
    d. 80%

91. On which financial statement might one find a gain or loss from discontinued operations?
    a. Income statement
    b. Statement of cash flows
    c. Balance sheet
    d. Statement of changes in owners' equity

92. Extraordinary gains or losses:
    a. Are shown separately on the income statement, after the effect of taxes
    b. Appear on financial statements much more frequently than does a change in accounting principles
    c. Include natural disasters (e.g., hurricanes, floods) regardless of the geographical location
    d. Require no footnote disclosures

93. When a company changes an estimate of some information built into the financial statements (e.g., the useful life of a plant asset that is being depreciated):
    a. It must immediately restate the past five years of financial statements to reflect the new estimate
    b. It is allowed to ignore the new estimate and continue using the old estimate
    c. It should use the new estimate in the year it occurs and subsequent years
    d. It reports the change in estimate expense on the income statement

94. According to the Association of Certified Fraud Examiners, of the three general categories of fraud, fraudulent financial reporting occurs the least but is the most costly.
    a. True
    b. False

95. Fraudulent financial reporting requires intent on the part of management to deceive the readers of the financial statements.
    a. True
    b. False

Which of the following statements is false?

96. Management may feel pressure to perpetrate fraudulent financial reporting to:
    a. Maintain or increase the company's stock price
    b. Obtain financing at better rates of interest
    c. Temporarily survive some short-term setbacks
    d. Appear to meet loan requirements, such as maintaining minimum benchmarks of certain ratios

97. Most frauds are detected by auditors.
    a. True
    b. False

98. Auditors have the same level of responsibility to detect material frauds as the responsibility to detect material errors (honest mistakes).
    a. True
    b. False

99. Which of the following is not one of the common methods by which to overstate revenues fraudulently?
    a. Record fictitious revenue
    b. Understate sales returns
    c. Hold the books open and recognize revenue early
    d. Overstate sales discounts

100. Researchers have coined the term *fraud rectangle* to describe the four elements necessary for fraud to occur.
    a. True
    b. False

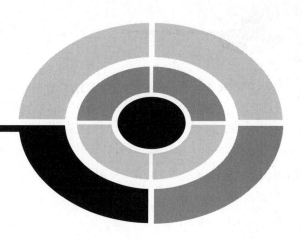

Answers to Quiz and Final Exam Questions

CHAPTER 1	CHAPTER 2	CHAPTER 3
1. b	1. b	1. b
2. c	2. d	2. c
3. a	3. b	3. b
4. d	4. c	4. b
5. c	5. a	5. a
6. c	6. b	6. c
7. d	7. c	7. d
8. a	8. a	8. a
9. c	9. a	9. d
10. b	10. d	10. d

CHAPTER 4
1. b
2. d
3. e
4. e
5. a
6. a
7. d
8. a
9. c
10. d

CHAPTER 5
1. a
2. d
3. d
4. a
5. b
6. d
7. a
8. c
9. a
10. b

CHAPTER 6
1. b
2. d
3. d
4. b
5. b
6. c
7. c
8. d
9. d
10. a

CHAPTER 7
1. c
2. b
3. b
4. a
5. b
6. b
7. c
8. a
9. c
10. a

CHAPTER 8
1. a
2. d
3. a
4. d
5. c
6. b
7. c
8. a
9. b
10. b

CHAPTER 9
1. c
2. b
3. a
4. c
5. d
6. b
7. b
8. b
9. a
10. b

CHAPTER 10
1. a
2. a
3. b
4. b
5. a
6. c
7. b
8. b
9. a
10. a

FINAL EXAM
1. d
2. a
3. b
4. b
5. c
6. c
7. b
8. c

9. a
10. c
11. c
12. b
13. a
14. a
15. b
16. b
17. a

18. d	46. d	74. b
19. b	47. b	75. b
20. a	48. b	76. b
21. b	49. a	77. a
22. a	50. d	78. a
23. d	51. d	79. b
24. b	52. d	80. a
25. a	53. b	81. a
26. e	54. d	82. a
27. b	55. a	83. d
28. d	56. e	84. d
29. b	57. d	85. a
30. e	58. d	86. a
31. c	59. c	87. b
32. d	60. d	88. c
33. b	61. a	89. a
34. a	62. b	90. a
35. a	63. a	91. a
36. a	64. a	92. a
37. b	65. c	93. c
38. d	66. b	94. a
39. a	67. b	95. a
40. b	68. a	96. c (this is a rationalization)
41. e	69. b	97. b
42. c	70. d	98. a
43. a	71. a	99. d
44. e	72. c	100. b
45. d	73. d	

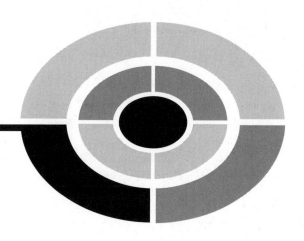

Index